D1452734

FIRE MANAGEMENT IN THE AMERICAN WEST

FIRE MANAGEMENT
IN THE AMERICAN WEST

Forest Politics and the Rise of Megafires

Mark Hudson

UNIVERSITY PRESS OF COLORADO

For Mara
and the mighty Quinn

Published by the University Press of Colorado
5589 Arapahoe Avenue, Suite 206C
Boulder, Colorado 80303

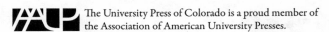 The University Press of Colorado is a proud member of
the Association of American University Presses.

The University Press of Colorado is a cooperative publishing enterprise supported, in part, by Adams State College, Colorado State University, Fort Lewis College, Metropolitan State College of Denver, Regis University, University of Colorado, University of Northern Colorado, and Western State College of Colorado.

∞ The paper used in this publication meets the minimum requirements of the American National Standard for Information Sciences—Permanence of Paper for Printed Library Materials. ANSI Z39.48-1992

Library of Congress Cataloging-in-Publication Data

Hudson, Mark, 1971 June 27–
 Fire management in the American West : forest politics and the rise of megafires / Mark Hudson.
  p. cm.
 Includes bibliographical references and index.
 ISBN 978-1-60732-088-3 (hardcover : alk. paper) — ISBN 978-1-60732-089-0 (e-book)
 1. Wildfires—West (U.S.)—Prevention and control—History. 2. Wildfires—West (U.S.)—
Prevention and control—History—Sources. 3. Forests and forestry—Fire management—West
(U.S.)—History. 4. Forests and forestry—Fire management—Political aspects—West (U.S.)—
History. 5. Forest products industry—West (U.S.)—History. 6. United States. Forest Service—
History. 7. Forest products industry—Environmental aspects—West (U.S.)—History. 8. West
(U.S.)—Environmental conditions. I. Title.
 SD421.32.W47H83 2011
 363.37'9—dc23
                               2011019915

Design by Daniel Pratt

20 19 18 17 16 15 14 13 12 11   10 9 8 7 6 5 4 3 2 1

CONTENTS

ACKNOWLEDGMENTS

This book has placed me in serious personal debt. First, I owe a great debt to Dr. Timothy Ingalsbee, who encouraged my interest in fire and whose passion for returning fire to the western woods was and remains relentless. His insights and perspectives on fire ecology and the "sociology of wildland fire" were a great inspiration, and he was extremely generous with his time, expertise, and resources. This may not be the book he initially pointed me toward writing, but he, more than anybody, was the one who set me on the path. I am responsible, of course, for where it has ended up.

I am also grateful for Dr. Bill Robbins's immense assistance at all stages of the project. His help navigating the archives, his suggestions on early drafts, and his path-breaking scholarship on the political economy of the timber industry were invaluable. I would also like to thank John Foster, Val Burris, and Richard York for their valuable advice and suggestions on previous drafts. Thanks also to the Forest History Society in Durham, NC, which provided a travel grant that enabled me to make use of the organization's wonderful archives. I am similarly grateful to the University of Oregon's G. Benton Johnson Dissertation Fellowship for financial support.

Peter and Suzanne Hudson contributed untold hours wading through early drafts and provided editorial suggestions that vastly improved the book's clarity and readability. Profound thanks also to members of the United States

Forest Service who took time out from their increasingly hectic lives to talk to an unknown graduate researcher. Without their insights, clarifications, and perspectives on contemporary fire management, the project would never have gotten off the ground. At the University Press of Colorado, thanks to Cheryl Carnahan for her stellar copyediting and to Daniel Pratt and Darrin Pratt. Finally, thanks to Mara Fridell for listening to me talk endlessly about forest fires for two years, for helping me think straight, and for her countless other forms of support. All of these people helped make this a better book. As usual, I remain solely responsible for any errors.

This book is based primarily on archival material from across the country. Materials from the University of Oregon in Eugene, the Oregon Historical Society in Portland, the Forest History Society in Durham, NC, Cornell University in Ithaca, NY, the National Archives in Washington, DC, the Federal Records Center in Seattle, WA, and the Minnesota Historical Society in St. Paul were used to develop an account of relations between the Forest Service and industry, as well as the debates among foresters and conservationists in the early twentieth century. Of particular value on the former count was the Archive of the National Forest Products Association, formerly the National Lumber Manufacturers Association, located in the archives of the Forest History Society. This collection contained extensive correspondence between Forest Service officials and members of the organized timber industry, as well as a great deal of material detailing forestry debates that took place internally among key industry activists on the subjects of regulation, public forest ownership, and fire management. Archives of the Society of American Foresters, also at the Forest History Society, and the Papers of the National Forestry Committee at Cornell University were also highly valuable in this regard.

The archival material is supplemented by interviews with Forest Service fire management professionals carried out during the summer of 2005. Managers across a range of ecosystem types in Oregon were interviewed before, during, and after the fire season. Professionals up and down the managerial chain of command were interviewed about the Forest Service's past, present, and future management of fire, organizational and societal enablers of and obstacles to the implementation of changing fire management policy, the specifics of fire management policy and practices in their respective national forests, budgetary constraints, and a range of other subjects.

Potential interview candidates were chosen from the USFS's online directory of officials, based on their professional titles and managerial responsibilities. An initial letter was sent to sixty-five potential candidates, inviting them to respond if they were interested in being interviewed or if they preferred not to be contacted again. Follow-up contact was made by telephone with those who did not respond. I ensured that I had permission to interview participants from a range of ecosystem types and along the chain of command ranging from top regional administrators to assistant fire managers. Once that requirement was satisfied, interviews were scheduled based on participants' location and availability during and immediately following the fire season. Interviews were conducted in offices and in the field, depending on the interviewees' schedule and preferences.

FIRE MANAGEMENT IN THE AMERICAN WEST

CHAPTER ONE

Introduction

Humans have a tortured relationship with fire. We are, in the terminology of relationship pathologies, "control freaks." We love fire if we feel we are in charge of it. Appropriately placed within the confines of the hearth, fire provides warmth and a sense of comfort, a shield both material and psychological against the encroachment of darkness. Fire in the right place and of the right scale is considered an indicator of progress, a seed of human civilization. When a small pile of sticks is set ablaze outdoors within the confines of a ring of stones, most of us are drawn to it, and not simply for the warmth it provides. We are, when fire is behaving in a socially appropriate way, deeply pyrophillic. But if fire gets uppity, the love turns to terror. Depending on our proximity, this fear is utterly rational. Having once caught my own hands on fire, I can attest that overly close encounters with uncontrolled flames are not to be encouraged. The many fatalities among wildland firefighters over the years provide much more profound and tragic testimony to the same point. However, over the past 50 to 100 years, humans' need for control has increased, in part because human populations continue to spread into what used to be considered "wilderness" and as part of a larger attempt at managing nature to suit our historically specific needs and wants. Even if we face no personal risk, we would much prefer to see fire bounded, enclosed, and managed. Fire that does not suit our needs has no place. Fire out of its cage is infernal. It is the tool of the mob, the invader, and the rioting masses. It is to be extinguished.

For those surveying the western landscape at the turn of the twentieth century, the fear of wildfire was primarily something to live with, not to act upon. While people would certainly fight to defend themselves, their families, and their homes from fire, the idea of eliminating fire to the greatest possible extent or controlling it would have seemed like a madman's dream. There was simply too much space and too many ignitions to make such an idea feasible. The mythological lesson of King Canute, who failed to hold back the tide by commanding the advancing waters to stop, would have seemed appropriate as a cautionary tale. Nonetheless, during the second half of the twentieth century, the United States Forest Service (USFS) seemed to be succeeding where Canute had failed. The relative absence of free-burning fire in US forests is an amazing result of that success, although one that westerners tend to take largely for granted.

In sheer scale, the magnitude of the project of fire elimination is astonishing. In the early twentieth century, when public lands were vast and prone to burn, even imagining that fire could be effectively chased out was in some ways courageous. Looming over this massive project in US forestry lore are some larger-than-life figures, most of whom sported the uniform of the USFS: Chief Gifford Pinchot, understood to have stamped the Forest Service with his utilitarian conservationism and to have set the organization's mission; Chief Henry Graves, who established fire protection as the first step toward real forestry; Chief William Greeley, who set the extent of fire suppression as the metric for progress in US forestry and fought tirelessly to gain the legal authority and resources needed to extinguish fire; and Ed Pulaski—symbol of the bravery and heroism of the ranger and frontline firefighter—who, in the face of a fast-approaching wildfire during the "Big Blowup" (a series of massive fires that raged throughout the West) of 1910, dragged his crew of forty-five men into an abandoned mine and positioned himself at the entrance with a pistol. He remained there all night, threatening to shoot any man who fled as the mineshaft timbers caught fire. He is credited with saving the lives of all but five of his men.

However, the lesson of Canute is beginning to appear menacingly relevant once again. Wildland fire is on the rise in the western United States. While successes continue in the US Congress for funding and resources, and heroics continue on the fire lines, westerners are facing a serious reckoning with wildland fire. As catastrophic fires become increasingly commonplace, all indications point to the reality that westerners are going to have to learn to live with fire.

A CATASTROPHIC SITUATION

This resurgence of wildfire in the US West is a catastrophe 100 years in the making. Whereas forest fires have crept and smoldered in the past, with only occasional blowups, conflagration now seems to be the norm. Fire intensity, frequency, and size are all on an upward trend,[1] along with the amount of money spent on wildland fire management.[2] Catastrophic wildland fire is the charismatic poster child of the larger "forest health crisis" the USFS has declared is afflicting the nation's woods. Eye-catching photos of flames blaze across the pages of newspapers and in evening news reports. Former president George W. Bush announced his forestry initiatives while standing "in the black"—on the charred remains of burned-over land. Bills are introduced and regulations enacted on the grounds of protecting communities from catastrophic blazes.

When I began writing this book in the summer of 2007, fire resources were stretched thin across the West as bone-dry forests and grasslands were ignited by dry lightning storms. During one week alone, on Friday 1,000 more fires were burning than had been burning the previous Monday. Around 15,000 firefighters were digging lines, lighting backfires, and dropping retardant as fire officials ratcheted up the wildfire alert level to its highest point. Seventy fires, each extending over 100 acres, were burning across twelve states, and ash was still floating down after Utah had suffered the state's largest fire on record. Evacuees were returning, and media coverage focused on the tragedy of torched homes, possessions lost, dreams gone up in smoke. By the summer of 2008 the costs of fire suppression nationally were approaching $1.6 billion, not because it was a bad fire season across the country but because of the particularly large and costly fires in California. We have come a long way from the early days of state-financed fire protection, during which flames were chased with considerable futility by a mule, a ranger, and his shovel.[3] By the end of June 2008, after a weekend storm had ignited 1,000 fires across the region, Governor Arnold Schwarzenegger asked President Bush to declare a state of emergency in California. By year's end, 1.33 million acres had burned in the state.[4] How did wildland fire become so fierce?

While many reasons have been suggested for the resurgence of fires—with various fingers pointing at climate change, logging, or real-estate development—policy, popular, journalistic, and academic discussions of fire share a high degree of consensus in one area. Their accounts overlap in claiming that the alarming recent trends in fire behavior are partly, if not largely, attributable to federal land management agencies' diligent suppression efforts, particularly those of the USFS.[5] An increasingly common narrative has emerged to explain the rise of catastrophic fire, featuring a largely autonomous state agency (the USFS) with a misguided missionary-professional ethic and an overconfident, pseudo-religious belief in the pursuit of human control over nature. The Forest Service's mania for fire prevention and suppression, it is argued, has resulted in more fire-prone and combustible forests. The USFS has spent its time and the public's money piling up fuel that now lies waiting for a spark. As a result of this narrative, politicians, environmental activists, and nervous homeowners across the US West have set their sights on reforming (or, in some extreme cases, abolishing) the Forest Service.

Blaming the state exclusively for the emergence of crises of various kinds is nothing new. Such a response has a great deal of cultural traction in the United States. In the 1930s and 1940s, for example, lumbermen blamed the size and structure of taxes for the massive deforestation wrought by industrial logging. The state, in its mythical status as a standalone institution, is held accountable for the low quality of education, the duration of the Great Depression, lapsing morality, environmental despoliation, welfare's failure, poverty, unemployment, the subprime mortgage meltdown, 9/11, unreliable trains, and so on. The trouble is that this tradition of blaming the government for crises is rarely, if ever, accurate. In many cases, blaming any actor exclusively for generating a crisis (e.g., economic, environmental, political) misses the boat. Rather, crises tend to emerge from relations between social actors operating within the constraints of a given context. This holds true for environmental, as well as economic, crises.

This book presents an alternative explanation for the genesis of catastrophic fire in the West. Drawing on correspondence between and within the Forest Service and major timber industry associations, newspaper articles, articles from industry publications, and policy documents from the late 1800s to the present, I argue that the state-focused narrative pushes much of the relevant action out of the picture. While a century of suppression has indeed increased the hazard of wildfire (again, along with human settlement patterns, changing land use, and, perhaps most alarming in recent years, climate change), the project of eliminating fire from the woods and the "blowback" of the increasing fire hazard do not stem from the USFS as an isolated, highly autonomous body. Rather, their roots are found in the Forest Service's relationships with other, more powerful elements of society—the timber industry in particular.

Within the activist ranks of many environmental social movements, the Forest Service is viewed as having a very comfortable, even friendly relationship with the timber industry. The USFS's relations with the timber business, however, have not always been amicable. During the 1930s and 1940s in particular, bad blood between the two deepened. As the Forest Service's periodic evaluations of the state of US forests generated ever bleaker forecasts, its leaders began to push for greater control over the business of lumbering, not only on public lands but on private lands as well. When the USFS began to publicly decry what it saw as managerial incompetence on the part of timber owners, resulting in forest devastation and the prospect of a deforested United States, business owners rallied in defense of the prerogatives of capital to conduct their affairs and dispose of their property as they saw fit. Commenting on a regulatory proposal floated by the USFS in 1940, for example, timber executive George F. Jewett of the Potlatch Timber Company in Idaho and an active member of the National Lumber Manufacturers Association (NLMA), unleashed a verbal assault on acting USFS chief Earle Clapp:

> I feel that managerial incompetence has been much less to blame [for the devastation of forests] than dumb or vicious public leadership. I use this last term advisedly for there are governmental leaders whose avowed purpose is to socialize the country. [Former chief] F. A. Silcox personally endorsed the pamphlet entitled "The Lower One-Third and the Forest Service" in which the proposed cure of our forest evils was to socialize enough of our forest area so that the private forests could be ruined by governmental competition . . . My objection to your general program is that whether intentional or not it plays right into the hands of those who would alter our way of life. This entitles them to the description "vicious." The National Socialist Party which dominates Germany professes just the ideals you propose: strict regulation of private property for the benefit of all the people. Allowing the government so much power destroys individual liberty just as effectively as the communist set-up of Russia. I believe men are more important than trees. If we have free men, they will take care of their trees when the time comes.[6]

Nearly a decade later, NLMA president A. J. Glassow expressed similar dismay at the continuing threats of government encroachment on the freedoms of business. Speaking to the nation's timber executives, Glassow gave a stirring "once more into the breach" address:

> My sole purpose in speaking to you today is to add my voice to those who would rouse every businessman in the country to action—action to protect the principle of freedom of enterprise . . . This freedom is hard to visualize—until it is suddenly and painfully restricted by Federal regulation . . . And if we think that the roots of freedom of enterprise are still firmly imbedded in our national economy and in present laws, we are not looking at the facts. The winds of socialization are blowing strong, and the soil of America has already

been sown with the seeds of federal control . . . Each year sees greater and greater extension of the power of the Federal bureaucracy over your economic freedom . . . There is the danger.[7]

The looming threat of a socialist takeover was a favorite theme of the timber industry during this period. When confronted with the fact that the industry's practices had, in fact, devastated US forests, workers, and communities in pursuit of private gain, executives took up a well-practiced refrain. "We are not the problem," they claimed. "Rather, turn your eyes toward the real destroyer of forests. Fire is the problem, and it is a hazard generated by the public, not the private owner. If you want to stop forest devastation, put out the flames." Jewett, testifying in 1940 before the Joint Congressional Committee on Forestry, which had a mandate to recommend forestry legislation, stated the case bluntly: "From your extended travels and the eight hearings held throughout the various forest regions of the United States, it is clear to you that nature will grow trees on over one-third of our continental area, if given the proper encouragement by man. This encouragement included protection against man-made hazards . . . The principal man-made hazard is fire."[8] Contrary to the dominant narrative's account, the picture that emerges from a close historical investigation is one in which fire is stamped out and rages back not as a result of the insulated policies of an overly muscular state agency run amuck but instead as a result of that agency's weakness relative to a highly organized network of timber capitalists.

The fuels of catastrophic fire are to be found in the tension created by the contradictory roles of state agencies operating within a context of predominantly capitalist social relations. Modern wildfire, in addition to being produced by the usual "fire triangle" of heat, fuels, and oxygen, is the result of a political-economic triangle made up of the commodification of forests, the strict requirements of profitable private forestry, and the very limited room for maneuver afforded the Forest Service in its efforts to implement "practical forestry" in the United States. Practical forestry, as George Gonzalez has pointed out, was an early euphemism in both timber and conservation circles for harvesting and growing trees in a manner that was practical in terms of the accumulation of capital.[9] Practical forestry was profitable forestry. The history of wildland fire management policy and its effects on the western landscape today, then, are best explained by looking at the context from which this policy emerged and in which land managers struggle to reform it. That context is an epic battle over two questions: for what purposes should US forests be managed, and in whose interest? These questions retain relevance today as environmental groups clash with timber companies and the state over forest management. Indeed, as Richard Behan has pointed out, the fight over the fate of the nation's forests is still bitterly contested, largely in the courtroom but also within managerial ranks, in the halls of the US Congress, and in the forests themselves when activists directly confront loggers.[10] But between 1930 and 1950, the state was likely to be the party clashing with timber interests in defense of forestry management for the public good, with its leaders angry and despondent about the devastation of the nation's forests.

ORGANIZATION OF THE BOOK

This book is intended to answer two questions. First, what are the origins of the current relationship between people and fire in the US West? Since that relationship is heavily conditioned by the actions of the United States Forest Service, a considerable portion of the book is dedicated to unearthing a history of how the USFS arrived at its longstanding policy and practice of trying to exclude fire from the woods. This history focuses on the period between the end of the nineteenth century (with the genesis of the Forest Service) and 1950. This is not to say that the contest over fire policy is contained within that period. Indeed, fire policy has been increasingly contested within the Forest Service since the late 1970s and on into the 2000s. These recent debates and political struggles have had a significant effect on contemporary fire policy, as discussed in chapter 2. However, the policy of fire exclusion that has so profoundly remade much of the western forest landscape has its roots in battles fought in the first half of the twentieth century. Second, now that it is widely acknowledged that this policy is neither ecologically nor economically sustainable (the National Park Service began reforming its fire policy in 1968, the USFS a decade later), why is the USFS having such a difficult time pulling back from suppression as its primary—almost exclusive—response to fire?

I begin by outlining the case for a sociological inquiry into wildland fire. While there is a growing social-scientific literature on the connections between culture, values, perceptions, and attitudes, on the one hand, and wildland fire on the other,[11] fire has been treated predominantly as a technical-managerial problem and is widely understood as a force of nature—a "natural disaster." As such, it may seem unlikely that sociology will offer much insight into why and how the human relationship with fire in the US West was formed. Chapter 2 thus sets out the case that today's wildland fires are just as social in content as they are natural. During this discussion, a broad overview of the social history of fire is recounted, drawing primarily on existing accounts of fire, fire protection,

US forestry, and conservation to address initial questions. How have Americans transformed the landscape through fire use? How has the pattern of forest fire changed since European settlement, as well as over the past century? What accounts for those changes? In chapter 2, I recount the institutional history of fire policy in the United States to provide adequate background so the reader is able to grasp and evaluate the remainder of the argument. This history relies heavily on secondary sources, providing only a surface accounting of actions the Forest Service has taken in its efforts to arrive at and implement a wildfire policy. I owe a great debt to Stephen Pyne, David Carle, and Ashley Schiff for their work in this area. The chapter also includes some assessment of the ecological consequences of the USFS's policy on fire and concludes by looking at the recent (re-)politicization of fire as it has come to dominate debates over land use and logging since about 2002.

In chapter 3, I review existing explanations for the emergence of the forest health crisis and for catastrophic wildland fire and unpack their implicit or explicit sociological content. I argue that existing explanations rest on specific assumptions about the nature and role of the state in capitalist society, its motivations, its tasks, and its relationships with the rest of society. With some oversimplification (to be remedied later in this book, I hope) for the sake of brevity, the dominant account of fire's turn for the worse contends that the Forest Service surveyed the nation's forests, saw them burning, perceived this as waste and injury to the potential human welfare to be derived from standing green timber, resolved to douse the flames, and then proceeded to do so. Catastrophic fire events early in the twentieth century played a role in galvanizing public support for suppression and acted as the crucible within which the Forest Service's views on fire were formed.[12] An addiction to fire fighting, born of the alleged tendency for bureaucratic budget maximizing, developed over time.[13] All of this, as we shall see, did in fact happen. However, the explanation is incomplete.

Its partial nature is the result of a contrived isolation of the Forest Service and its actions in the realm of fire protection from the larger context of the state's role in ongoing struggles over access to US forests. Through an exclusive focus on the agency's actions in creating a culture, economy, and technical capacity for fire suppression rather than on the dynamics of conflict over the fate of the forests, a causal explanation emerges that is implicitly or explicitly built on a very particular theory of the state. Blame is heaped on Forest Service bureaucrats and their misguided mania for demonizing and extinguishing flame. A picture is drawn of an overly muscular, insulated, highly autonomous, scientifically minded corps of forest managers hell-bent on stamping out every last spark in the woods. The Forest

Service, in this explanation, autonomously generated the will and capacity for the long-held policy of fire suppression in a gambit to maximize the productivity and efficiency of US forests. The Forest Service itself, in its many recent policy reviews and introspective publications, has engaged in a confessional brand of hand-wringing that centers its own actions in the deterioration of national forests. In short, the dominant narrative of fire in the United States is highly and indefensibly state-centric. State-centered explanations are those that emphasize the centrality of the state in shaping history, claiming that the state has its own set of interests—distinct from those of other social actors—and the capacity to realize those interests. A review of relevant sociological debates on the nature of the state, its degree of autonomy, and its role in capitalist societies points to one aspect of the larger social-theoretical significance of the problem of wildland fire. Chapter 3 concludes by identifying important questions that the state-centered explanations advanced to date fail to answer and that thus demand another look at the social dynamics that produced the policy of full suppression. Most pressingly, I ask why the USFS was apparently able to act with such autonomy with regard to fire policy, given the widely recognized fact that it showed a complete lack of autonomy on other forest management issues.

In chapter 4, I argue that we can much better understand the social component of catastrophic wildfire by highlighting the political-economic context of capitalism in which the USFS has operated. Historical evidence is presented that calls into question the high degree of autonomy attributed to the USFS and that highlights the role of class-based actors in determining fire policy. Of key relevance on this front, given that an autonomous agency should be able to realize its wishes, are the assessments by Forest Service leaders and employees concerning the steps necessary to halt the devastation of forests by commercial timbering on private land and the USFS's inability to undertake those steps. In this chapter I examine in particular the fate of efforts to gain federal regulatory power over private timbering and to nationalize a much greater portion of forestlands than those held within the National Forest System. Key members of the USFS viewed these initiatives as vital to address what they saw as the major threat to the nation's forests: overexploitation and the looming specter of timber famine. This struggle took the form of a series of regulatory and legislative initiatives championed by the USFS. While the state's relationship with timber capital fluctuated from cozy collaboration in the period leading up to the New Deal to outright conflict, one thing remained constant: every regulatory or nationalizing initiative was either defeated outright or altered significantly at the behest and in the interests of timber capital. Failing in its efforts to secure the power to regulate private forestry, the

Forest Service fell back time and time again on a quid pro quo arrangement with timber capitalists, in which the state was to provide fire suppression in exchange for conservation-oriented logging reform by private owners.

Given this history, I argue in chapter 5 that a crisis-theoretic approach to understanding the USFS's actions over the course of the twentieth century best explains the emergence of catastrophic wildfire. Based predominantly on Marxist and neo-Marxist theories of crisis (primarily, but not exclusively, those of Karl Marx, James O'Connor, Claus Offe, and John Foster), I argue that the current "forest health crisis" is an exemplar of Offe's "crisis of crisis management."[14] That is, we can best understand the emergence of catastrophic wildfire as a regular feature in the western United States in light of the state's absorption of environmental crisis generated by capitalist industrial forestry and its inability to adequately manage that crisis given the ongoing tension between its role as the political guardian of the conditions of accumulation and its role as a defender and promoter of the public good. I also characterize the removal of fire as an instance of "metabolic rift"—a rupture in the basic ecological processes that reproduce forest ecosystems—and argue that the theory of metabolic rift, in contrast to other Marxist theories of environmental crisis, better positions us to consider the role of the state in mediating the interaction of humans and nature that occurs in the labor process. In short, in chapter 5, I argue that fire as conditioned by human intervention, no less than other elements of forest ecology, is a relational product. It cannot be dumped exclusively on the doorstep of a mischievous or malicious nature, an overly powerful state agency, or rapacious capital.

In chapter 6, I examine the question of ecological modernization as it is hypothesized to be occurring among the state apparatuses of industrialized nations. Ecological modernization theory (EMT) suggests that the tensions alluded to in chapters 4 and 5 can be transcended. In their place, EM theorists see the development of a win-win scenario that combines ripe conditions for accumulation and a successful defense of the public good (in this case defined as the maintenance of ecological systems as "conditions of life").[15] The USFS's recent policy shift away from total fire suppression toward a policy that vows to allow fire to reoccupy, to the greatest extent possible, its old ecological role in the forests presents a promising case study for EMT. It is suggestive of a classic process of ecological modernization, in which negative side effects of resource management strategies become evident over time through scientific inquiry, resulting in the appropriate adjustments to those strategies.

Data from interviews with USFS and Bureau of Land Management fire managers are triangulated with trends in agency spending to evaluate the extent to which the Forest Service is undergoing a process of ecological modernization with regard to wildfire. Interviews served as a ground-truthing exercise, and my understanding of the practice and policy of fire management was greatly expanded and clarified by those with whom I spoke. In addition, the interviews provide a window into the organizational process of ecological modernization and allow some assessment of the extent to which this process is proceeding, the obstacles to its progress, and fire managers' attitudes and opinions about both the policy directions and practical operations of the nation's primary forestland management agency. The chapter concludes that, while policy is changing and has in fact been shifting since the late 1970s, the tensions inherent in the state's contradictory roles within capitalism have not been transcended, and practice remains largely unchanged. Factors both internal (planning processes, managerial risk calculations, and incentive structures) and external to the organization (real-estate development, budgeting shortfalls, a "fire-industrial complex," and public perceptions of fire) have prevented change on the ground, despite altered guidelines for practitioners and formal policies. In terms of the ecological consequences—the bottom line of any test of ecological modernization—USFS fire management remains highly problematic, as practitioners in the field are well aware. I argue—against an assumption implicit in EMT—that the state's managerial practices are highly constrained not only by social forces in the present but also by its own past management. Because of this, past ecological blunders, such as the removal of fire, are not easily undone.

I conclude by connecting questions of ecological modernization and theories of the state. While an emergent literature is hypothesizing the development of "environmental states" as part of the broader process of ecological modernization, the question of how such an emergence might either contradict or complement the state's role in capitalist society has not been well addressed. I argue that the state in a capitalist context is incapable of becoming environmental in any meaningful sense. As long as the state is restricted to the management of environmental and economic crises created by capitalist social relations and by the labor processes those relations demand, it is likely to continue to produce new forms of crisis. That is, the lack of state autonomy relative to capital even as the state attempts to manage economic and ecological crises generated by the latter precludes the emergence of a genuinely environmental state.

CHAPTER TWO

THE SOCIAL DIMENSIONS OF WILDFIRE

> The Forest Service sounded the note of progress. It opened up the wilder-
> ness with roads and telephone lines, and airplane landing fields. It capped
> the mountain peaks with white-painted lookout houses, laced the ridges and
> streams with a network of trails and telephone lines, and poured in thousands
> of firefighters year after year in a vain attempt to control forest fires . . . Is it
> possible that it was all a ghastly mistake?
>
> *Elers Koch, USFS, "The Passing of the Lolo Trail," 1935*

NATURAL? DISASTER?

On December 11, 1987, during its forty-second session, the United Nations—
taking a controversial stance in opposition to earthquakes, tsunamis, land-
slides, and other "calamities of natural origin"—declared the 1990s to be the
International Decade for Natural Disaster Reduction. Included in the long list of
natural disasters to be "reduced" by the international community over the course
of the decade, along with plagues of locusts and floods, was wildfire. But is wildfire really a "natural disaster?"

We might do well to question both the adjective and the noun in this characterization of wildfire. Regarding the noun, the social content is unquestionable.
As Ted Steinberg demonstrates forcefully in *Acts of God*, "disaster" is inextricable
from, and defined by, its social context.[1] Weather, for example, is disastrous only
when it rips up a housing development or floods a town. Rain at one time of the year
is a boon, at another a catastrophe. Patterns of residential development, driven by

profit and frequently abetted by state and federal governments, determine which groups specifically will be hardest hit by heavy rains, tornadoes, and hurricanes.[2] Hurricane Katrina's devastation of New Orleans and the US federal government's response laid bare the racial and class content of disaster for television news audiences around the world. In the realm of forestry, the United States Forest Service (USFS), the timber industry, and the Ad Council have spent millions of dollars[3] creating the perception that fire in a forest is a disaster. Indigenous inhabitants saw it otherwise, as did many early white settlers, and fire ecologists—some in the employ of the USFS—have been questioning the equation of fire and disaster for decades.[4] Clearly, the designation "disaster" is contingent on the ideological, political, and economic dominance of specific groups that have specific interests. The social geography of race, class, and gender determines where and upon whom disaster falls.

But what about the social content of the adjective? A "natural" disaster, as we commonly understand the term, is a potentially harmful effect produced by geological, chemical, or climatic processes beyond human control. Nobody standing in the wreckage of a tornado-shredded home goes looking for the perpetrator, although we would do well to ask why that home so often belongs to a poor person or a member of a racial minority and why it was placed knowingly in harm's way. Fire is unquestionably a "natural" phenomenon. It is technically a chemical process of rapid oxidation resulting from the interaction of heat, fuel, and oxygen. Once fuels enter the flaming stage of combustion—that is, once a stick is on fire—the fire's behavior is dictated largely by the distribution and condition of additional fuels, weather, and topography. Heating often takes place as a result of a lightning strike generated by one of the 44,000 thunderstorms that occur worldwide on any given day.[5] All of this can and does take place in the absence of humans. Fire precedes us.

Thus, at first blush it may seem like another tricky slight of the sociological hand to portray fire as "socially constructed." However, a fire is not a fire is not a fire, just as a flood is no longer a flood, given the industrious beavering of the US Army Corps of Engineers over the past 200 years.[6] Fire's character, distribution, frequency, and effects are all heavily conditioned by the human hand. In this respect, Smokey Bear—love child of the Forest Service and the Ad Council—has been right all along, in his own reductionist way, in blaming "you" for forest fires. Fire and its effects on landscape and ecology materialize as they do because of a multitude of social-historical factors, including land-use decisions, technology, public perceptions, values, and economics. Each of these, in turn, is conditioned by changes in the pattern of fire, as we shall see. It is a relationship well captured by Karl Marx's aphorism that "the history of nature and the history of men mutually determine each other so long as men exist."[7]

Thus contrary to the UN categorization, we ought to dispense from the outset with the notion that fire is a "natural disaster." It might be (or have been) one or the other, but it is certainly not both. In the United States, the foundations of modern fire were laid when the westward expansion of the US empire violently removed the original, fire-wielding inhabitants of the land, moved white settlers into an environment sculpted through fire, and, over the course of a long century, created organizations to mediate citizens' relationship with this seemingly destructive process. While human efforts to corral fire were initially highly limited in their geographic reach and effectiveness, by the 1930s a massive reservoir of surplus labor was released into the woods in the form of the Civilian Conservation Corps (CCC), and the process of significantly altering the pattern of fire in the US West—and thus the region's ecology and landscape—was set in motion. The current regime of wildland fire, no less than that associated with indigenous burning practices, is an element of "second nature,"[8] a "produced" nature inseparable from the social relations from which it emerged.

THE FALL OF WESTERN FIRE

How, then, is wildfire different today than it was 50 or 150 years ago in the western United States? Fire was ubiquitous in many western ecosystems prior to European settlement. In addition to lightning-caused fires, indigenous land-use practices involved frequent anthropogenic burning for a wide variety of purposes. Landscapes were manipulated with fire for purposes of war, agriculture, and hunting—creating, according to fire historian Stephen Pyne, "a mosaic of anthropogenic fire regimes as complex as the historical geography of the cultures themselves."[9] Nancy Langston describes how indigenous burning practices helped create a variety of different landscapes in the West, from ponderosa parkland forests to grasslands and prairies.[10] William Robbins relates that European explorers encountered a "charred and blackened landscape" produced by indigenous burning in Oregon's Willamette Valley.[11] He stresses that in addition to having a significant effect on the Willamette Valley's landscape, "Native burning played an important part in shaping the ecology of other fire regime settings,"[12] including the Blue Mountains and the Cascade Range. In 1878 John Wesley Powell recognized the Native American influence on the landscape when he advocated removing Indians as a mechanism to contain wildfire and thereby increase the acreage of standing timber.[13]

While a deeply entrenched myth has developed about indigenous populations "living lightly on the land," the extension of that myth to the belief that
Native American groups were incapable of altering their environments to any
significant degree has been foreclosed by the incontrovertible evidence of indi-
genes' widespread use of fire to shape the landscape in ways favorable to Native
livelihoods. The rule in many western ecosystems was frequent fire, both naturally occurring (ignited by lightning strikes) and anthropogenic. Fire ecologist
James Agee estimates that in an average pre-settlement year, 184,737 hectares
(465,495 acres) burned in the area that is now Washington and Oregon.[14] Such
figures, combined with the knowledge that human hands held the torch for
many of these fires, effectively quell the ailing myth of the early US West as wilderness. The western ecosystems encountered by whites, while seeming to their
eyes untouched, had in fact been modified through human labor and for human
needs, no less than those impacted by the farmers' fields, mines, and ranches that
soon dotted the landscape. This is not an argument that the transformative activities of indigenous groups were ecologically equivalent to those of Europeans, in
either quality or scale.

Euro-American expansion into the West profoundly affected that region's
ecology and landscape. One element of this transformation—one whose significance is only now becoming clear—was the effect of European settlement on the
pattern of fire, as Pyne thoroughly describes.[15] This is not, however, a simple case
of European colonists with no understanding of their new home and a genetically
encoded fear of fire moving in and having to stomp out the flames (although some
of this occurred). Many of the early settlers in the West either adopted elements of
Native burning practices themselves or grumblingly accepted that fire was a part
of the landscape, regardless of whether it was a help or a hindrance.[16] According
to a California forester in 1904, "The white man has come to think that fire is a
part of the forest, and a beneficial part at that."[17] In the Pacific Northwest, the
arrival of white settlers actually resulted in an increase in the number of anthropogenic burns.[18] Railways, logging, and land clearing combined to produce the
conditions for more frequent, larger, and more intense fires by strewing both
slash and sparks across the landscape.

The project to eliminate fire from the woods reached the western United
States, as it did other colonial peripheries, not just with the arrival of settlers
but also with industrial forestry[19] and the resulting commodification of forests.
Wholesale capitalist exploitation of forests followed the exploitation of labor as
it laid steel rails into the West. Mill towns sprung up along the tracks. Both the
railways and mill towns demanded fire protection "at least sufficient to get the

logs out of the woods in a form other than smoke and ash."[20] However, to say that the project of fire exclusion began with the arrival of industrial forestry and the resulting demand for protection overstates its antiquity, since desire and ability were distant cousins at best until the 1930s (around 125 years after Lewis and Clark arrived at the Pacific), and they only grew close following World War II, with the mechanization of fire fighting. While many foresters, both public and private, saw (or presented) fire as a menace beginning at least at the turn of the twentieth century, their distaste for burning was more than matched by their limited capacity to act on it. In 1900 an estimated 30 million acres of forest and grassland burned across the United States.[21] Dr. Greg Aplet of the Wilderness Society estimated that between 1930 and 1939, an average of 40 million acres burned annually.[22] In the 1960s that number ranged from a low of 2.6 million acres to a high of 7.1 million acres.[23] The majority of the reduction took place in the fifteen years between 1940 and 1955.[24] Significant reductions in burned area, then, are a recent phenomenon.

These impressive reductions were the stuff of early foresters' dreams. While debate over the role of fire in the forests simmered and occasionally flared during the first quarter of the twentieth century, by 1921 a dominant position (the evolution of which is the basis of chapters 3 and 4) emerged that fire was an unmitigated evil in the woods and that forestry would never get off the ground as long as the flames roamed unchecked. However, the development of an apparatus sufficient for the task—undertaken primarily by the USFS—took a long time. The Forest Service *Use Book* that served as the code for forest management in the very early years (up to 1911) sheds some light on the rudimentary nature of the federal agency's early fire-fighting apparatus. While admonishing rangers that "insurance against the destruction of property, timber resources, and water supply by fire"[25] was the greatest benefit to the community derived from the establishment of forest reserves (national forests) and that, accordingly, "officers of the Forest Service have no duty more important than protecting the reserves from forest fires,"[26] the book is sketchy on the details of fighting fire. The organization of citizens' brigades is mentioned briefly, but the *Use Book* is geared to a ranger patrolling his enormous territory on foot or horseback. Under the heading "How to Fight Fire," the book instructs him to carry an ax, a mattock, and a shovel and when he encounters a fire (it is hoped, while it is still small) to dig trenches, throw dirt on the flames, and, if necessary, light a backfire.[27] When one early ranger was asked on a Forest Service exam how to handle a crown fire (a fire that has moved into the canopy), he reportedly responded, "There's only one way: I'd run like hell and pray for rain."[28]

While this may be an honest assessment of the chances of stopping a full-blown crown fire today, as in 1905, the Forest Service—once dependent on its ability to roust barflies from local taverns to fight fires—has developed an infrastructure for fighting fires that is a paragon of industrial scale and efficiency and that runs from no fight. Today, the shovel-wielding lone ranger (possibly at the head of a posse) has been replaced with an army of trained, Nomex-clad, Pulaski-bearing firefighters, rolling engines, bulldozers, and a full-fledged (if dated) air force. On average, during the five years between 2000 and 2005, fire agencies (led by the USFS) annually mobilized 1,318 tactical crews, 1,241 engines, 15,000 overhead personnel, 446 helicopters, and 173 air tankers.[29] The Forest Service's ability to get resources where and when they are needed has become the standard by which other disaster management organizations are measured. The organization today successfully attacks and suppresses 98–99 percent of unwanted fires.[30] As a result, fire has become a fugitive, reduced to a small fraction of its former ecological influence.

SMOKEY AND ALL THAT: HOW THE USFS PUT(S) OUT FIRES

The story of how this came to be has been told elsewhere.[31] Its broad outlines are worth reviewing briefly here, however, in part because the story provides a foundation for the analysis in the chapters that follow and in part because it demonstrates more clearly the social content of fire. In addition, it reveals an important hole in the narrative. The account that follows, while strong on explaining the development of the state's capacity to put out fire, leaves unaddressed the question of why the Forest Service—which started out as a highly marginal, poorly resourced state agency—was given the means and the directive to undertake a war on fire.

We can very roughly divide Forest Service wildland fire policy into two periods: the declaration and escalation of the war on fire, running from the turn of the twentieth century to 1978, and the period of diplomatic détente, from 1978 to the present. Along the way, a number of policy milestones were passed that have become emblematic of the nation's relationship to fire. As we shall see, both the ideas underlying the US Forest Service's understanding of fire and the organizational resources that enabled its policies are inextricably connected to broader social events and forces.

Declaration and Escalation of War

The context for early efforts at fire suppression in the West was the hurly-burly of land grabbing, rail laying, mine blasting, and timber cutting through which white America helped itself to "fresh territory" following the Civil War. Historians have variously described this process as "feverish exploitation,"[32] an "orgy of resource abuse,"[33] and a "rape of gargantuan proportions."[34] The swath of the ax and the fires that followed were wide and bright enough to raise eyebrows, and a movement arose pushing for a more rational and efficient use of national resource wealth. As both Samuel Hays and William Robbins have pointed out, many of the corporations and capitalists involved in resource extraction, including timber capital, were perfectly amenable to the suggestion.[35] Their major concern, after all, was to bring stability to the frontier wildness and the economic unpredictability of the period.[36]

While European conservation measures in the United States date back at least to William Penn's demand that, on land he granted, one acre of woods be retained for every five cleared, they were largely un-enforced and ineffective. Most state involvement in forests was limited to moral support for planting trees, occasional surveys of the forests, and holding back enough standing oak to continue to float a navy.[37] Most historians set the blocks for the forest conservation race at Franklin B. Hough's address to the American Association for the Advancement of Science (AAAS) in 1873 on "the Duty of Governments in the Preservation of Forests." The AAAS was taken enough with Hough's message that it resolved to appoint a committee to "memorialize Congress and the several State legislatures upon the importance of promoting the cultivation of timber and the preservation of forests, and to recommend proper legislation for securing these objects."[38]

As it turned out, Hough was advocating for his own future job, since four years later, with a $2,000 appropriation from the US Congress (slipped in as a rider), he was hired to undertake a study of the "national wants in regard to timber, the probable supply for future wants, [and] the means best adapted to their preservation and renewal."[39] In 1878 Hough published his first of three *Reports on Forestry*, the last of which (published in 1882) focused on forest fires. Hough's report recommended a public reservation policy for timber. His suggestion was supported by the young American Forestry Association (AFA), a conservation organization in which Hough was also active. While on the surface this seems to indicate a push by an agency of civil society against the unfettered right of capital to exploit nature, the AFA—a flagship organization in the early conservation movement—was deeply penetrated by extractive capital.

In 1913 and 1914, right-wing Representative William E. Humphrey attacked the conservation movement (and the Forest Service) in the US House as a vehicle for the concentrated control of resources and markets by big capital at the expense of small capitalists. While Humphrey's goal was to smear the Forest

Service in an attempt to affect the opening of national forests to unrestricted private exploitation, his research is instructive in revealing the character of the conservation movement and the AFA specifically at the turn of the twentieth century. Humphrey filled two-and-a-half pages of the 1914 Congressional Record with small print bearing the names and short biographies of key members of the AFA, revealing that "a reading of the list of officers and members for years past is like reading a directory of the vested wealth of the United States and Canada." He reported that "a large proportion of the officers and membership is and has been for years made up of representatives of Pennsylvania coal and iron companies, New England manufacturing interests, electric and water power interests, the wood-pulp interests, the land-grant railways, and the great timberland barons and great lumber-manufacturing interests of the country."[40] Foresters concerned about the AFA's position on conservation and forestry issues reinforced Humphrey's concerns. Forester Raphael Zon, whose politics were on the far side of the spectrum from Humphrey's, referred to the predominance of timber capitalists in the AFA when he claimed that "it is not a secret, but the association is now under the influence of people who do not care to advance the cause of forestry in any shape or manner."[41] The AFA was undoubtedly saturated by the influence of resource capital.

The first incarnation of the modern Forest Service was established as the Division of Forestry in the USDA under Hough in 1881 and given legal recognition as a government agency in 1886, when it was taken over by the Prussian forester Bernhard Fernow. Four years into his tenure as division chief, Fernow famously cast the "fire problem" of US forestry as "one of bad habits and loose morals."[42] Fernow believed US incendiarism could be dealt with by passing and enforcing stricter laws against burning, as existed in Europe and Japan. A lax attitude toward the destructive nature of fire, Fernow held, was the key issue; he claimed "there is no other reason or necessity for these frequent and recurring conflagrations."[43] In this at least, Fernow was a pioneer, pointing toward US forestry's future view of fire as a troublesome menace, threatening both profitability and resource conservation (a rhetorical pairing laboriously forged by the timber industry). At its 1886 meeting, the AFA resolved that "fire is the most destructive enemy of the forest, and that most stringent regulations should be adopted by the National and State and Territorial governments to prevent its outbreak and spread in timber stands."[44] Almost fifty years later, the AFA repeated the claim that fire remained a problem because of "public carelessness and irresponsibility," which had "not been adequately dealt with by the states and the Federal Government."[45] This was and remains the message at the root of the Smokey Bear campaign.

For ten years the Division of Forestry was essentially a scientific rather than an administrative unit. While it encouraged the practice of forestry on private lands to some extent, the federal government had no forests of its own to administer. It was not until 1891 that the US Congress took Hough and the AFA to heart and authorized the establishment of the forest reserves that would eventually form the beginning of the National Forest System. Through a process that remains murky to historians (primarily because the papers of John W. Noble, then-secretary of the interior, seem to be lost),[46] a Section 24 was added in committee to what came to be known as the Forest Reserve Act authorizing the president to reserve forestlands. One year later President Benjamin Harrison used this power to set aside 13 million acres of land in fifteen reserves. Today, the National Forest System comprises 192 million acres.

While the origins and passage of Section 24 remain somewhat obscure, the real struggles regarding the forest reserves were not over their establishment but instead over who would manage them and for what purposes. The question of purposes was a struggle over preservation or use. The secretary of the interior understood and interpreted the 1891 Forest Reserve Act as a preservation effort. The 1897 Pettigrew Amendment to the Sundry Civil Appropriations Bill, which for the first time provided guidance for managing reserves, fell on the side of use by not specifically precluding it. According to Hays, the 1897 act "paved the way for federal officials in the future to permit grazing, commercial lumbering, and hydroelectric power generation within the forests, and to establish the national forest program clearly as one most concerned with rational development."[47]

The question of specific purposes was raised again in Gifford Pinchot's quest to wrestle control of the reserves away from the General Land Office of the Department of the Interior—a crusade that stretched from 1898, when Pinchot took over from Fernow as chief of the Bureau of Forestry, to 1905. In the end, Pinchot's promises to more fully open the forest reserves to commercial harvesting, mining, and grazing and his efforts to prevent them from becoming game parks proved effective.[48] By insisting that the forests be put to greater commercial use, he garnered key support from previously resistant western congressmen, as well as the American National Livestock Association, the Great Northern Railroad, the Northern Pacific Railroad, and the National Lumber Manufacturers Association.[49] At times, Pinchot is said to have "built up the National Forest System despite the hostility of western senators and representatives."[50] This is simply not the case. While there were occasional bitter tirades against the Forest Service (Senator Weldon Heyburn of Idaho was a famous antagonist), the birth and early development of the National Forest System enjoyed the support of the resource extraction industries and their many representatives and allies in the US Congress. Without the support of these organizations, won through the promise to keep forestlands accessible to exploitation, Pinchot's agency would never have been able to build the National Forest System. Despite (or perhaps, in the case of the AFA, because of) the commercial shift that gained industrial support, the AFA and the Sierra Club also supported the transfer.[51]

Having been assured that it would continue to have access to nature as a raw input, timber capital perceived the biggest threat to the perpetuation of the resource to be fire, and the USFS concurred. Having forcibly removed Native Americans from the land and then set aside significant acreage from settlement by whites, the Imperial state was obliged to appear a capable steward. Early Forest Service chiefs were tireless exponents of the "facts" that fire control was possible (a contention many found dubious),[52] wise, and indeed the foundation and sine qua non of forestry. The theme that fire protection—which, in the discourse of both the Forest Service and "progressive" lumbermen, meant a program of full suppression—was the "preliminary... essential first step" for forestry was pushed relentlessly by both the USFS and timber capitalists. In 1910 Chief Henry Graves published Bulletin 32, "Protection of Forests from Fire," in which he claimed unequivocally that "the first measure necessary for the successful practice of forestry is protection from forest fires."[53] Graves's successor, William B. Greeley, echoed the sentiment, stating that under his watch the progress of forestry in the United States would be measured by "smoke in the woods."[54] Pinchot had earlier warned that "like the question of slavery, the question of forest fires may be shelved for some time, at enormous cost in the end, but sooner or later it must be met" if the nation were to shift the production of timber from a mining to an agricultural model.[55] Just a dozen years later he optimistically asserted that "today we understand that forest fires are wholly in the control of men."[56]

Less frequently revealed is the fact that leading figures within the private sector were equally vociferous in connecting fire suppression with the adoption of forestry by private lumbermen. Wilson Compton, a key figure among politically organized timber capitalists and secretary-manager of the National Lumber Manufacturers Association, wrote in 1925 in *The Washington Post* that "the first step in any policy looking toward the conservation and perpetuation of forests is the prevention and control of forest fires." Never one to waste an opportunity to pitch for a subsidy, he added, "Primarily the responsibility for fire control must rest upon Federal and State agencies. The public must help."[57] Similarly, F. E. Weyerhaeuser claimed that the three great obstacles to the profitable reproduction of timber (and thus, in the timber industry's view, to forest conservation in the United States) were time, fire, and taxes.[58] Fire, he had argued before the US Congress in 1908, was primary among these: "To save the forests, the main thing is to make laws to prevent fires."[59]

Despite the rhetorical declaration of war on fire by the USFS, it had little capacity to act. While district foresters and rangers could do their best to be vigilant against fire in the national forests, there was no national fire policy, and cooperation among the federal agency, the states, and private owners was limited. Forest fire was monitored and controlled primarily by private associations of timber owners, states, and frontier townsfolk. It was not until the passage of the Weeks Act in 1911 that the USFS was authorized to cooperate financially and administratively with states and private landowners in the suppression and prevention of fire in forests that protected the watersheds of navigable rivers (navigability was broadly interpreted to mean any river down which a log could be floated, hinting at the real purpose of fire protection). This authority was expanded in 1924 by the Clarke-McNary Act, which removed the restriction of cooperation to those particular watersheds. These two acts made up the backbone of a national fire policy administered and controlled by the USFS, and the Clarke-McNary Act set the tone for the "cooperative" relationship between the Forest Service and the forest products industry for decades to follow.[60]

Following the Great Fires of 1910 (discussed in chapter 3) and up until the passage of the Clarke-McNary Act, the USFS wrestled both internally and with outside interests over the fire issue. The debate was reduced to a binary choice between reliance on light-burning "folk practices" and a no-holds-barred assault on fire.[61] Favoring the latter for a variety of reasons to which I return in chapter 4, the Forest Service sought a philosophical and practical framework for a national fire policy that could win the day against the doctrine and practices of its light-burning opponents.

This quest for a way to cope with fire coincided with the emergence of Frederick Winslow Taylor's scientific management as a revolutionary approach to maximizing industrial efficiency. Taylor's scientific management held that if managers could break tasks down into tiny parts and apply scientific principles to reduce the amount of time each part consumes, enormous efficiency could be attained. Taylor's ideas were mostly about controlling the movement of human bodies, turning workers into machines that would perform exact, repetitive motions in the act of production to increase profits. While it is questionable whether Taylor would have been so well-received in a society not dominated by the profit motive, his principles caught the imagination of all kinds of managers, not just those worried about profit. The Forest Service drew inspiration from his scientific management and applied it to fire protection. The guide that resulted was called *Systematic Fire Protection in the California Forests*, written by California forester Coert DuBois and published in 1914. It is a Taylorist masterpiece.

Just as the industrial engineers who applied Taylor's ideas to factories obsessed over tiny intervals of time, looking at how long it took a worker to complete a full swing of a hammer, DuBois's book made time the key variable in measuring the success of fire protection: the faster someone could see a fire, report it, reach it, and attack it, the greater the success in minimizing burned acreage and costs of suppression. The lesson from *Systematic Protection* was that all effort was to be put toward minimizing that interval of time. When the science of management became accomplished enough to reduce that time sufficiently, the war on fire would be won, and there would be no need to debate the pros and cons of quaint folkways involving the irresponsible and unrefined application of the torch to the woods.

DuBois's guide was time-obsessed. He presented charts on the speeds one could expect from horses' various gaits relative to the customary "flat-footed walk," noting the minutes one could save by urging the horse into a brisk trot, lope, or fast lope.[62] He emphasized that accurate recording of elapsed times for fire detection, reporting, and response was critical to improving efficiency, suggesting that "the supervisor should make arrangements for synchronizing the timepieces throughout the Forest organization. Standard Forest time should be given out from the Supervisor's office twice a week . . . The watch carried by the average ranger will not vary within this period to a degree which will render time figures unusable." His assessment of the degree of control over fires that could be attained and that in fact the public would demand was astonishingly optimistic: "In a very few years 10 acres will represent a protection standard that is too low. The people will demand that no fire be allowed to cover over 2 acres, and they will be willing to pay for that degree of protection . . . Any fire over 10 acres in size will be the subject of a most searching investigation to fix responsibility."[63] Minimizing the time between ignition and response was equated with maximizing efficiency in terms of both resources lost and dollars spent. While a competing model held that suppression should be regulated by a net present value calculation that weighed the costs of suppression against the value of resources preserved, the complications of valuing standing timber (given wild price fluctuations over time and the slipperiness of non-timber values) made doing so impractical.

Within the private sector as well, timber industrialists drew on Taylorism in their deliberations on how to cope with fire. In the early 1900s the Western Forestry and Conservation Association (WFCA), a key organization in the network of organized timber capitalists, formed a Standardization Committee dedicated to sharing experiences and ideas related to fire and coordinating fire suppression activities. Much of this mission boiled down to collecting the accumulated experience of private fire association workers in the field and distilling it into a uniform "approved digest" for use by all fire protective associations. There was great concern that current forest workers' skills and experience would be lost if they quit or retired or should themselves "be lost."[64] While some committee members argued the difficulty of reducing field experience to a codified and universally applicable system of rules and practices that any worker could execute, the committee's main spokesman urged the importance of the task. Walter D. Humiston, in his reflections to the WFCA on whether to continue the work of the Standardization Committee, quotes approvingly and at length the work of Harrington Emerson, a disciple of Frederick Taylor and the founder of the first generalized consulting agency in the United States. Emerson propounded the principles of efficiency and applied them not just to specific engineering problems but to organizational and managerial problems as well. His key contribution was the idea of optimizing the sum of the net benefits of several factors to come up with a way "elements can be combined so as to secure the best results." To accomplish this, a single task, or goal, had to be expressed. In this case, the task was "to protect the timber of the Pacific Northwest from forest fires."[65]

At the Mathers Field Conference in 1921—the first national conference held by the Forest Service—DuBois's model of time-based suppression planning was made doctrine, and in the eyes of the USFS the public debate over light burning was finished. Time of suppression was to be the key measure of fire protection's success. This idea was responsible in part for the push of infrastructure into the backcountry of national forests—the process Elers Koch lamented in "The Passing of the Lolo Trail," quoted at the beginning of this chapter. If time was of the essence, the USFS wanted people in the backcountry as soon as it could get them there; it wanted people in place to spot fires as early as possible, and it wanted communication systems to sound the alarm. Hence the incursion of roads, trails, lookout towers, and telephone wires deep into the backcountry. This focus on the need to minimize the time between ignition and control was fully cemented in 1935 with the 10 AM Policy, which decreed that the Forest Service should plan and mobilize to suppress any fire by 10 AM the day after it was spotted. If that was not accomplished, the goal was to put it out by 10 AM the next day, and so on. This policy had remarkably long-lasting appeal, surviving a policy review in 1967, only to be finally abandoned as official policy in 1978.

Establishing a policy is one thing; gathering the necessary resources to carry it out is another. While the Forest Service had won the legal capacity to deficit spend for emergency suppression in 1908 (a policy put to the test and proven solid in 1910, when the USFS handed the US Congress a bill for $1.1 million for the Idaho and Montana fires), it lacked anything near the resources required for both backcountry fire fighting and preparedness. As a result, the 10 AM Policy would only have been so much chatter had it not been for the fact that the United States was in the throes of a massive economic crisis that left the country with a huge supply of surplus labor. The stock market crash in 1929 and the Depression that followed were highly felicitous events for the USFS, as the agency attracted more than its share of the government-mobilized unemployed in the form of Emergency Conservation Works (ECW) crews and, later, the Civilian Conservation Corps. The CCC and ECW crews were assigned to both public and private lands.[66] Their work in the forests consisted primarily of fire protection, both direct (fighting fires) and indirect (constructing breaks and infrastructure).[67] The Forest Service administered 80 percent of all ECW work projects and benefited as well from the Public Works, Civil Works, and Transient Relief Programs. In 1936 Chief Forester Ferdinand "Gus" Silcox reported that "more than one and one-half million young men" had taken part in forest conservation as members of the CCC.[68]

Without this release of surplus labor into the woods, the policy of all-out suppression would certainly have lacked the necessary infrastructure on both federal and non-federal lands. On just the latter, in their first year of operation CCC crews from hundreds of camps scattered throughout the forests strung 6,878 miles of telephone line, cut 14,279 miles of firebreaks, built 15,298 miles of roads and trails, erected 213 lookout towers, and constructed 53 lookout houses.[69] The State Commission of Forestry for Alabama reported that "through the operation of the CCC we have been able to obtain for the more heavily forested localities of the State detection, communication, and transportation facilities which would have required years to secure otherwise."[70] Mobilization of men under the Forest Service's ECW programs took place with time-based performance in mind, and the results seemed a vindication of DuBois's model of systematic protection. The 60 percent reduction in acreage burned and reduced loss of commercial timber value between 1932 and 1933 were attributed to the "presence of hundreds of Emergency Conservation camps in the national forests on forest improvement jobs."[71] This was an odd reversal of trends elsewhere in the world where surplus labor has been vented into forested lands. In Brazil and Indonesia's massive transmigration programs, for example, surplus workers were encouraged to migrate to

FIGURE 2.1. "Our Carelessness: Their Secret Weapon" was one of several wartime posters intended to tie forest fire prevention to national defense. Artist unknown. US Department of Agriculture, 1943. Available at http://www.nh.gov/nhsl/ww2/ww30.html; accessed May 5, 2009.

the rainforests to colonize and farm. In both cases this led to massive increases in agricultural burning. As labor was turned out into the forests, rivers of flame followed its path. In the case of the United States, where millions of unemployed were mobilized, fire was smothered as detection, communication, and transportation systems were pushed ever further into the backcountry to ensure a minimum elapsed time between ignition and an effective suppression response.

This massive injection of manpower dried up quickly, however, with the arrival of World War II and the end of the New Deal programs. To sustain the commitment to full suppression embodied in the 10 AM Policy, the USFS drew upon relationships forged with the US military during the war to mechanize the process. During World War II, wildland fire became tied to the rhetoric and systems of national defense as the Forest Service established cooperative agreements with the Office of Civil Defense and the Department of Defense.[72] Figure 2.1 illustrates a typical articulation of wildland fire and national defense. Appropriations for fire preparedness were made for strategic national areas under the banner of defense, first from Germany and Japan and then in the context of the Cold War. The Cold War and the threat of nuclear warfare prompted an injection of fire research funding into the Forest Service, which studied the physics and control of mass fire of the type the Allies had unleashed on Dresden and the United States had ignited over Hiroshima and Nagasaki.

FIGURE 2.2. Smokey and before. Available at http://www.smokeybear.com/
vault/default.asp ("Death . . . ," "Please . . . ," and "This . . .") and at http://www.
state.sc.us/forest/posters.htm ("Thou . . ."); accessed May 14, 2006. Smokey Bear
images used with the permission of the USFS.

In addition to funding for preparedness and research, the other great boons that resulted from the Forest Service's military connections were access to surplus machinery and equipment development. The military conducted joint tests with the USFS to check the capabilities of helicopters and air tankers for wildland fire fighting.[73] Once their potential was established through field experiments (such as the creatively named "Operation Firestop"), they became a mainstay of backcountry fire suppression. As Pyne reported, "After the Korean conflict, an immense storehouse of war-surplus equipment became available, to which the Forest Service and its collaborators had priority access. Its sudden mechanization, most spectacularly with aircraft, allowed fire suppression to extend its reach over the countryside . . . It was a golden age for equipment development and scientific research."[74] During this period the Forest Service and its allies in the private sector and among state foresters were also able to triple the appropriation for Clarke-McNary funds, thereby infusing the cooperative programs with new funding.

The final hurdle for a policy of full suppression, which the agency had committed to organizationally and gathered the required resources to implement, was to bring what was perceived as a careless or even downright incendiary public onside. Drawing on the resources of the Wartime Advertising Council and the cultural reach of Walt Disney (through "Bambi"), the Forest Service launched one of the most successful ad campaigns in US history. The USFS icon, Smokey Bear, is among the most recognized figures in the US cultural landscape, and many can recite his message without prompting. However, the struggle to represent fire as an unmitigated evil in the woods actually got under way decades prior to Smokey's invention by the admen of the Foote, Cone, and Belding Agency. Poster campaigns, print advertising, special issues of magazines and trade journals, radio spots, and a roaming evangelical-style troupe (the AFA-sponsored Dixie Crusaders) were all employed to mobilize the nation into a posture of vigilant guardianship against fire in the woods.[75] From the beginning, the propaganda war against fire attempted to tap into resonant themes of patriotism and Christian piety (figure 2.2). The editors of a 1939 issue of *American Forests*, dedicated to fire prevention, recalled Revolutionary America:

> America needs a rebellion of consciousness to bring to life a public will to stop forest fires . . . to bring to bay with guns of public opinion a national enemy that is dropping fire brands somewhere in our land at the rate of one every three minutes day and night . . . Patriotism in America may lack the virility of old and with some it may be out of fashion, but it is not dead. There are still millions of people who . . . are ready and eager to become Paul Reveres on the

public opinion highways of our country. By those highways only can we ever hope to attain a public will to prevent forest fires.[76]

For use in its campaign in the South in 1937, the Forest Service cobbled together a pamphlet on "Forest and Flame in the Bible," pulling out such divine support for fire prevention as "a fire devoureth before them; and behind them a flame burneth: . . . behind them a desolate wilderness, yea, and nothing shall escape them. –Joel 2:3."[77] Once Smokey came on the scene, as the posters in figure 2.2 amply demonstrate, themes of patriotism and piety remained strong.

This campaign has been highly successful. Advocates of the Smokey program (administered as part of the Cooperative Forest Fire Prevention program) repeatedly posited a causal relationship between Smokey's long reach[78] and the declining number of fires and acres burned.[79] Social scientific research in the 1970s confirmed that the USFS and its partners' public relations efforts had been effective. William Folkman's early research into public perceptions of fire demonstrated a strong negative perception of forest fire and strong support for all-out suppression.[80] A survey of relevant research by Gary Machlis and his colleagues, however, suggested that the effects of anti-fire propaganda may not be so deep-seated in the US psyche. Their review of the literature on public perceptions of wildland fire showed that "the public has grown more knowledgeable about wildland fires and their effects, understands the benefits of wildland fires, and supports management practices that allow wildland fires."[81] At least, the public is supportive until the prospects of wildland fire escaping prescription or damaging property are raised, at which point support seems to waver.[82]

Détente?

Machlis and his colleagues' summary of conclusions is reflective of a retreat from the Forest Service's all-out war on fire and a new public relations emphasis on fire as an ecological process vital to forest health. The death knell of the 10 AM Policy sounded in 1978, when the new *National Forest Manual* dictated a "pluralistic" approach to fire, including the use of the once-heretical tool of deliberate light burning (now labeled prescription burning) and increased discretion by fire managers regarding the initiation and continuation of suppression actions.[83] The National Park Service had cleared the way for this transition a decade earlier, with its own prescribed fire and "let burn" policy provisions,[84] and the USFS began dabbling in natural fire experiments in 1972.[85] More recent fire policy reviews have reiterated and strengthened the Forest Service's commitment to fire "management," as opposed to fire "suppression." In 1995 a Federal

Wildland Fire Management Policy was adopted by all federal land management agencies. Updated in 2001 and still the lodestar of fire management, the policy makes firefighter safety the top priority and claims that "fire as a critical natural process will be integrated into land and resource management plans and activities on a landscape scale across agency boundaries. Response to wildland fires is based on ecological, social, and legal consequences of the fire. The circumstances under which a fire occurs, and the likely consequences on firefighter and public safety and welfare, natural and cultural resources, and values to be protected, dictate the appropriate response to fire." Further, the policy claims that "wildland fire will be used to protect, maintain, and enhance resources and, as nearly as possible, be allowed to function in its natural ecological role."[86]

This policy seems a far cry from the bad old days of the 10 AM and 10 Acres Policies, allowing supervisors and managers the flexibility to make judgments about whether, when, and where to reintroduce fire as a key ecosystem process. However, a somewhat grim assessment of progress in implementing this policy emerged in 2000: "Although the current policies of all four wilderness management agencies clearly recognize the importance of fire as a natural part of wilderness ecosystems, implementation of wilderness fire programs varies greatly between agencies and is far from what would be required to restore natural fire regimes."[87] J. Boone Kauffman contributed to the gloom by noting that "about 3 out of every 1,000 [fires] were managed under the policy of wildland fire use" between 1998 and 2002.[88] Since these assessments, further progress has been made on the paper front in enabling a more flexible approach to fire management, moving the USFS further from the strict 10 AM Policy. New implementation guidelines for the 1995 Federal Wildland Fire Management Policy were published in 2009, enshrining for land management agencies the principle of Appropriate Management Response. With the realization that this might imply that previous management responses had been *in*appropriate, the language was changed to Response to Wildland Fire. These guidelines enable fire managers to manage the same fire for different resource objectives and to adopt different management options over space and time. Thus a fire might be aggressively suppressed on one front, where it threatens a community or a structure, while on another front it might be allowed to burn to accomplish fuels reduction goals.[89]

Given the novelty of these implementation guidelines, it is too early to tell what kind of difference they will make in terms of tactical action on the ground. The unit chosen as the vanguard for putting the new guidelines into practice was the Sequoia/Kings Canyon National Park, with the 2008 Tehipite and Hidden fires. Indeed, the park employed a variety of management responses on the two fires, hitting the Hidden fire full force where it threatened to escape the park boundary and allowing it to accomplish some restoration goals on another patch of acreage. With the Tehipite fire, the key consideration was the firefighters' safety; after several injuries, a determination was made—accounting for geography, distance from developed areas, and weather conditions—not to attempt to immediately suppress the fire. It is difficult to tease many lessons from this test that might enable us to predict its implications for Forest Service or Bureau of Land Management (BLM) fire management, in part because the Fire Management Plan for Sequoia/Kings Canyon already allowed for a very flexible management response. The Sequoia/Kings Canyon plan contains no full suppression zones or wildland fire use zones but enables almost any management response anywhere in the park. Park officials have stated that they would not have responded to the fires any differently prior to the new policy. What the policy does do, according to the park's fire management officer, is enable a thoughtful, non-rationalized (in the Weberian sense that it reduces the system's highly formalized, rule-bound nature while enhancing the role of human decision-making) response to fire on federal lands and enable multiple agencies to operate under a single planning document.[90]

Further limiting the lessons the USFS can learn from the Sequoia/Kings Canyon trial run is the fact that the USFS and other land management agencies have different missions than the National Park Service and different geographies of land ownership and development surrounding their lands. So it remains to be seen whether the 2008 implementation guidelines will make a significant difference in fire management practices. I return to the problematic intersection of policy and practice in USFS fire management in chapter 6. For now, the important point is that efforts to reorient the approach to wildland fire in the West strain against the bonds of history. The manifestations of a century-long war—infrastructural, organizational, economic, legal, cultural, and ideological—prevent a simple restoration of fire to its natural role in forest ecosystems. What has this meant for nature in the West?

ECOLOGICAL IMPLICATIONS

The ecological consequences of containing fire vary enormously from place to place. Different forest types and tree species have evolved in different fire regimes, and the removal of fire will accordingly have different results. I do not intend to review here the literature on fire ecology in the West, but the interested reader has no shortage of excellent resources to consult.[91] The relevant issue for this book is

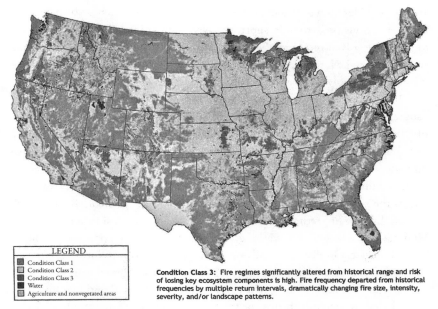

LEGEND
- Condition Class 1
- Condition Class 2
- Condition Class 3
- Water
- Agriculture and nonvegetated areas

Condition Class 3: Fire regimes significantly altered from historical range and risk of losing key ecosystem components is high. Fire frequency departed from historical frequencies by multiple return intervals, dramatically changing fire size, intensity, severity, and/or landscape patterns.

FIGURE 2.3. Fire regime condition classes. Source: USFS Fire Regime Condition Class Map, 2000. Available at http://www.fs.fed.us/rm/pubs/rmrs_gtr87/rmrs_gtr87_pg37.jpg; accessed March 9, 2010.

that ecologists across the board agree that the drive to remove fire from the forests is akin ecologically to removing sunlight or rain. Burning is a key ecological process that both shapes and is shaped by the structure and character of the forest. Fire's frequency, distribution, and intensity will affect the distribution and health of forest types and tree species, and some tree species are highly dependent on fire—either at frequent or infrequent return intervals—for their reproduction. Ponderosa pine (*Pinus ponderosa*), for example, relies on frequent, low-intensity burns to wipe out less fire-resistant competitors. Coastal Douglas fir (*Pseudotsuga menziesii* var. *menziisii*), on the other hand, counts on high-intensity, infrequent fires to help it out-compete more shade-tolerant species.[92]

Vegetative structure and distribution have major effects on the size, distribution, and viability of wildlife populations as well. Contrary to the message conveyed by the teary-eyed critters depicted on Smokey Bear posters and the terrifying imagery of Walt Disney's Bambi, forest fires kill and harm relatively few animals, since most can either flee or find shelter with considerable ease.[93] Once the fires have passed, new habitat is created in dead and downed trees, and new growth provides food for small mammals, deer, and elk—which, in turn, provide prey for various predators. In short, the plant and animal communities we see today have evolved in tandem with the shifting pattern of fire and forests that emerged after the last Ice Age, about 11,000 years ago. The removal of that process has predictably had major but differentiated consequences.

To gain a firmer grasp of what ninety years of suppression has meant for the flammability and health of western forests, fire scientists have attempted to classify the extent of departure from historical fire regimes (pre–European settlement)[94] using the concept of the Fire Regime Condition Class (FRCC). This is a three-tier classification system (FRCC 1 through 3) in which FRCC 1 represents the least difference between current and historical conditions and FRCC 3 represents the most difference. On lands labeled FRCC 1—particularly those with historically long fire-return intervals (such as on the western side of the Cascade Mountains in Oregon and Washington)—the history of suppression has made little difference. On FRCC 3 lands—often those with historical fire regimes that have a frequent fire-return interval (0–35 years)—the difference is significant (as, for example, is the case in central and southern Oregon) and may also have been altered by logging, grazing, or the introduction of exotic species. FRCC 3 lands are defined as those at high risk of losing key ecosystem components. The USFS has classified 26 percent of National Forest lands as FRCC 3 and 41 percent as FRCC 2. In short, the Forest Service has declared that 132 million acres (of a total of 197 million acres) are at moderate or high risk from wildland fire.[95] Figure 2.3 depicts a coarse-scale map of FRCCs for the United States. While the USFS uses such data to assist it in targeting its fuel management priorities, for our purposes it can be understood as a broad-brush illustration of the social content of wildfire beginning with European settlement. Black areas indicate FRCC 3, and dark gray indicates FRCC 2.

RESURGENT FIRE?

There are signs, however, that despite its massive apparatus, the Forest Service's grip on fire is beginning to slip. Data on the size and frequency of large fires show a disturbing (to some) upward trend—one also reflected in the cost of suppression (figure 2.4). Total appropriations for wildfire protection in 2005 were $2.9 billion. In 2000, 2002, and 2003, suppression costs alone topped $1 billion. In 2002, the year in which three western states had their largest fires on record (the Biscuit fire in Oregon, the Hayman fire in Colorado, and the Rodeo-Chediski fire in Arizona), the relevant agencies spent a combined total of $1.6 billion, with

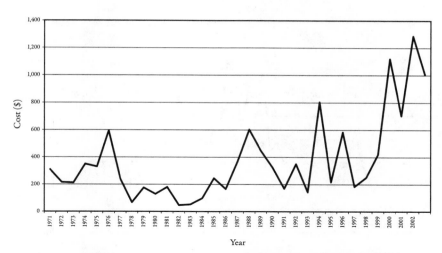

FIGURE 2.4. Suppression costs for the USFS, 1971–2002, show a remarkable upward trend from the low levels of the late 1970s and early 1980s. Data sources: United States Forest Service Central Accounting Data Inquiry (to 2000) and Foundation Financial Information System (2000–2002). Courtesy, Krista M. Gebert, USFS economist.

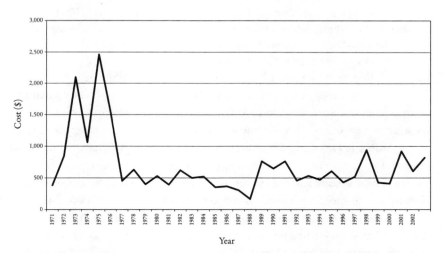

FIGURE 2.5. USFS suppression costs per acre burned have not risen dramatically since 1971. Data sources: costs: United States Forest Service Central Accounting Data Inquiry (to 2000) and Foundation Financial Information System (2000–2002); acres burned: National Interagency Fire Management Integrated Database. Courtesy, Krista M. Gebert, USFS economist.

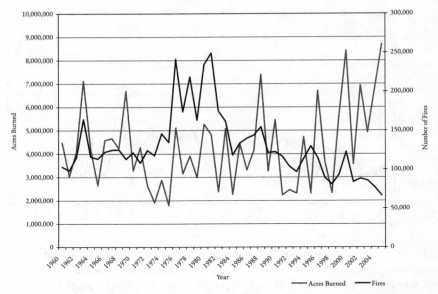

FIGURE 2.6. Number of fires and acres burned, all public lands, 1960–2005. A relatively close correlation between the two variables breaks down after 1987, as acres burned trends upward and number of fires trends downward. Data source: National Interagency Fire Center, Wildland Fire Historical Statistics, Total Fires and Acres, 1960–2005. Available at http://www.nifc.gov/stats/wildlandfirestats. html; accessed March 16, 2006.

the USFS alone spending $1.1 billion on suppression.[96] Following the expensive 2000 season and a critical assessment of wildland fire management carried out by the General Accounting Office in 1999, congressional attention came to bear on what was perceived to be an uncontrolled rise in suppression expenditures.[97] In response, the Forest Service undertook internal reforms aimed at controlling costs and putting in place more transparent accounting.[98]

However, research by Forest Service economists shows that despite claims about wasteful spending and the skyrocketing costs of fire suppression, the per-acre costs of suppression have not increased significantly since the 1970s (see figure 2.5). Rather, the pattern is one of expenditures moving in tandem with the size and frequency of large fires.

The changing fire pattern is linked primarily to changing climate, with the period 1987–2003 exhibiting longer and more severe alternating wet and dry periods. Fine fuels (the most flammable vegetation) build up during wet periods and become ripe for ignition during long dry spells. David Calkin and his colleagues, using data for Forest Service lands only, suggest that this phenomenon, in interaction with an already existing overabundance of fuels from fire suppression, has led to the increase in fire size and severity.[99] A review of data for all fire-reporting public land management agencies confirms the pattern. The correlation between the number of fires and the number of acres burned breaks down after 1987 ($r = 0.33$ for the period 1968 to 1986, while $r = -0.05$ for the period 1987 to 2005; see figure 2.6).

THREATS, DEVASTATION, AND DANGEROUS PLANS: THE (RE-)POLITICIZATION OF FIRE

Numerous scholarly, journalistic, and technical/managerial publications have commented on this shift toward bigger, more severe blazes.[100] They all acknowledge that shifts in forest structure as a result of land-use decisions have contributed to the change in fire behavior. However, commentators vary considerably in their assessment of exactly what kinds of land uses are to blame and what should be done about the problem. The Office of the President has suggested that the problem lies with "radical changes during the last century due to the suppression of fires and a lack of active forest and rangeland management."[101] President George W. Bush clarified what he meant by "a lack of active management" during the 2004 presidential debate in St. Louis when he said that "what happens in those forests, because of lousy federal policy, is they grow to be . . . they're not harvested . . . And as a result, they're like tinderboxes."[102] Others blame the USFS's bureaucratic "scientific-managerial" approach to fire, rooted in Progressive-Era notions of control over nature[103]—a claim that, as we shall see, provides a partial but far from complete explanation. Still others blame logging, road construction, urban development, livestock grazing, and habitat fragmentation.[104]

In short, the result of the big fires in recent years has been a renewed politicization of fire management. Under the cover of debates about "what ought to be done with fire" lurks the larger debate about "what ought to be done with the forests." Rhetorical struggles over access to the nation's forests are taking place increasingly on the field of fire management—a terrain deeply structured by fear. Antagonists in the struggle over forest policy are at pains to associate their projects with a reduction in the risk of catastrophic wildfire that now looms over every western city, town, hamlet, and subdivision. This holds true across the spectrum, from the president and members of the US Congress,[105] timber trade associations,[106] and libertarian think tanks[107] to conservation organizations[108] and wilderness preservationists.[109] The USFS now covers much of its management activities—from timber sales to habitat restoration—under the protective shroud of fuels management and wildfire hazard reduction.

The politicization of wildfire has been particularly visible in two major areas of forest policy: fuels management and post-disturbance logging. The first of these came out of the technical realm of the Forest Service and into the public eye during the buildup to the Healthy Forests Initiative (HFI, 2002) and the Healthy Forests Restoration Act (HFRA, 2003). President Bush, standing in the blackened aftermath of the Squires Peak fire in Oregon in 2002, repeatedly invoked the dangers of catastrophic fire in announcing the HFI, liberally deploying the language of fear (fire "devastates," "kills," "rages," "threatens," and "ruins") as he laid out the case for exempting thinning projects from environmental review and appeal. According to President Bush's speech that day: "Our policy has not had the health of our forests in mind. The hands off policy that have [sic] contributed to this environmental crisis have [sic] been well-intentioned; no question about that. Nobody is questioning the intentions of those who have helped put this policy in place. But they're dangerous—dangerous plans. And we've got to do something about it."[110]

The initial thrust of the president's efforts to "do something about it" involved a heavy reduction in avenues for public oversight of USFS fuels management projects that involved forest thinning. The logic behind the HFI and the HFRA was that forests were overcrowded as a result of professional land managers' inability to actively manage them. This inability, in turn, was cast as a product of overzealous and litigious environmental groups that used the National Environmental Policy Act (NEPA, 1970) and the courts to block much-needed fuels management projects that involved logging.[111] Many of the USFS and BLM fire managers interviewed for this project agree with this assessment. Research by the US General Accounting Office (GAO) into the claim that litigation—particularly "frivolous" litigation by environmentalists, as President Bush's administration framed it—is the source of the problem suggests that the claim is exaggerated. The GAO found that of 818 Forest Service decisions on fuels management in 2001 and 2002, only 3 percent were litigated. Only 24 of the 818 decisions were appealed, and of those, 79 percent were processed within 90 days.[112] The Bush administration tied fuels reduction and fire protection to promises of increased harvesting of old-growth timber in the Pacific Northwest.[113] Mark Rey—USDA undersecretary for natural resources and the environment, former timber industry lobbyist, and the man directly in charge of the Forest Service at the time—proposed allowing increased commercial harvesting in return for licensees doing some of the thinning. "If we're going to be able to do this [restore forests to a less fire-prone structure] in anything less than forty years, we're going to have to find ways to encourage investment by partners who will help defray the costs," Rey explained.[114] Environmental groups, in response, charged that the increased threat of wildfires was a product of past logging practices facilitated by the Forest Service and that while forest restoration was indeed a vital goal, including some thinning, the USFS was using it as a cover to open up more public lands to commercial logging, which would do nothing to reduce the wildfire hazard.[115]

A similar struggle has erupted over the issue of post-disturbance (which includes post-fire) logging in the national forests—so-called salvage logging. This has been a bone of contention between much of the environmental community and the USFS ever since the establishment of the Emergency Salvage Timber Sale Program (the "salvage rider") as part of the Emergency Supplemental Appropriations and Rescissions Act in 1995. This piece of legislation—authored largely by Mark Rey, then-aide to Idaho senator Larry Craig—exempted post-fire timber sales from administrative appeal, reduced their environmental planning requirements, and limited the period for judicial review. The program expired in 1996, with Al Gore later lamenting its signing as the biggest mistake the Clinton administration made.

A similar piece of legislation, the Forest Emergency Recovery and Research Act (FERRA), was making its way through the US Congress in 2005–2006. FERRA followed on the heels of the HFI and HFRA as a second flashpoint in the debate over fire management on public lands. While the HFI and HFRA address the issue of forest management pre-fire, FERRA dealt with post-fire management. Specifically, it attempted to codify into law the idea that active post-disturbance management, including timber sales to extract downed and dead timber or standing trees with a high probability of mortality up to five years from the event, is both economically and ecologically advantageous. This claim was and remains highly disputed, particularly with regard to the ecological consequences of post-fire logging. Numerous studies present the alleged ecological benefits of post-disturbance harvesting as either dubious or actively detrimental to forest recovery.[116] Given that somewhere between 35 and 50 percent of logging on the national forests would have fallen under the categories exempted from NEPA and the Endangered Species Act (1973) under FERRA,[117] its passage would have represented a very significant shift in power over the determination of forest management, from the public (through its use of the review and appeals processes) to forest supervisors within the USFS. While FERRA passed in the US House of Representatives, it was never voted on in the US Senate.

Fire management, then, is the new frontier in the struggle over US forests. Forest policy and the practice of forestry on the national forests now take place largely within the overarching context of the "forest health crisis" and the priority of fuels management. Two major initiatives aimed at opening up the national forests to increased timber harvesting have been proposed either in response to or under the cover of the rise of catastrophic wildfire. Conservationists and preservationists resist these initiatives on the same basis. In the midst of this struggle, the question has inevitably arisen: who or what built this potential inferno around westerners? Regardless of the fact that Americans have moved, and continue to move, into ecosystems that have repeatedly burned for at least hundreds of years (and probably more), the emergence in the last several years of what appears to be an increasingly volatile and severe fire regime has caused many to turn an accusatory eye toward the nation's federal foresters.

CHAPTER THREE

FORESTER-KINGS?

Fire Suppression and the State

> From Gifford Pinchot on, the chiefs of the Forest Service have been as
> monarchs on the richest areas of the public domain. It is a field of authority
> which Presidents and departmental secretaries seldom invade, in which even
> Congress treads with care.
>
> *From "The Lumber Business," unpublished manuscript by James Stevens and Robert E.*
> *Mahaffey, public relations counsel to the West Coast Lumbermen's Association, 1946*

As Americans, and westerners in particular, started to hear about the "forest
health crisis" and fires began to take on more spectacular proportions, a dominant narrative emerged to explain how it all went wrong. The specific mix of
culprits responsible for the increasingly unmanageable behavior of wildland fire
varies and in some cases is hotly argued. Two hundred years of fossil fuel combustion and the associated carbon dioxide emissions resulting in climate change
must take some of the blame. Climate, however, reacts with an altered landscape
to produce current fire patterns. Primary responsibility for the production of that
landscape, and thus for catastrophic wildfires and declining forest health in general, has been laid largely on the shoulders of the nation's public land managers
in the USFS. Most versions of the history frame the situation as a tragedy: a case
of noble intentions thwarted by a fatal flaw—usually cast as a misguided belief
in human domination of nature.[1] For the dean of US fire history, Stephen Pyne,
the story is one of technocratic rule by a Forest Service forever scarred by the
experience of the Great Fires of 1910, discussed later in this chapter.[2] A few inter-
pretations see the situation in slightly more malevolent shades, highlighting the

politically motivated suppression of a sound but heretical science[3] or presenting it as a simple case study on the evils of public meddling in affairs better dealt with by the private sector.[4]

In this chapter I examine these accounts of fire history and unpack their sociological and political assumptions. In particular, I look at three elements held in common among accounts of US fire policy: (1) the extraordinary degree of autonomy accorded the USFS, (2) the argument that fire policy was a product of technocratic rule by an organization with too much faith in its own scientific expertise, and (3) the argument that fire policy was rooted in an ideology of conservation that was drilled into a highly professionalized and missionary USFS corps and that had the support of a group of northeastern elites. Together, these three claims form the backbone of the dominant narrative of fire in the United States expressed in scholarly, journalistic, activist, and policy/technical literatures.

Without explicitly doing so, this narrative draws upon and reinforces a specific theory of the state. While this may seem like a completely academic issue, it has enormous implications for the way activists, scholars, and practitioners approach the important question of fire policy reform. Reformers both inside and outside the Forest Service are actively shaping their strategies and making demands with an unacknowledged model of state behavior, capacities, and goals in the background. We need to ask whether this model accurately reflects the history of fire and forest policy. Are the wildfires of today really the product of an agency executing its own ideologically motivated agenda? Furthermore, does the underlying theory contain an accurate assessment of the scope for autonomous action by a state agency in the United States? If it does not, then strategies for reform need to be reshaped with a more realistic (empirically verified) assessment of how the state is likely to behave within the political-economic context of capitalism.

The next section briefly reviews state-centered theory. Those familiar with this body of work or those interested primarily in the history of fire management might wish to skip to the section "The Fire Narrative: State-Centered Commitments."

STATE-CENTERED THEORY: A BRIEF REVIEW

The theory of the state supporting (and drawing support from) the dominant narrative of fire can be broadly characterized as "state-centered." That is, in contrast to theories of the state that see elements of civil society acting through the state to pursue economic and political resources ("society-centered" theories), state-centered theories suggest that the state matters in and of itself. Policy outcomes, in the state-centered approach, are causally affected by the structure of political institutions (parties, bureaucracies), the intentional and unintentional effects of the behavior of state actors, or both. Within this theoretical framework, the state is an effective and significant actor in its own right, with interests and agendas specific to the various agencies and institutions that compose it. This theory contends that the state is not an agent of some other social principal; nor is it merely an institutionalized space in which various interests struggle. In the words of an early proponent of centering the state in political analysis, Eric A. Nordlinger, "the preferences of the state are at least as important as those of civil society in accounting for what the democratic state does and does not do; the democratic state is not only frequently autonomous insofar as it regularly acts upon its preferences, but also markedly autonomous in doing so even when its preferences diverge from the demands of the most powerful groups in society."[5]

State-centered political theory as a "self-conscious"[6] field of scholarship emerged in the 1980s, largely in response to perceived shortcomings in Marxist, elitist, and pluralist approaches to theorizing the state. In particular, scholars who became associated with the state-centric approach were critical of Marxist and neo-Marxist conceptions of the state as an instrument of capitalist class power and were equally critical of pluralists for understanding the state as an arena in which interests struggle over the allocation of government "outputs."[7] According to state-centered theorists, both pluralists and Marxists, along with the rest of western social science, failed to recognize the "explanatory centrality of states as potent and autonomous organizational actors."[8] In response, an eruption of scholarship began in the late 1970s and attained full flow during the 1980s and 1990s, in which a number of dependent variables—mostly policy outcomes— were explained primarily by reference to the structure of political institutions associated with the state (e.g., parties, bureaucracies) and with the will and capacity of state actors and organizations.

Scholars in this tradition staked out their claim to sociological legitimacy based on the canonical figure of Max Weber who, writing in turn-of-the-century Germany, had made the initial claim for the centrality of the state, both as an expression of domination through (legitimated) violence and also in structuring relations between elements of civil society itself.[9] Weber also argued that the power of a bureaucracy relative to those it "serves" (here he used as an example a state bureaucracy in the service of either a democratic or an aristocratic ruler), while theoretically up in the air, is "always great, under normal conditions overtowering."[10] In making this argument, Weber located the basis of this power in the bureaucrat's control over knowledge of both systems of administration and their objects.[11] There is undoubtedly much ambiguity in Weber's discussion of state bureaucracy with regard to its autonomy and power, particularly in that while he claimed that in the modern era rulers are increasingly dependent on the bureaucracy and that the bureaucracy contains its own "pure power interests" (which are not necessarily in line with the interests of those who formally rule), he also discussed the bureaucracy as a "highly developed power instrument in the hands of its controller"[12] and claimed that the economic effects of the structure of bureaucracy vary largely in accordance with the economic interests of the ruling class.[13]

The recent surge in state-centered theory following this Weberian path has been most empirically active in the areas of social policy—especially the development of the welfare state[14]—industrial policy,[15] and revolutions.[16] This largely comparative and historical work presents claims more unequivocal than Weber's: that the state—both in its organizational structure and its willful actions—significantly affects policy outcomes in ways that do not allow those outcomes to be attributed to either class-based interests (as they allege Marxists would have it) or the relative power of other non-state interest groups (as they allege the pluralists would have it).

A classic example is the contribution of state-centered theorists to the debate over the passage of the National Labor Relations Act (NLRA, or "Wagner Act") of 1935. Theda Skocpol and Kenneth Finegold argue in this context—against Michael Goldfield's class-based account[17]—that the form and timing of the state's response to increasing strike militancy in the 1930s cannot be explained except through reference to state autonomy from class interests. In Skocpol and Finegold's analysis, class conflict, manifested in the militant mobilizations of radical and communist organizers, is seen as having infinitely less influence on the formation of the NLRA than the internal machinations of state-employed lawyers and economists. Furthermore, they argue that New Deal labor legislation, far from an attempt on the behalf of capital to chill radical labor organizing and militancy, actually facilitated growth in union membership (and was an intentional effort by state actors determined to fill the void in labor relations left behind by the collapse of the National Industrial Recovery Act and "helped to make industrial workers more amenable to radical organizers than they otherwise would have been."[18]

Similarly, in another study Skocpol rejects class conflict as a significant cause of the early emergence of "social provisioning" in the United States. In *Protecting Soldiers and Mothers*, Skocpol dismisses arguments that attempt to explain this emergence using the strength of organized labor in class struggles, the "enlight-ened self-interests" of welfare capitalists, or the subordination of the state to capi-talist class interests.[19] She also sets aside non-Marxist explanations based on the particular character of "national values" alone or the mechanical unfolding of welfare along with industrialization and the rise of wage labor.[20]

Rather, she argues that each of these society-centric models of policy develop-ment erroneously sees the state as an arena of conflict or as the agent of other social interests rather than as an agent with its own goals and capacities for autonomous action. She thus argues, in putting forward her own "structured polity" approach, that any theory of policy formation must take into account the ways political action is mediated by the interests, structures, and capacities of the state.[21]

Her argument is based on the historical development of Civil War, widows', and mothers' pensions in the United States and the failures of labor-led attempts to gain "paternalist" social provisioning (provisioning attached to participation in the wage labor force—a predominantly male role). The argument privileges the agency of middle-class activists and professionals in policy formation. According to Skocpol's account, particular characteristics of the US state (its loosely feder-ated structure, women's complete exclusion from the franchise, the male working class's early inclusion in the same, and the drive to move away from party patron-age) lent themselves to provide leverage for federally organized voluntary asso-ciations of middle- and upper-class women in their drive to extend a maternally and domestically based version of morality into the public sphere. She states: "Longstanding political structures—including early democratization for white males, along with a federal state that divides authority and gives legislatures and courts pivotal policymaking roles—have not encouraged U.S. industrial workers to operate as class-conscious political forces. The operations of political parties have also persistently discouraged class-consciousness, even though parties have become less patronage-oriented during the twentieth century."[22] On the other hand: "National and local groups claiming to speak for the collective interests of women were able to mount ideologically inspired efforts on behalf of mater-nalist social policies. Patterns of exclusion from—and temporary incorporation into—electoral politics shaped the possibilities for women's political conscious-ness."[23] Thus the key political actors in Skocpol's analysis include not only class-based actors (they are present, but they take on a much diminished role relative to Marxist and power elite accounts of policy development) but also politicians, reform-minded professionals and intellectuals employed by the state, and power-fully organized associations of the middle class—in this case, organized around gender.

The claims of most state-centered theorists have mellowed somewhat since the early flourish of strong language represented by Nordlinger's formulation. Rather, a central claim has become not that the state is always and everywhere autonomous but instead that state autonomy varies historically, even within capitalism, a single nation, or a single agency. Gregory Hooks, for example, argues that the United States Department of Agriculture (USDA) set up the conditions for its own "capture" by societal interests (in this case, the American Farm Bureau Federation), resulting in a loss of autonomy between the New Deal Era and the immediate postwar period.[24] Even as early as 1985, in her introduction to *Bringing the State Back In*, Skocpol was introducing a more nuanced approach to state-centered theory that backed away from blanket claims that the state was always and everywhere autonomous. Reflecting on her research with Finegold, which also focused on the relationship between the USDA and the American Farm Bureau Federation, she claimed: "In short, 'state autonomy' is not a fixed structural feature of any governmental system. It can come and go." This is true, she argued, because "the very *structural potentials* for autonomous state actions change over time, as the organizations of coercion and administration undergo transformations, both internally and in their relations to societal groups and to representative parts of government."[25] In a similar vein, C. Edward Paul has suggested that state autonomy should be understood as an interstitial phenomenon, with its potential located between the tensions of pluralist, democratic pressures and the power of the ruling elite. As such, Paul argued, the state's autonomy will vary widely across issues and decisions.[26] Claims have, in fact, been watered down to the extent that G. William Domhoff felt justified in stating that by advancing her "structured polity" approach in *Protecting Soldiers and Mothers*, Skocpol had sucked the content out of state autonomy theory and stuffed its empty husk with pluralism.[27]

State-centered theorists, however, claim otherwise—they claim that they hold to a distinct set of theoretical commitments, apart from those of society-centered scholars. Hooks painstakingly set out the distinctions between society- and state-centered theories.[28] I have adapted his table by distinguishing between Marxist and pluralist variants of society-centered theory in table 3.1.

Scholars in the state-centered tradition held to these basic commitments as their agenda began to shift toward explaining not only the consequences of state autonomy (such as the passage of the NLRA or the reorientation of industrial research and development) but the causes of its variation across time and place.[29] State-centered theorists have presented a number of hypotheses in their pursuit of this research agenda. Michael Mann, for example, suggests that the

TABLE 3.1. Commitments of society- and state-centered theories

Conceptual Issue	Society-Centered Theoretical Commitments		State-Centered Theoretical Commitments
	Marxist	*Pluralist*	
View of the state	State is a tool or partner of the capitalist class	State is an arena	State is potentially autonomous
Origin of policy Agenda	Defined by ruling-class interests	Defined by interest groups	Defined by state officials
Source of power of state officials	Power derived from organization of conditions for accumulation	Power derived from society, especially interest groups	Power derived from occupation of state offices
View of politics	Reflective of class struggle over exploitation, surplus, labor process, and so on	Struggle waged by organized interest groups over allocation of resources	Frequently involves a struggle over institutions and rules of process
Dynamics of transformation of the state	Shaped by the relative strength of contending classes	Shaped by changing balance of power in civil society	Shaped primarily by the balance of power internal to the state

Source: Adapted from Gregory Hooks, "From an Autonomous to a Captured State Agency: The Decline of the New Deal in Agriculture," *American Sociological Review* 55 (1990): 31, table 1

degree of state autonomy depends upon the growth of state capacities (because of the state's functionality for powerful groups) and the powerful groups' subsequent loss of control of state agencies (because of the latter's increasing ability to access and mobilize resources).[30] He argues that the increase in state capacities in the industrialized West has not enabled states to overcome the power of the capitalist class.[31] Drawing heavily on organizational theory, Bruce Carruthers approaches the causality question by suggesting three major determinants of state autonomy: homogeneity of personnel group affiliations (especially class background), the state agency's structural dependence on elements within its operational environment, and "possession of recognized expertise"[32] that allows states to produce their own independent definitions of problems and solutions. To this, Carmenza Gallo, in the context of arguing that power is an attribute not of organizations (such as the state) but rather of relationships, adds that autonomy vis-à-vis an economic elite is more likely if the state has access to other powerful allies.[33]

THE FIRE NARRATIVE: STATE-CENTERED COMMITMENTS

The dominant narrative of fire in the United States rests on a number of the theoretical commitments listed in Hooks's schema (see table 3.1) and suggests a variety of sources for the Forest Service's autonomy that reflect state-centered theorists' broad classification of causes. First, the state is held to have an extraordinarily high degree of autonomy, in that the policy agenda of fire suppression originates with state managers and is carried out despite opposition from timber owners, livestock producers, and the agency's own scientists. Second, the bases of the Forest Service's autonomy are its "recognized expertise" in the field of forestry, its control over a large portion of the nation's timberlands, and its control over the funding for fire research. USFS autonomy is enhanced through the development of strong organizational loyalty among employees, at the root of which is a missionary ideology of conservation. This ideology was shared by influential northeastern elites who shored up the Forest Service's power relative to timber capital. Third, the USFS successfully developed the infrastructural power to accomplish its policy agenda, after which it grew even more insular and autonomous, escaping effective oversight by the US Congress and eschewing input from external sources on the issue of fire protection. These three claims, which clearly put the state at the center of the action, form the backbone of the dominant fire narrative. Each is treated in turn in the next sections.

Extreme State Autonomy

First, the Forest Service displays an extreme version of autonomy in the dominant fire narrative, in line with Nordlinger's early formulation. This makes for an odd split in assessments of the Forest Service's autonomy. On the one hand, many authors recognize the USFS's deep interdependence with, and in some cases subservience to, outside interests when it comes to timber, recreation, and grazing.[34] On the other hand, most accounts of fire policy specifically are focused heavily on the organization, ideology, and behavior of the agency acting in relative isolation. In the dominant account, from the beginning the Forest Service has not only executed fire policy but has also *determined* it. This has allegedly been the case despite opposition to USFS policy by a number of constituencies, including the immediately affected public (those who inhabit the fire-prone and fire-adapted landscapes of the West), class-based interests (private timber and ranching industries), and other state elites (particularly in the Department of the Interior).

For example, David Clary's critique of the Forest Service's perpetual fear of "timber famine" makes an unequivocal claim for the organization's general autonomy. "Convinced that it was right, fired with a sense of mission, and free of interference from others, the Forest Service addressed the national forests," he declares.[35] Robert H. Nelson, after noting the pervasive nature of fire in the pre-settlement West, summarizes the complexities of wildland fire policy: "Then, early in the twentieth century, the federal government introduced a policy of active suppression of fire . . . As a result, over the course of the twentieth century, fire was largely eliminated from most western forests."[36] He goes on to make the case that given this colossal blunder by the USFS, 80 percent of US national forests should be handed over to state, local, or private managers.[37] David Carle, while unearth-ing a history of dissent over fire policy from within the USFS and other federal agencies, similarly claims that the war against fire was "declared . . . by the young profession of American forestry" embodied in the ranks of Pinchot's agency.[38] The Forest Service's view of fire as an unmitigated evil became institutionalized following the massive 1910 fires in the northern Rockies, according to Carle. Carle is re-treading ground already crossed by Ashley Schiff in his organizational study of the USFS, *Fire and Water: Scientific Heresy in the Forest Service*, in which he claims that "to the Service, the Coeur d'Alene conflagration of 1910 con-firmed the necessity for absolute protection; fire, man's universal enemy, would be attacked with equal vigor on all fronts."[39] Stephen Pyne adds the weight of his formidable scholarship to the dual consensus that all-out fire suppression in the United States had its genesis organizationally within the Forest Service and his-torically in the events of the 1910 "Big Blowup." Pyne makes particularly strong claims for the role of the 1910 fires in setting federal fire policy on the fixed rails of suppression. He argues that the "memory of the 1910 fires," as experienced by key USFS personnel, "became embedded in institutional fibers through statutes and manuals and bureaucratic records . . . The Big Blowup [a particularly intense period of the 1910 fires from August 20–21] persisted in influencing the Forest Service because those who experienced it continually reminded the Service by waving, as it were, the bloody red shirt of 1910."[40]

In his deeply researched *Fire in America*, Pyne takes a more structural approach to explaining fire, although he is less concerned about explaining the Forest Service's original commitment to the policy of total suppression than he is with the historical variation in the particular "fire problem" to be addressed. His explanation for the shifts in the USFS emphasis from the problems of "fron-tier fire" to "backcountry fire" to "mass fire" to "wilderness fire" rests on the agency's access to various kinds of available surpluses (land, money, manpower, machinery, information).[41] Still, Pyne contributes to the dominant fire narra-tive's foundation in state-centered theory by focusing on the particular people and organizational structure of the Forest Service to explain fire policy. Nancy Langston, in her classic work on forest management in the Blue Mountains of Washington and Oregon, focuses as well on the Forest Service's championing of fire suppression—whose apotheosis was the USFS's 10 AM Policy—against the opposition of local land users and industrial foresters.[42] All of these accounts suggest that the Forest Service developed and successfully pursued a policy of out-and-out fire suppression in the face of opposition from all sides.

Accounts focus in particular on the debate, with its epicenters in California and the South, over "light burning," which the Forest Service presented as a dangerous and backward practice that—like its Native American practitioners—should be removed from the land without exception. The colonial imagery the Forest Service deployed during this debate was striking. Fire suppression was equated with the march of civilization. Burning, on the other hand, was primitive, ignorant, and equated with the imagined savagery of aboriginal peoples. Henry Graves and William Greeley both disparagingly referred to light burning as "Paiute forestry" in their public salvos against the practice.[43]

Indeed, it is not surprising that the Forest Service mobilized a racist, colonial discourse, given the intellectual soil in which US forestry took root. US forestry's genealogy runs through the foundational figure of Gifford Pinchot back to his mentor, Dietrich Brandis, reported as having had "a more profound influence on Gifford both as a forester and as an individual than anyone except his family and Theodore Roosevelt."[44] Brandis was a German-trained forester hired by imperial Britain to manage the forests of Burma and its "crown jewel," India. The British crown's goals in forest management followed the logic of colonialism: to extract the maximum value possible from the reserves it had established, and to use the raw resource for its own strategic needs (particularly during World War I, during which India's forests were heavily deforested for military purposes).

While celebrated as pioneers of environmentalism by Gregory Barton in *Empire Forestry and the Origins of Environmentalism*,[45] British colonial forestry was just as much an act of enclosure as a policy of forest conservation, since it reserved access to nature for the colonizing state at the expense not only of logging interests but often also of local populations, whose use of the forests the Imperial state saw as wanton. "Empire forestry's" first task was to catalog and inventory the forest resources of new colonies to rationalize appropriation by the Imperial state, generally under a system of scientific management. The latter, according to Barton, had its origins in the cameral sciences, "a system of science applied to governmental offices attempting to devise a profit to the state through methods of strict quantification and regulation."[46] In the case of India under the

British, forestry's primary motive was initially the reservation of wood supplies for military use and then, during the heyday of the Indian Forest Service, the establishment of a system of forestry designed to generate a perpetual stream of revenue. According to James Scott, it is only a slight exaggeration to claim that "the crown's interest in forests was resolved through its fiscal lens into a single number: the revenue yield of the timber that might be extracted annually."[47] The scientific forestry championed by Barton was founded in a logic of accumulation that could do nothing but reduce forests from multifunctional complexes of ecological processes to an "abstract tree representing a volume of lumber or firewood."[48]

US forestry replicated this model—including its commitment to apply the principles of industrial scientific management to nature—in establishing its own forest reserves, although forests were reserved to ensure the perpetuation of capital's access to raw inputs rather than for the generation of use or exchange value by the state itself. Pinchot, in his autobiography, expressed his desire to replicate in the United States Brandis's accomplishments in Burma and India. The earliest US-trained foresters absorbed their lessons from the *Manual of Forestry* written by Brandis's successor in the Indian Forest Service, William Schlich. Part of the European colonial legacy to US forestry was the idea that the Imperial state, in order to be seen as a responsible steward of its resources, was obligated to protect them from wasteful use and destruction. Primary among the agents of the latter was fire. As Pyne related,

> Foresters know fire as it threatened their trees, a danger bred by pastoralists, slash-and-burners, travelers, charcoalers, and miscellaneous transients, and those other competitors for the woods, such as gatherers of honey, nuts, and medicinal plants. Foresters feared and detested flame. Thrust into fire-blasted colonies, they became nearly apoplectic with outrage. Nothing could be done about honest forestry until fires were controlled.[49]

According to the dominant narrative of fire, the Forest Service took on this burden of control wholeheartedly and worked diligently—and, in the long run, mistakenly—to establish a policy of fire exclusion and the means to carry it out even deep in the backcountry. As the dominant narrative presents it, lined up against the USFS's push for fire eradication was an array of opponents ranging from local ranchers,[50] lumbermen, and "practical foresters" led by such figures as T. B. Walker and George Hoxie[51] to the Department of the Interior,[52] prominent political figures such as John Wesley Powell,[53] and even a small cadre of the Forest Service's own scientists.[54] Many of the light-burning advocates, particularly ranchers and lumbermen, established their own racialized discourse of fire, referring to light burning as "the Indian way" and appealing to the effectiveness of Native American burning practices in reducing the threat of big summer fires.[55]

As related in chapter 2, the Forest Service nailed down the lid on light burning at its Mathers Field Conference in 1921, committing to run instead with DuBois's hours-based full-suppression model of fire protection; from there, the USFS embarked on building up its infrastructural capacities. In an encapsulation of the lines drawn in the struggle over fire policy by the weavers of the dominant narrative, Carle explained: "On one side were lumbermen and ranchers who had historically burned their privately held lands to control wildfire or to clear lands for grazing. The fire control bureaucracy ultimately succeeded in suppressing those light burning advocates."[56]

The story, then, is of an overly powerful, independent state agency trampling the practically grounded, experiential folk knowledge of private producers, with disastrous results. It is a familiar discourse of state villainy in the United States, one vigorously propounded by capital—not least by elements within the timber industry. Whenever relations between the USFS and timber capital became rocky, the latter would raise the Weberian specter of bureaucracy run amuck. To take just one example, R. A. Colgan, executive vice president of the National Lumber Manufacturers Association, argued before the Agricultural Subcommittee of the House Committee on Appropriations that the Forest Service was becoming too powerful and expansive. "I have witnessed the gradual and progressive development of this department into a strong and powerful organization. Each year I have been able to watch its development into a more domineering and expanding bureau," Colgan stated. "The accelerated increase in the size and scope of the Forest Service, its constant efforts to expand its activities and influence beyond limits set by Congress, have raised the question in many minds as to the ultimate purposes of this governmental organization. Is its real purpose to serve the interests of the country by working sincerely with all agencies interested in the perpetuation of our forest resources, or," he insinuated, "is it aspiring to take over and control one of our basic industries?"[57]

The State's Interests: Conservation, Efficiency, and the Domination of Nature

State-centered theories of political outcomes, in addition to having to demonstrate the state's willingness and ability to formulate and execute its own policy agenda, require an explanation of motivation. Marxist theories of the state view the state's motivation either as a mediated reflection of particular capitalist class interests or as based in the structural requirement to maintain conditions for the accumulation of capital. Pluralist models tend to cleave to a rational choice motivational model in which interest groups struggle to maximize their access to political and economic resources. State-centered theories, on the other hand, suggest that politicians and bureaucrats have their own distinct interests. Having made the case that the Forest Service was able to exercise its will independently and indeed, in some cases, against the grain of capital's expressed preferences, the dominant narrative of fire must also answer this question: why was the Forest Service so hell-bent on what seemed to many a useless, expensive, and quixotic campaign to purge the forests of fire?

The interests of the Forest Service, in the dominant account, are derived almost entirely from the culture and ideology propagated by its leadership and successfully cultivated within the ranks of its employees. A material interest is related as well, based on the agency's addiction to wildland fire suppression funds, but it does not come into play until late in the story, and it is always secondary. The genesis of fire protection, in the dominant narrative, is a tale of state-based ideological fervor. The ideology in question is said to have two major, intimately related elements: a belief in the scientifically informed human domination of nature, and a belief in the righteousness of a utilitarian version of conservation.

The theme of fire protection as a product of human pretensions to dominate nature carries loud echoes of Carolyn Merchant, who, in *The Death of Nature*, stressed the power of metaphor in shaping not only our understanding of nature but also nature itself. The shift from an organic to a "clockwork" nature—from seeing nature as maternal to viewing it as a machine to be controlled—is decisive in Merchant's view, having lifted the moral constraint the image of nature as a "nurturing mother" had imposed on its unrestrained, utilitarian use.[58] Merchant thus lays out a historical movement from a relationship with nature characterized by maternal reverence and restraint to one characterized by a utilitarian preten-sion to control through scientific rationality, with its embodiment in the new sci-ences of environmental management, whose flagship was forestry. For Merchant, the controlling aspirations of modernity for order and progress are brought to bear on nature, as they are on all spheres of life.

In the literature on fire, this metaphorical shift is given pride of place. According to Nelson, for example, "the campaign against fire was . . . a campaign against nature out of human control. If the forests were to be deliberately man-aged to achieve goals for human use, the destructive actions of fire would have to be controlled. This would be a task that depended on the application of the expert skills of the forestry professionals newly staffing the Forest Service."[59] Langston, while arguing persuasively that the "forest health crisis . . . is political more than ecological,"[60] goes on to place the explanatory weight for forest management on the ideology of domination: "The troubled history of land management has its roots not in ignorance but in American visions of the proper human relationship to nature. Americans shaped the western landscapes according to a complex set of ideals about what the perfect forest ought to look like and what people's role in shaping that perfect forest ought to be . . . in other words, this is not just an ecology story; it is a story about the complex metaphors people use to mediate their relationship to nature."[61] Domination was presumed to follow from scientific knowledge—a presumption usually traced back to Francis Bacon—and the Forest Service is held up as a leading example of the state's penchant during the Progressive Era to push a technocratic model of administrative governance over both laissez-faire economics and democracy. The proponents of progressivism, and its champions in the Forest Service, "believed in science with all the fervor of a religion . . . and sought to elevate scientific expertise to a controlling role."[62]

The complement to this ideology of domination within the dominant narrative is an ideological commitment to activist government in the service of the public. The state, it is argued, viewed itself as the sole agent capable of undertaking the subjugation of nature to human ends while simultaneously ensuring that doing so was in the service of the public good rather than of particular interests. A 1905 letter that outlined management guidelines for the national forests, signed by Secretary of Agriculture James Wilson but actually written by Gifford Pinchot, supports this interpretation: "In the administration of the forest reserves it must be clearly borne in mind that all land is to be devoted to its most productive use for the permanent good of the whole people, and not for the temporary benefit of individuals or companies . . . Where conflicting interests [between potential users] must be reconciled the question will always be decided from the standpoint of the greatest good of the greatest number in the long run."[63]

The assumption that the USFS's policy decisions were driven by a religious commitment to these guidelines—which are said to embody the principles of the conservation movement and progressivism more broadly—runs deep through the literature on the Forest Service and on fire. Christopher Klyza, for example, argues that "the drive for autonomy by the forestry agency during this period [1898–1907] was based on a coherent conception of the public interest. The idea was that the public interest was best served by having the government retain ownership of large tracts of forest, and that these forests be managed for the greatest good of all society by foresters."[64] Pyne argues similarly that the "philosophy of conservation" was responsible for not just the US practice of reserving forests but for that of other colonial powers as well. In this understanding, it is the imperial state's belief that it and only it can successfully manage resources for the "commonwealth" that leads it to reserve and protect forests.[65]

Not only did the philosophy of conservation provide a basis for the policy of full suppression, but it is also claimed to have played a pivotal role in maintaining the Forest Service's autonomy relative to timber, mining, and grazing interests. Much is made in the literature about the USFS's focus on instilling both a missionary zeal for conservation and a deeply held professionalism among its employees. This fits well with state-centered theory, in that the development of an ideologically committed professional corps within the state—one without personal or economic ties to the dominant class—is theorized to increase the autonomy of the state and help it avoid capture.[66]

Pinchot, in building up the trained workforce required to manage the national forests (and to push the practice of forestry among private owners), undertook a number of measures to increase the professionalism of the USFS. He refused to undermine the merit-based application system for USFS positions by giving way to patronage appointments[67] and expected that "passing a civil service examination, after undergraduate and perhaps graduate study, would reinforce the professional ethos that he expected to dominate the service's actions."[68] Pinchot was said to have "moved vigorously to keep any taint of political favoritism from his agency, making it distinctly different, to his mind, from the corrupt General Land Office" from which he had wrested the forest reserves.[69] In addition, he drew on his parents' fortune to underwrite forestry education in the United States with the establishment of the Yale Forest School in 1900. Here, as in foresters' summer assistantships in the woods and their early employment with the service, they had the ethic of professionalism whipped into them. Yale provided every Forest Service chief up to 1940, and its graduates populated the faculties of other colleges of forestry throughout the United States.[70] Finally, Pinchot was responsible for setting up the Society of American Foresters in 1900, with an initial meeting of seven members in his office. Through these institutions, Pinchot pushed the ideology of conservation on his employees, and it came to infuse the practice of federal forestry. Langston outlines a view of the way the ideologies of conservationism and domination wrapped the young Forest Service in an insulating layer woven of professionalism and belief:

> Gifford Pinchot's foresters were extraordinarily optimistic. They shared with
> Pinchot a firm faith that science would allow them to understand everything
> worth knowing about the world. Redesigning wild nature as an orderly, effi-
> cient machine was at the heart of their efforts . . . Science, conscious purpose,

and human reason would engineer a new world out of the chaos of laissez-faire economics and short-term selfish interest. The conservationists felt theirs was an almost sacred mission: to perfect nature and civilization both . . . As scientists who had the interests of America and American forests at heart, they felt they were beyond criticism. Their very enthusiasm and faith—qualities that made them extremely effective—fostered an arrogance that often blinded them to the consequences of their actions.[71]

The Forest Service, although it came to represent an active manifestation of the conservation movement, did not represent the entire movement. In the dominant narrative of fire, the USFS's autonomy was bolstered by strong public support—which it actively generated through its public relations efforts—in particular by the support of a corps of elite northeastern intellectuals devoted to the cause of conservation, not the least of whose members was President Theodore Roosevelt. Roosevelt was a committed conservationist and a great friend of Pinchot's. It was only after he took over as president following William McKinley's assassination that the US Congress eventually authorized the transfer of the forest reserves to the USDA. McKinley had been reluctant to support the transfer in the face of initial western opposition, whereas Roosevelt recommended the transfer within three months of taking office.[72] In addition to powerful allies in the executive branch (who included Secretary of Agriculture James Wilson and Secretary of the Interior Ethan Hitchcock—the two departments involved in the proposed transfer), the Forest Service drew on the support of "progressive reformers" in the East, who saw Pinchot and the Bureau of Forestry as exemplars of the progressive spirit.

Klyza cites gushing editorials in publications such as *The Atlantic* and *The New York Times* as evidence for public support in the East.[73] According to Samuel Hays, this eastern support began to rally strongly behind conservation and the Forest Service in 1908 and was based in the ranks of "middle- and upper-income urban dwellers. Most of the organizations recruited their members and obtained their financial support from urbanites, and many of their leaders had been active in other types of urban reform."[74] Hays specifically cites the prominent role of women's organizations, such as the General Federation of Women's Clubs and Daughters of the American Revolution, in the conservation movement.[75] These groups—concerned about the rising preoccupation with all things material in the United States at the expense of the aesthetic, moral, and spiritual—lobbied hard for conservation and were great supporters of the Forest Service. This alliance may have been fully cemented by the fact that Gifford Pinchot's mother was chair of the Daughters of the American Revolution's Committee on Conservation.

Thus the forest health crisis is laid at the feet of a well-meaning but mis-guided state with an ideological conviction that it should and could act in the interests of the public as a whole. The poor state of US forests flows directly from the problems of technocratic environmental and social engineering by govern-ment agents. Flush with unfounded optimism about the possibilities of scien-tifically guided manipulation of nature and of its own ability to perform that manipulation in the service of human progress, the Forest Service became blind and deaf to dissenting opinions about the ecology of forests—both scientific and experientially grounded. As a result, forests are in a state of decay, overcrowding, and sickness—the natural equivalent of a misbegotten urban housing project. The primary pathology of the ecosystem is the absence of fire.

The commitment to fire suppression, springing from the connected ideolo-gies of control/domination and conservation/efficiency, was then hardened in the crucible of the 1910 fires, in which all USFS chiefs up to Ferdinand Silcox (whose tenure ended with his death in 1939) played some role.[76]

State Resources and Capacity

With its course set, the Forest Service embarked on a century-long crusade to clean the smoke out of the forests, becoming more and more insulated from other elements of civil society as it became the dominant national force in fire research and protection. According to Pyne, "The Forest Service came to domi-nate the national fire establishment by virtue of its mandated responsibilities, its disbursement of Clarke-McNary funds, its supervision of the Cooperative [Forest] Fire Prevention Program (Smokey Bear), its control over the production of essential information and research, and its responsibility for fire equipment development and distribution."[77] The Forest Service had fought to accrue all of these responsibilities unto itself; as such, it presents a strong case for the notion of state autonomy. Having successfully positioned itself as the arbiter of human-fire relations in the US wildlands, the USFS worked to maintain its legitimacy in the face of challenges that arose in the late 1960s and 1970s from fire ecologists and a new wilderness-based environmental movement. The Forest Service's response to these challenges as they have mounted since that time is the subject of chapter 6.

A final explanation for the USFS's interest in full suppression, one usu-ally relegated to the back pages in the narrative of fire,[78] is that fire suppression opened up what appeared to be a limitless reservoir of money and resources for the Forest Service. In 1908 the US Congress authorized the USFS to deficit spend on emergency forest fire suppression. This authorization was put to the test two years later, when the Forest Service handed Congress a bill for a whopping $1.1 million resulting from the 1910 Big Blowup. Congress obligingly handed over the money. This had enormous implications for the Forest Service's approach to fire, providing an incentive to spend less on prevention and more on suppression after-the-fact. The USFS is normally allocated an amount for emergency suppression based on a five-year average funding model. If requirements exceed this amount, as they do in above-average years, the Forest Service transfers funds from other budgetary pots, and Congress has never failed to make an additional appropriation to pay the money back.[79] The Forest Service, some argue, became addicted to these seemingly "free" emergency suppression funds, and without a fiscal check on its pursuit of fire, the agency is prone to spend lavishly on putting out fires. As Pyne put it, fire protection grew around the 1908 deficit-spending provision "like crystals on a string."[80] He has argued that "the 1908 act made fire management what it became: the agency went with the money. It did what it was paid to do, which was suppression."[81] Indeed, a commonly advanced theory about state bureaucracies is that their interests are largely reducible to budget maximizing. The Forest Service's budget, as well as its accrual of other kinds of resources (labor and machinery in particular, as discussed in chapter 2), has benefited enormously from the war on fire. Appropriations related to the fire war now account for about half of the Forest Service's budget. The agency's interest in fire suppression, then, does go beyond the ideological in the dominant narrative of fire. It is argued that as a maximizing state bureaucracy, the USFS has an interest in pursuing the war on fire, just as the Department of Defense has an interest in pursuing war on people.

UNANSWERED QUESTIONS IN THE NARRATIVE OF FIRE

How well does the dominant narrative of fire explain the development of fire policy within the Forest Service? There is no question that the Forest Service chiefs were forceful advocates for fire suppression; nor is there any doubt that the agency built itself (both financially and in terms of the development of an identity) on the back of its provision of that service—both directly and through cooperative arrangements—on public and private lands. It is starkly clear that the USFS worked effectively within the US Congress to gain the capacity to chase smoke into the most remote corners of the backcountry. I do not dispute that the Forest Service had considerable success in infusing its employees with a sense of pure purpose and of their place in the great struggle for conservation. Nor do I dispute that the Forest Service drew on Pinchot's connections to the northeastern elite to shore up its struggles with other state agencies and with the US Congress. However, the tale of the USFS as the primary actor in the narrative of fire in the United States raises troublesome questions.

First, why was the USFS able to act with such autonomy with regard to fire policy, given that it showed a complete lack of autonomy on other forest management issues? How was the Forest Service able to win its battle over light burning and successfully institutionalize the policy of full suppression, especially against the interests of timber barons and railroad companies?

The fact that the USFS is seen as a highly autonomous actor, its chiefs as "monarchs of the public domain," is surprising, given the well-known and well-documented intimacy of the agency's relationship with the timber industry.[82] There are some organizational accounts of the Forest Service that argue for its autonomy from special interests,[83] but as Paul Hirt points out, these studies pay no attention to the broader political context in which the USFS operates.[84] Herbert Kaufman's classic *The Forest Ranger*, for example, focuses on how the Forest Service produces compliance among its geographically dispersed employees with a centrally determined policy. He provides no analysis of what or who actually makes the policy in the first place. Paul Culhane also focuses on the local level, looking at how the Forest Service, in making specific resource allocation decisions, plays special interests against one another to maintain its autonomy. Again, this is about the USFS's ability to implement policy in the face of local resistance rather than about the establishment of policy and purposes at a higher level.

Christopher Klyza has looked at the higher level of political struggle, and he argues that the Forest Service displayed a high degree of autonomy during the decade 1898 to 1907, as evidenced primarily by its ability to facilitate the transfer of the forest reserves from the General Land Office of the Department of the Interior to the USDA and its ability to free itself from the US Congress by generating its own revenue. However, he demonstrates that the Forest Service was able to accomplish its goals only after radically changing the extent of commercial exploitation of the forest reserves that would be allowed to appease western resource-extracting capital and its allies in the US Congress.[85] Initial legislative efforts to affect the transfer had failed in 1901 and 1902, foundering on the shoals of western opposition. The deal succeeded in 1905 only after key capitalist organizations had agreed to support the transfer based on promises of continued access to the reserves, proclaiming their support at the 1905 American Forestry Congress.[86] The bill's final modifications prior to passage addressed mining interests' concerns about their ability to access timber.[87] This certainly calls into question the claim of "autonomy." While a convincing case can be made that the USFS created some wiggle room for itself vis-à-vis the US Congress by freeing itself temporarily from dependence on annual appropriations, history is less supportive of a claim of autonomy from capital. Furthermore, Klyza argues that the "window of autonomy" enjoyed by the USFS closed in 1907, well before it became a major player in US forestry.[88]

In an opposite view, scholarly accounts of the Forest Service that focus on forestry's broad historical and political context suggest that the agency was captured by the timber industry[89] or that from the beginning the agency and the industry were characterized by a unity of ideology and purpose.[90] Even the Forest Service's greatest champion, Gifford Pinchot, as early as the 1890s, saw the danger of capture lurking in the close ties between the timber industry and the public forestry agency. By 1914 (several years after his tenure as chief of the Forest Service had ended), he was convinced that his fears had come to pass. As Char Miller points out in his biography of Pinchot, "Although as chief he too had been interested in cooperative programs with the timber industry, and had sought ways by which to encourage the creation of a mutual agenda because of the power that lumbering lobbyists held in Congress, he was now [in 1914] convinced that accommodation meant capitulation."[91] Another key figure in the early political battles over forestry agreed. Raphael Zon, a close friend and ally of Pinchot's following the latter's departure from the USFS, argued in a letter to diehard conservationist Major George Ahern that "there was a time when the Forest Service and the progressive elements in Congress were fighting side by side. Today the leaders of the reaction and conservatism are the friends of the Forest Service. The Service must regain its independent position and rely upon popular support, instead of the support of [National Lumber Manufacturers Association secretary-manager] Dr. Compton and similar pillars in the lumber industry."[92] I return to the actual degree of autonomy the USFS enjoyed up until the postwar period in chapter 4.

Despite widespread recognition of the timber industry's influence on the Forest Service generally, when it comes to analyzing the history of fire policy, there is a marked tendency to either claim or assume that the USFS had both the will and the capacity to unilaterally develop and execute a policy of total fire exclusion. The class-based interests vanish from the picture as the focus moves to a detailed account of organizational struggles within the USFS and the power of the agency's ideological convictions about the control of nature. Among spinners of the dominant narrative, only Pyne offers concrete explanations of how fire policy was institutionalized against the preferences of "the vast majority of the American public." His explanation, however, resorts to the "immense conviction" of suppression's advocates in the USFS and the agency's alignment with the general "sentiment of the nation at large" in favor of activist government during the Progressive Era.[93]

Immense conviction among proponents, it must be admitted, cannot explain victory or defeat in the political arena, particularly since the policy's opponents were equally firm in their own conviction. Equally, the "sentiment of the nation" in favor of activist government in the Progressive Era is a fairly thin string on which to hang an explanation. As we shall see in chapter 4, all of the Forest Service's proposals for activist government in the realm of timber harvesting and forest management more generally during the Progressive Era, the New Deal Era, and the early postwar period were soundly beaten back, despite the agency's strong conviction that the proposed measures were vital and its alleged monopoly over forestry expertise. Why, then, did fire suppression alone sail through so successfully on the winds of national sentiment? The issue was highly contentious. There was no national consensus, either scientific or in public opinion, on the issue of fire, as Carle, Schiff, Pyne, Steen, and Langston have taken pains to establish. As a result, the eventual policy outcome must have been the product of power. The basis of the Forest Service's power in the establishment of fire policy remains unclear.

It could be argued that fire was viewed as an insignificant part of the Forest Service's role in forest management more broadly, and as such it flew under the radar of forest politics. However, nearly everybody agrees that fire was *the* central organizational task of the Forest Service, at least following the 1910 fires, and was seen as a foundational prerequisite for the viability of timber growing rather than timber mining. The historical record certainly supports this argument. Both the USFS and the major voices of timber capital saw fire protection as key to the fate of the forests. Thus the question as to why the Forest Service was permitted to do what it wanted over the opposition of capital (timber and ranching in particular) in one area and not in any others needs a more robust explanation than the dominant fire narrative has offered.

A second troubling question is, why did an organization with such a strong ideological commitment to science as the guiding force for public policy suppress its own scientific research? Both Carle and Schiff describe in great detail the internal struggles within the Forest Service over the science of forest fires. They conclude that the USFS steered scientific research and its conclusions toward support for a preexisting commitment to fire suppression.[94] This suggests that the Forest Service's mania for fire suppression was not simply a product of an ideological commitment to scientifically guided human control over nature. Those within the USFS pushed for a national policy, despite the fact that scientists both within and outside the agency told them that this plan was misguided and that different forest ecosystems required different approaches to fire. Herman H. Chapman, an assistant professor at Yale; Harold Biswell, former Forest Service scientist and then a forestry professor at Berkeley; and Harold Weaver, a Bureau of Indian Affairs forester, have been singled out for their role in pursuing research on the benefits of fire in forests, and they all faced difficult institutional barriers in publishing their research. They were all attacked by the Forest Service for their advocacy of an ecosystem-specific approach to fire.[95] In the face of practical evidence from the southern longleaf pine forests and California's dry forests that fire was vital to the rejuvenation of some forests, the Forest Service pursued a policy of fire eradication.

Why would an organization so committed to the scientific mastery of nature refuse to acknowledge its own researchers' results? If science was not to dictate USFS fire policy, then what was? The obvious response of an "ideological commitment to conservation" holds no water, since research had demonstrated that in some ecosystems fire was key to the growth of new timber—the very thing the USFS claimed to be supporting with its policy of full suppression. An agency ideologically committed to the most efficient use and perpetuation of resources, and one characterized by technocratic rule, would not have been so selective and biased in its attention to science. Fire suppression was not the policy most reflective of the best available science on the conservation and perpetuation of forests—even reduced as they were to units of merchantable timber. This was a fact many in the Forest Service were well aware of before, during, and after the public debates over fire suppression and controlled burning.

It would be rash to argue that the actions of the USFS were irrelevant to the current state of US public forests and even more so to generalize from this case and suggest that the state simply does not matter. Work within the "state-centric" tradition by people such as Peter Evans, Gregory Hooks, Jeff Goodwin, and others have put that idea to rest.[96] In some ways, the case of fire provides additional support for the idea that the state matters. Undeniably, the decisions taken by USFS leaders, and their translation into practice, have greatly transformed many western landscapes. The question of autonomy, though, begs more than this rather simple conclusion. A full inquiry requires us to investigate fully the context in which state managers operate. We need to examine the limits of their power. To what extent can the state be understood to have distinct interests? To what extent are state agencies able to develop an agenda and have that agenda recognized as constituting the legitimate set of political questions and objectives, to the exclusion of others? To what extent is the state able to influence the preferences and expressed interests of other parties? Finally, to what extent are state administrators able to exert their will and realize their preferences over those of others? Answers to these questions will help establish a context for state action. When it comes to the question of state autonomy, then, the key question is not so much *what* the state does (and its results) but *why*.

These questions must prompt a deeper look into the historical, social, political, and economic contexts in which fire policy developed. The politically important question of how we ended up with conflagrations like the Biscuit and Rodeo-Chediski fires—and thus how we might cope with them or change course in the face of their cautionary tales—seems only partially answered by references to the isolated figure of the Forest Service. In chapter 4, I propose an alternative explanation. Rather than focus on the internal organization of the Forest Service as it pursued the policy of full suppression, I advance a more relational explanation—one that takes seriously the idea that policy outcomes, and in this case the landscapes one such outcome has created, are the products of power and interaction. Rather than a powerful state agency rushing headlong into the backcountry with its Pulaskis and air tankers, chapter 4 documents the struggles of a state agency as it negotiates the tensions of its required functions of accumulation and legitimation in a capitalist society.

CHAPTER FOUR

MANAGING IN THE WAKE OF THE AX

A small bunch of foresters cannot buck the march of economic events . . . We can be a thousand times right but our voice will not prevail . . . I cannot see how we can put over regulation of the lumber industry—the only thing that I am convinced will stop forest devastation.

Raphael Zon, Letter to Maj. George P. Ahern, 1929

To address the unanswered questions posed at the end of Chapter 3 (namely, why was the Forest Service seemingly able to unilaterally and autonomously set fire policy, and why did it massage scientific research to support a policy of full suppression), we need to look at the political-economic context in which the USFS, and forestry[1] more generally, was expected to operate in the United States.

This inquiry is connected to yet another unanswered question within the dominant narrative of fire. While there is a great and, given its history of reductionism, fairly reasonable vilification of scientific management as the paradigmatic approach to forests, this begs a question on which most current managerial, journalistic, and scholarly accounts of wildland fire are silent. That is, to what purposes is management put?[2] Management and its ends are inextricable, but they are not identical. Conflation of the two obscures, either by accident or intention, the material interests that determine the form and character of human transformations of nature. To shed light on the question of how we ended up with forests in crisis, we need to ask: what were the goals of US forest policy?

PROFIT: THE ENDS OF (AND MEANS TO) US FORESTRY

"A Letter to Foresters"

An exchange in the Society of American Forester's (SAF) house publication in 1930 provides a useful entry point. A letter signed by seven SAF foresters, among them Gifford Pinchot, exhorted the profession to support a program of federal regulation of forests and expanded public ownership of forestlands. In the authors' eyes, only such a program would be sufficient to halt "forest devastation" in the United States.[3] The journal simultaneously published four dissenting responses to the letter, each of which lays out in no uncertain terms the boundaries and purposes of US forest policy. Rufus C. Hall wrote: "There is enough to do for the cause of forestry . . . without wasting enthusiasm and energy in chasing the rainbow of federal regulation. It is well to face the fact that forestry will be effectively practiced by private owners only when and where forestry will pay them a reasonable return."[4] Royal S. Kellogg, director of the American Pulp and Paper Association (APPA) and a leading figure in the ranks of organized timber capital, derided the letter as propaganda unfit for discussion within a scientific organization such as the SAF. He proclaimed, "There can be no one solution and no one policy" for "the forest problem." Rather, "There is and can be progress through study, research, and invention with the results intelligently applied in the light of ascertained economic conditions."[5] F. W. Reed, a onetime USFS district ranger who later headed the Forestry Department of the National Lumber Manufacturers Association (NLMA, an umbrella organization of regional lumbermen's trade associations and the heart of timber capital's political activity; it later became the National Forest Products Association), argued that "the forester inevitably must look upon forestry as a business proposition, to be practiced with a due regard for financial profit, rather than a public cause to be striven for with something akin to a religious zeal."[6]

The final letter, by C. Stowell Smith, who also left the USFS to work as a private forester, spun an agricultural analogy. "When conditions change in farming," Smith argued, "it simply means that the farmer must buckle down and revise his methods to suit what markets are available. If he cannot produce a profit on corn, maybe he can on rabbits . . . I have absolute faith in the forestry profession and its ability to take full advantage of its opportunities. But it, like the farmer, cannot afford to grow corn where rabbits are the profitable product."[7] While the analogy raises some vexing questions (what are foresters to grow if not trees?), the intended moral is clear: forest policy must serve the profitable production of trees for harvest. Of all the themes that emerged from the twentieth-century debates on forest policy, this one springs out the most clearly. Unpublished responses to the letter, some from foresters within the Forest Service to whom the letter was circulated prior to publication, also reflect how deeply the connection between forestry (and, with it, conservation more broadly) and profit ran in the minds of foresters. To take one example, a letter entitled "A Voice from the Wilderness" (ironic, since it parrots the line of many public foresters and the entire timber industry) argues that "forest construction will take place under dynamic, sane, thorough leadership of foresters who understand business, finance, and economics as well as silviculture and are able to bring profit from the work . . . It is *not* the duty of the foresters to *stop* forest devastation. It is our professional privilege to make forest construction profitable."[8]

Indeed, given the tone of the responses to the letter, one would think its authors were hostile to the idea that forestry should be a paying proposition. Some of them, notably Robert Marshall and Raphael Zon, likely did not think that profit should be the driving force behind forest management. However, among those the letter's critics were scolding was the progenitor of the idea that forestry must pay: Gifford Pinchot. While Pinchot became a tireless battler for public regulation and ownership of the nation's forestlands later in life, his shift away from optimism regarding the prospects of sustainable private forestry occurred only after he left the Forest Service. During his tenure as chief of the USFS, Pinchot was determined to adapt what he had learned about European forestry to the political economy of the United States. He argued forcibly that forestry in the United States would never take hold unless it could fit within the confines of an accumulative regime. Timber owners viewed European forestry as uselessly theoretical and unworkable within the different US market and political contexts. The Forest Service thus took it upon itself to make forestry "practical," which is to say profitable.[9] The struggle to make forestry—as opposed to "cut-and-run" timber harvesting—profitable, and thus attractive to private lumbermen, was the core mission of the fledgling Bureau of Forestry and its later incarnation as the United States Forest Service under Pinchot. His successors as chief of the USFS continued his efforts.

"Will It Pay?"

Pinchot had laid out his goals for US forestry even prior to taking the helm of the Division of Forestry. Employed at age twenty-six as manager of the forests on George W. Vanderbilt's massive Biltmore estate, Pinchot wrote in *Garden and Forestry* that his work there "should do much to remove forestry from the

anomalous and often illogical position into which the mistaken zeal of some of
its friends have forced it, and to ground its roots in the solid Earth of business
common sense . . . [My work] asserts a proposition which must ultimately lie at
the base of forest preservation in this country: namely, that it is not necessary to
destroy a forest to make it pay."[10]

Once Pinchot was ensconced in the offices of the Division of Forestry, he
wasted little time before attempting to convince private landowners of the profitability of "conservative logging." In the early years, most of the agency's time
and money were dedicated to servicing private lumbermen's requests for working
forestry plans. Circular 21, issued by the division only three months after Pinchot
took office, offered the agency's expertise to private operators who wanted to
implement forestry on their land. For small owners, the Division of Forestry paid
all costs. For large ones, the division paid its agents' salaries, and the owner paid
their expenses. J. Girvin Peters, a forest assistant with the division who assessed
the program in 1904, described the agency's terms of cooperation with owners as
"extremely generous."[11] The idea behind the circular, according to Pinchot, was
to "get down to the brass tacks of spreading the gospel of practical Forestry by
creating practical examples in the woods."[12] In assessing the impact of Circular
21, which private timber owners both large and small took up to such an extent
that it strained the capacity of the tiny agency, Pinchot claimed (somewhat gran-
diosely): "It wasn't gilt-edged German Forestry by any means . . . But it did pay, it
did stop forest devastation, and it did provide for a second crop."[13]

The order of priority in Pinchot's assessment accurately reflects the hierarchy
of purpose in US forestry. Conservation as practiced and preached by the Forest
Service, far from a movement antagonistic to the management of resources in
the service of accumulation, was, as others have pointed out, aimed explicitly at
ensuring that management of resources would turn a profit—not just at that time
but into the future as well.[14] The parallels with the current discourse of sustainable development are obvious. Pinchot summed up the singular problem of US
forestry on private lands in an address to the National Wholesale Lumber Dealers
Association: "It is all based on the primary question, Will it pay?"[15]

President Theodore Roosevelt—heralded as a champion of forestry and conservation—underscored Pinchot's mission to make forestry profitable in a 1903
speech to the Society of American Foresters, published in *Forestry and Irrigation*
in conjunction with Pinchot's declaration of faith in the idea of conservation
through profit, cited in the previous paragraph. Roosevelt began by drawing a
connection between forestry and US wealth: "The primary object of the forest
policy, as of the land policy, of the United States is the making of prosperous

homes."[16] By this, Roosevelt meant not the actual construction of homes out of wood but the generation of wealth through capital accumulation. "[Foresters'] attention must be directed not to the preservation of the forests as an end of itself, but as a means for preserving and increasing the prosperity of our nation," Roosevelt declared. The *purpose*, then, of scientific forestry in the United States was profit. It turned out that profitability was also the *means* by which conservation would emerge on private lands. According to Roosevelt, the forests "can be renewed and maintained only by the cooperation of the forester with the lumberman." The bottom line, Roosevelt argued, was that "the attitude of the lumberman toward [foresters'] work will be the chief factor in the success or failure of [that] work." He demanded that foresters "keep their ideals and yet seek to realize them in practical ways,"[17] sticking to the established code in which "practical" meant profitable and "cooperation" meant (as Pinchot later realized) capitulation to the lumbermen's will.

Pinchot's successor, Henry Graves, who returned from his stint as dean of forestry at Yale University to lead the Forest Service after Pinchot was fired by President William Taft, followed his predecessor's lead in signaling that the agency was there to facilitate, not to regulate, forestry on private lands. In 1915, in a speech advocating the expansion of public ownership of forests (a position many in the industry favored at the time as a measure to reduce the overproduction that plagued the industry),[18] Graves carefully maintained the Forest Service's position on its role vis-à-vis capital. Treading a careful line between assuring business that the Forest Service was there to facilitate accumulation for the industry as a whole and assuring the public that the USFS was acting as a steward of resources in the public interest, Graves explained:

> The cooperation of the public in aiding this industry to a better footing cannot be secured if specific private interests are made dominant and the welfare of the public at large [is] overlooked or subordinated. But cooperation which seeks broader public ends, benefiting the industry to the same degree as it benefits the country at large, will succeed from the beginning ... The forest service has sought to maintain this constructive attitude toward the lumber industry, looking always to the public interests which the industry must serve.[19]

In the USFS's thinking, however, the public interest turned out to be much in line with the private interest: "It is certainly of benefit to the public to have the important industries of the country prosperous; and there is a definite public loss if they are not."[20] Forestry, and more generally the conservation of resources, was to be brought about by making reforestation profitable. The science of forestry—

which the Forest Service claimed as its arena of expertise—was to be deployed on private lands not in the service of forests but rather to ensure timber's lasting profitability. Graves's views on this topic were consistent with those he voiced in *The Forester* while he was at Yale:

> A demonstration of silviculture which . . . makes financial considerations of incidental interest alone does an injustice to forestry, especially at this time when the science is on trial as really practical for business men . . . The measures which the forester as a silviculturalist would like to use are modified by financial considerations. The American forester must devise systems of management which will accomplish the owner's object and at the same time maintain the productiveness of the forest.[21]

Fire and Taxes: The Limits of Legitimate Government

By 1905, the year of the forest reserve transfer, the timber industry's organized element was convinced that the federal forestry agency was well-disciplined enough that the industry would support it. Nelson W. McLeod, president of the National Lumber Manufacturers Association, addressed the American Lumber Congress (which Pinchot credited with having sealed the reserve transfer) with a gushing endorsement of the Bureau of Forestry:

> Such as assemblage [of state and private foresters] . . . would have been impossible ten years ago. The lumberman and the forester were then far apart. So long as forestry was regarded as merely scientific, but little progress was made; but as it came largely through the influence of our Bureau of Forestry to be more clearly understood as a Business matter, the prospect has brightened rapidly . . . In developing an American system of forestry founded upon sound business principles and adapted to local conditions, the Bureau of Forestry is doing a very important work.[22]

In 1905 the American Forest Congress was, as George Gonzalez has pointed out, essentially a mobilization by capitalist trade associations designed to publicly demonstrate their strong support for the Bureau of Forestry—support that had been won with promises of increased access to forest reserves for the extractive and grazing industries.[23] The organized element of the timber industry continued to proselytize for cooperation both among its own members and with the Forest Service. Edward T. Allen, a former USFS employee who later worked for the Western Forestry and Conservation Association (WFCA)—another key node of the lumbermen's political network—stated his view of the only way forward for forestry. "In my opinion," he wrote in *West Coast Lumberman*, "forestry will never succeed in the United States until it is so closely allied with lumbering that neither forester, lumberman nor [the] public makes any distinction."[24]

This is not to say that the timber industry was a perfectly cohesive fraction of the capitalist class. There were those who strongly resisted any government incursion into what they saw as their exclusive realm. There were ideologues of a libertarian persuasion who saw every Forest Service overture for "cooperation" as an insidious plot in the direction of totalitarianism and the erosion of the national character. This was particularly the case during Ferdinand Silcox's leadership of the USFS in the 1930s, but it was also evident in the 1920s and continued through the Cold War heyday of the 1950s.[25] However, the NLMA, headed by Dr. Wilson Compton (as secretary manager), together with the WFCA (headed by Allen) and the West Coast Lumbermen's Association (WCLA, with former USFS chief forester William Greeley as head), acted as venues for timber capital to work out and publicize a unified political agenda. In discussing a matter of conflict between loggers and mill owners, for example, L. C. Boyle (counsel to the NLMA) wrote Compton that "one of the outstanding advantages of the National [NLMA] is that it can be used as a forum wherein its members can frankly discuss industrial problems and reach equitable conclusions as to trade relations, etc."[26] Correspondence between Compton at the NLMA and lumbermen across the country, bearing on a wide range of regulatory and legislative measures, supports Boyle's claim.

The agenda pushed by organized timber was generally one of moderate conservatism, allowing for limited government intervention (particularly in cases in which such intervention could help stabilize the market) in specified areas. David T. Mason, manager of the Western Pine Association, laid out the industry's view of the government's legitimate roles in forestry at the 1936 meeting of the Society of American Foresters. While claiming that "there appears to be rather general agreement that in the solution of our forest problems there should be realization to the maximum extent practicable upon private ownership, management and operation," Mason conceded that the state could help the industry in its quest for conservation by acting "to remove unreasonable economic obstacles and to create reasonably favorable conditions for further private forestry." This essentially boiled down to reducing taxes on standing timber and providing fire protection. Mason also allowed that the state would be within reasonable limits if it purchased "forest lands of such character as to be impracticable for private ownership and management."[27] The leaders of the timber industry's policy planning network were unified in their belief that "cooperation" with the Forest Service in this limited set of affairs was the best way to stave off a more regulatory and antagonistic approach by the federal foresters. As we shall see, relations were not always silky between the industry and the Forest Service, particularly when the USFS pushed hard on the issue of federal regulation of private logging. As William Robbins has argued, however, the dominant tilt of the relationship has been toward Forest Service "cooperation" with industry.[28]

From the beginning, then, the USFS was not an organization designed primarily to protect the environment from the depredations of capitalism; rather, its purpose was to ensure that timber would remain available for profitable exploitation into the future. For all the weight placed on scientific hubris as primarily responsible for the contemporary forest health crisis, it was recognized from the outset—as Graves's comments (cited earlier) and Pinchot's distrust of "European forestry" attest—that science would have to take a backseat to the maintenance of profitability. While the application of scientific management to forests has indeed had disastrous consequences, what set the forests on a path of deterioration was management's gross reduction of the forest ecosystem into a manipulable space for the maximized production of a single commodity.[29] I will resist invoking the cliché about forests and trees, but it would be apt. Foresters were not instructed to see a set of mutually supporting and interdependent processes, as an ecologist would view the forest. Rather, they were taught to see actual and potential board feet of timber. Neither science nor "management" per se dictates such extreme reductionism.[30] Rather, the specific political-economic context, and even more specifically, the requirements of profitability and growth endemic to capitalism, determined the purposes for which managers would attempt to regulate the human relationship with nature. From 1898 onward, the federal forest agency was saddled with the contradictory tasks of conserving the nation's forests (both public and private) while simultaneously ensuring the ability of capital to profit from their exploitation.

THE GENESIS OF FIRE PROTECTION: CONFLICT OR COOPERATION?

The primary tool in the forester's box necessary to make forestry profitable was the elimination or minimization of the threat of fire. Chief Graves put it succinctly, arguing immediately after the historic 1910 fire season that "the main reason why forestry is not more widely practiced is the danger that the required investment may be lost or seriously impaired by subsequent fires."[31] The question is, was the state solely or even primarily responsible for making fire suppression its central task, as state-centric theory would suggest? Were lumbermen, grounded in their practical experience of fire as either helpful or inevitable, generally opposed to fire suppression as a means of protection? Were they steamrolled by the crusading, scientifically dogmatic state?

Myth of the Bully State: Fire Exclusion as a Capitalist Project

It was indeed the case, as related in the dominant narrative, that some "practical lumbermen" in California and many in the South stuck by the practice of light burning, refusing to cede to state efforts aimed at fire's exclusion. Small timber owners in the South in particular resisted the doctrine of fire suppression, and for many years the Forest Service viewed the South as something of a problem child. However, there is also no question that the large, organized segment of the lumber industry—the segment that was most active and effective in politics—was steadfastly in favor of all-out fire suppression and, in fact, was actually the vanguard in both practicing fire protection and advocating for a stronger government role in its provision. Interestingly, the most accurate accounts of the genesis of fire policy are found in historical works that deal with US forestry more broadly rather than in those that focus on fire policy specifically. Harold Steen's history of the USFS and William Robbins's *American Forestry* and "The Good Fight" are particularly strong in highlighting the growth of fire protection as a relational phenomenon that sprang from the interaction of the Forest Service and timber capital rather than being a product of the bullying USFS alone.[32]

On the practical side, rather than starting with the state, organized fire protection in the West began with voluntary associations of timber owners jointly funding patrols of their lands. States had to be pressured into facilitating fire protection, which they did first by requiring contributions from private owners to fire protection associations and then by funding those associations from the public purse. Rather than pinpoint the 1910 fires as the pivotal moment in western fire history, as do most histories of fire in the United States, Robbins and Steen look eight years earlier at another set of conflagrations—the ones that swept through private timberlands on the west side of the Cascade Mountains from Washington to southern Oregon. The most severe of these 1902 fires was the Yacolt burn in southern Washington. As a result of the economic losses suffered in the 1902 fires, timber owners rallying under the banner of Lane County, Oregon's, biggest timber holder, the Booth-Kelly Lumber Company, created a cooperative fire patrol.[33]

These kinds of private protective associations proliferated in the West, with eight major "pioneer" protective associations active in Oregon, Washington, and

Idaho by 1908. George Long, the western manager of Weyerhaeuser's vast holdings and a leading figure in the early organization of protective associations, bragged in 1908 (with considerable overstatement) that as a result of these associations, forests in Washington were for the first time in history "systematically patrolled and the public mind educated to the importance of saving the forest from fire."[34] The WFCA was founded on the basis of an "Outline of Organization for Work" written by Long in 1909. Primary among the tasks listed was to "bring all persons owning timber, or interested in timber supply, together in a forest fire protective association."[35] These associations came into being largely as a result of the timber lobby's slow progress in its struggle to obtain public funding for fire protection. In that area as well, however, the organized lumbermen eventually demonstrated their legislative clout—exercised in no small part through the WFCA.

Focusing their efforts on the Pacific Northwest, where the last great forests remained and huge holdings were at risk from fire, lumbermen argued that the public had an interest in the prevention and suppression of fires because of the economic significance of the lumber industry and, further, that the state should thus shoulder some, if not all, of the burden. Essentially, timber owners sought to externalize costs by socializing the risk to their investments by getting the state to pick up the tab for fire protection. This campaign was started at the state level immediately following the 1902 fires, with Long taking the point position for the industry. Attempts to obtain state funds for the protection of private timber failed in Oregon in 1903. A Washington bill that same year, although approved, was much weaker than the industry wanted; it only contained provisions for county commissioners to appoint a few fire rangers and to issue burning permits. The Oregon bill, while stronger and actually passed by the legislature, was vetoed by the governor, largely because he thought owners should pay their own costs for protection.[36]

However, by 1905 the timber industry—in part by gaining a greater direct foothold in state legislatures with the election of a number of lumbermen after 1903[37]—managed to massage bills through to passage in both states. In Washington, the industry gained support for a state forest fire commission. In Oregon, it managed only (as a result of Governor George Chamberlain's continued resistance) to pass an act establishing a court-appointed fire patrol, financed by timber owners. In 1907, under the same governor, financial responsibility for the fire patrol was finally shifted to the state. This legislative push came, not coincidentally, in the midst of a massive buy-up of forested land in the West and Pacific Northwest by the major timber companies. Between 1890 and 1910, these companies purchased huge swaths of land in Washington, Oregon, Northern

California, Idaho, and western Montana; they needed to have those investments protected.[38] While the timber companies were active in pushing for state-level subsidization of fire protection on public lands, they were initially less active on the federal level. Organized timber capitalists were, and remained throughout the numerous battles over forest regulation, vehemently opposed to federal involvement. If government had to be involved in the forest industry's affairs, they argued, let that involvement at least be "home-grown."

Organized timber's distaste for the possibility of federal meddling in forestry was also notable in the passage of the 1911 federal legislation—the Weeks Act—that first gave the Forest Service the authority to fund fire protection on state and private lands. Organized lumber was remarkably absent in the public debates over the Weeks Act, which contained two primary provisions: one allowing for the purchase of eastern lands for inclusion in the National Forest System, and the other authorizing the Forest Service to cooperate with state and private landholders on fire protection for forests surrounding navigable streams. George Morgan has argued that organized lumber's silence on the Weeks Act resulted from a provision, later struck from both the US House and Senate versions of the bill, demanding that to be eligible for federal funds, private owners had to submit to federal regulation of their harvesting and transport methods.[39] Even the more moderate, organized lumbermen who had advocated for a state role in fire protection could not tolerate this provision, and they withheld support. Their lack of enthusiasm was likely the reason the provision was removed. However, following the Weeks Act's passage, industry support for federally provided fire protection grew stronger as lumbermen realized the benefits of this kind of "cooperation." Without federally subsidized or otherwise publicly provided fire protection, the timber barons argued, private forestry would never come to pass. Why replant cut-over lands or take on the expense of reproducing timber after logging when the definite prospect existed that fire would wipe out the investment before it could be liquidated? The Forest Service, true to its mission of lifting the barriers to profitable forestry and cognizant of an opportunity to expand its powers, took up the challenge.

Private lumbermen's support for federal "cooperation" on fire protection bore fruit thirteen years after the Weeks Act went into effect with the passage of the Clarke-McNary Act in 1924. William B. Greeley, the US chief forester at the time of Clarke-McNary's passage, viewed it as his most significant contribution to forestry. Indeed, the act marked a precedent-setting victory for the doctrine of cooperation with industry over a competing push for government regulation of private lumbering. In the face of proposals to regulate private logging, organized lumbermen repeatedly invoked the "spirit" of cooperation embodied in Clarke-McNary in an effort to push back the threat. Greeley, once he took his position at the helm of the West Coast Lumbermen's Association after leaving the Forest Service, was among those most vocal on this front. Fire protection, and the eventual victory of an ecologically short-sighted full-suppression model, was less the product of scientific debates over the merits of excluding fire, as authors like David Carle[40] would have it, and of a scientifically obsessed bureaucratic juggernaut, as Robert Nelson[41] suggests, and more a product of the debate over whether and how private logging would be regulated by the state.

Crisis Management: The Struggle to Avert "Timber Famine"

How can we understand the state's position vis-à-vis the timber industry on the issue of forest regulation? The argument—often heard in activist circles—that successive Forest Service administrations were voluntary tools of the industry are difficult to reconcile with the wild fluctuations in the state of goodwill between the USFS and lumbering interests over the course of the twentieth century. Relations were generally very good between the two during the reigns of Pinchot, Graves, and Greeley—probably reaching a high point with Greeley, who was unabashedly pro-industry, anti-regulation, and vehement in his pursuit of "cooperative" relations with lumbermen. After this point relations definitely soured, as the USFS came under the direction of chiefs who strongly believed in the need for regulation and the promise of forestry for addressing other societal woes (unemployment in particular) during the 1930s and 1940s. Both Ferdinand Silcox and Lyle F. Watts were demonized by industry representatives as heavy-handed, "non-cooperative," and, in some cases, socialist or fascist menaces to the American way of life. When Richard McArdle took over as USFS chief in 1952, the push for federal regulation of private lands died out and has not been seriously resurrected.[42] Conflict between the Forest Service and private operators today has more to do with timber sales on national forests than with any threat of federal intervention on private land. So despite the friendly relations early on and the tight consensus between industry and the Forest Service from the mid-1950s onward, relations have at times been fairly antagonistic between the USFS and the timber industry.

One would have a difficult time advancing a simple instrumentalist interpretation of the Forest Service's relation to timber capital, given the history of conflict and occasional hostilities. Administrations have not universally accommodated the policy wishes of timber capitalists. In this regard, the argument for the state's "autonomy" is irrefutable. The state did attempt on several occasions to move against the industry's wishes. It developed proposals for regulation and recommendations for legislation that in some instances were quite radical and oppositional to the timber capitalists' economic interests. The state often did so with the assistance of scientific and civic organizations such as the Society of American Foresters (or at least some of its members) and the American Forestry Association. The historical record is thus more in line with a structuralist theory of the capitalist state, in which the state strives to maintain the general conditions of profitability even against the interests of specific companies or individual capitalists. However, the truly relevant questions when it comes to an evaluation of any state agency's autonomy, if "autonomy" is to have any meaning whatsoever, are what were the *purposes* of the state's attempted actions (with careful consideration of the intended beneficiaries), and was the state *able* to pursue the agenda it thought was necessary for those purposes?

The answer to the first question has been partially answered. Ensuring the availability of standing timber for harvest was the Forest Service's bottom-line purpose, and it continued to be so well after the introduction of the concept of "multiple use" that was supposed to position timber on equal terms with other forest uses, such as recreation.[43] The assumptions that this timber should provide US industry with the inputs it required for production, as well as offering timber harvesters a profitable opportunity, were unquestioned. The timber industry, particularly in the early years of the Forest Service's existence, was doing everything in its power to log the country bare in as short a time as possible. The rapid deforestation of the eastern and lake states gave rise to fears that a completely laissez-faire approach to timber harvesting would soon leave the United States with a treeless landscape.[44] From its inception, the Forest Service's mandate was to stave off the possibility of "timber famine." Its goal was to manage the problem of forest devastation caused by unrestrained industrial logging and the potential supply-side crisis that practice presented. The USFS's fears with regard to the future of timber supplies in an unmanaged market mirror the hazards James O'Connor suggested in his "second contradiction of capitalism" thesis.[45]

Capitalist production relies on what O'Connor calls the "conditions of production." They include the existence of labor power, available external physical conditions such as natural resources and pollution sinks, and accessible and productively useful arrangements of space and infrastructure. O'Connor argues that these are "fictitious commodities."[46] As theorized most explicitly by Karl Polanyi regarding labor, land, and money, under capitalist relations of production fictitious commodities are not produced and reproduced by and for sale on the market but rather are treated as though they were.[47] Forests, for example, are appropriated, and their value-bearing elements are sold as though they had been factory-produced. On the buyer's side, the ideal is a uniform product delivered when and where required in the appropriate quantity, as though there were no ecological or biological constraints on the "production" of forests. As a result, O'Connor contends, there is a chronic tendency within capitalism to "underproduce" the fictitious commodities labor power, nature, and space. Individual capitalists are in a position whereby they have both the opportunity and the motive (cost competitiveness) to externalize the costs of production of fictitious commodities. At the same time, capital requires that the natural conditions of production be reproduced sufficiently to ensure their continued availability. The fact that this reproduction fails to take place in an unregulated market, leading eventually to a supply-side crisis, is O'Connor's "second contradiction." He suggests that the only way out of the contradiction is through the mediation of an "independent" agency assigned to regulate access to nature and to ensure the adequate reproduction of the conditions of production. According to O'Connor, "This agency can be no other than the capitalist state."[48]

The Forest Service undoubtedly saw its mission in exactly these terms. This is not to say that the USFS struggled to maintain and restore healthy, functioning forest ecosystems in the wake of timber capital's heavy axes. Rather, within its own reductionist view of forests as an empty space in which to maximize the production of board feet of timber—a legacy of its colonial heritage—the agency saw that unregulated private cutting would leave the country without timber of its own. A constant Forest Service refrain was that of impending timber famine—an obsession David Clary has identified as the USFS's core belief and the underlying rationale for all its actions.[49] On this point, Pinchot was a committed doomsayer, repeatedly predicting an imminent supply-side crisis as a result of deforestation. In 1910 he claimed: "The United States has already crossed the verge of a timber famine so severe that its blighting effects will be felt in every household in the land. The rise in the price of lumber which marked the opening of the present century is the beginning of a vastly greater and more rapid rise which is to come."[50] In 1919 the tune remained constant, this time from Chief Graves. His article "Private Forestry" outlined a long series of economic crises unfolding or predicted to unfold as a result of regional deforestation in the lake states and the South as supplies dwindled and mill closures appeared imminent. He also addressed the threat to national security posed by timber famine, drawing on the experiences of England and the United States during World War I as cautionary tales. Had the war come fifteen years later, Graves warned, the nation would have had great difficulty obtaining the timber it required for the war effort.[51] Pinchot, still very active in the forestry movement after President Taft removed him from the Forest Service, supported Graves's assessment: "The recent addresses of the Chief Forester [Graves] . . . give so thorough an analysis of the effect of uncontrolled lumbering upon wood-using industries and local communities, and present the argument so convincingly, that no unbiased person can fail to appreciate the social and economic menace of our present policy."[52]

That same year, the Society of American Foresters appointed a Committee for the Application of Forestry, chaired by Pinchot and composed of eight other prominent foresters (including SAF president Frederick E. Olmsted and future USFS chief Ferdinand Silcox), to recommend steps to halt "forest devastation" on privately owned timberlands. In the preamble to its report (under the subtitle "The Facts") the committee proclaimed: "The beginning of timber shortage is here already, and cannot but grow worse for many decades to come. In item after item the price of lumber and other forest products is already almost prohibitive. We are consuming nearly three times more wood than we are producing. As with any other crop, wood cannot be consumed faster than it is produced without exhausting the supply. At the present rate, our saw-log timber will be gone in about fifty years."[53] Four years later, in 1923, Chief Greeley predicted to the Senate Forestry Committee that "without change in present conditions of regrowth and depletion, American Forests will be exhausted in 30 to 40 years." Greeley went on to claim that timber famine was already plaguing the major lumber markets as a result of "high freight rates caused by the long distances of the remaining forests from the consuming centers."[54] Ten years later a USFS report mandated by Senator Royal S. Copeland (the so-called Copeland Report), which outlined a proposed national forestry plan, also highlighted the fact that forest "drain" considerably outweighed forest growth and identified "forest deterioration" as "one of our major national problems."[55] In 1939 Secretary of Agriculture Henry Wallace was again warning of the dangers of timber famine. "Less than 35 percent of our forest land now bears trees big enough for saw timber," he lamented to a Joint Congressional Committee on Forestry. "More than one-third of our remaining saw timber forests are economically unavailable. Annual growth in usable saw timber forests is one-half less than the annual drain from them. As a Nation we are, therefore, still depleting our capital stock of soil resources."[56]

During World War II, Chief Lyle F. Watts predicted that postwar lumber needs would remain as high as wartime needs, which were greatly draining forest resources.[57] Watts estimated that losses during the war exceeded new growth by 50 percent.[58] According to the chief, "Only by the most aggressive measures can we hope to bring saw-timber growth in line with needs."[59] While the Forest Service's major assessment of US forests in the 1950s—the Timber Resource Review—did not invoke the language of timber famine, it did suggest the likelihood of a supply crisis for high-quality saw timber, particularly given the rapid harvesting of old growth.[60] Supply-side fears continued into the 1960s, with a price spike for wholesale lumber in 1967 and 1968 and the publication of a Forest Service study on the supply of Douglas fir in the Pacific Northwest claiming that harvesting was outstripping growth, with future declines in softwood timber availability likely the result.[61] Here, then, we have a half-century's worth of fear revolving around O'Connor's second contradiction. These fears clearly played a major role in shaping the Forest Service's mission. There was a clear understanding that the economics of lumber in an unregulated environment was producing a strong disincentive to reproduce the industry's conditions of production. Lumbermen argued publicly that they had neither the means nor the responsibility to reforest or even to cut in such as way as to facilitate natural regeneration. According to lumbermen, it fell to the public to deal with the aftermath of timber harvesting. The USFS complied. The variable factor over time was not the USFS's imperative to manage the consequences of environmental degradation that resulted from industrial logging but instead the means by which the Forest Service sought to do so.

Fire protection was viewed as one necessary requirement to ensure that the nation would continue to enjoy a steady supply of timber and was held up vigorously by capitalists as the master key to forestry in the United States. In their historical review of forest and range policy development, Samuel Trask Dana and Sally Fairfax state flatly that "fire control is the most dramatic contribution to economically viable forestry."[62] However, the Forest Service (or its employees) occasionally argued that fire protection alone was not sufficient. At various points, the USFS held that two other remedies were necessary: vastly increased public ownership of forestlands, and federal regulation of private forestlands. At other points, while the Forest Service's leadership pushed for cooperation, elements within the broader forestry community—often led by Pinchot—struggled for public ownership and federal regulation. Conflict over the latter perceived requirements recurred until the 1950s, when Chief Richard McArdle dropped them in the face of both total industry opposition and a hostile White House administration. From McArdle onward, the managerial approach to dealing with fears of timber shortage focused on "getting the cut out" of the national forests by increasing harvest levels through intensive management.[63]

Prior to this, and beginning with Circular 21's offer of technical assistance to private landowners, the focus was on establishing forestry practices on private lands, which still represented the vast majority of timberlands in the United States. The Forest Service put much of its political effort into changing the way logging was undertaken on private lands. The major conflicts among the USFS, conservationists, and the timber industry broke out over this managerial thrust, not over fire protection (which, as we have seen, was industry's baby, although one the Forest Service willingly adopted). If the Forest Service was, as the dominant narrative of fire suggests, a powerful and largely autonomous agency with a respected monopoly on forestry expertise, it should have been able to push its policy agenda for regulation and public ownership successfully, just as it allegedly steamrolled the opposition on the wisdom of fire suppression. The record of conflict between the USFS and the timber industry, however, suggests that the Forest Service was severely constrained in the avenues it was allowed to pursue in its management of what it saw as widespread forest devastation and deterioration.

COOPERATION VS. REGULATION: THE BUILDUP TO CLARKE-MCNARY

The Clarke-McNary Act, which drastically expanded the authority for federal funding of fire protection on state and private lands, was eventually passed in 1924—to the delight of Chief Greeley, who described what a thrill it was to be "in on the kill." The Forest Service was an ardent supporter of the bill and had worked hard to ensure its successful passage through the US Congress. Greeley, along with the industrial allies who had helped him secure the bill's passage, viewed Clarke-McNary as the ultimate preventative against any "radical" schemes to regulate private timber harvesting. Instead, the bill validated, codified, and provided precedent for the industry's mantra of "cooperation, not regulation."

Regulatory Threat

Interestingly, though, Clarke-McNary was the culmination of a process begun by Greeley's predecessor, Henry Graves, when he began to push the idea of public regulation of private forests toward the end of his tenure as chief. He proposed this idea to the community of foresters in 1919 but had previously discussed public regulation with Royal S. Kellogg, his former colleague at the Forest Service. It was Graves who proposed that the federal government provide funding to the states for the protection of private timber holdings, although with regulatory strings attached.[64] Stressing the predominance of private holdings in the makeup of the nation's forestlands ("Private owners own four-fifths of the standing timber in the country"),[65] Graves claimed that the perpetuation of the timber resource required timely steps toward private forestry, which had not been accomplished through the cooperative approach the Forest Service had taken to date.[66] Kellogg rejected the idea, suggesting that regulation was pointless if it forced private capital to undertake unprofitable measures. Launching a theme that would stay afloat for decades among industry associations, Kellogg advocated increased fire protection funding and public purchase of cut-over land, with no other government intervention in lumbermen's affairs.[67] The SAF weighed in that same year by establishing its Committee for the Application of Forestry, which not only warned of impending timber famine but laid the blame squarely on the shoulders of private owners who were still, with a very few exceptions, cutting and running. According to the committee,

> It is these privately owned forests which are being devastated. It is their devastation which must be stopped. Although they insist that they [privately owned forests] are essential to the safety and prosperity of the Nation, the forest industries have taken no steps to ensure their own perpetuation, have made no effort to put an end to forest devastation, and have persistently avoided all responsibility for maintaining a dependable supply of forest products. In its own behalf, and for its own protection, the public must intervene.[68]

The committee offered for consideration a far-reaching slate of federal legislation aimed at ending forest devastation on private lands. Purchase of lands and federal control over production and the production process were key elements of the recommendations. In an article in which he supported the committee's program, Pinchot presented as fantasy the idea that private lumbermen could be baited into forestry. "Forest devastation will not be stopped through persuasion, a method which has been thoroughly tried out for the past twenty years and has failed utterly," argued Pinchot. "Since otherwise they will not do so, private owners of forest land must now be compelled to manage their properties in harmony with the public good."[69]

In fact, the committee recommended government control not just over cutting but also in modifying the institutions that governed the relationship between owners and workers in the timber industry. Included in the committee recommendations was a provision for the establishment of an institutional venue for the "interchange of views and the adjustment of differences arising between labor,

82

management, and the public."[70] This reach beyond silvicultural matters into the wage relationship, along with the suggestion of regulated logging, provoked the sharpest criticism from the industry, as well as from some public foresters. The recommended legislative action was for the establishment of councils composed of workers' and employers' representatives who, along with government representatives, would work out such issues as wages, hours of work, overtime, leave, housing, board, and "the participation of employees in matters relating to conditions of employment."[71] One committee member, J. W. Toumey, signed the document only on the condition that his specific objections to this provision would be published. This was a radical program for a group of US foresters—one of whose members had only a decade earlier been the lead voice for "forestry that pays." It was also an amazing recognition of the fundamental connection between the exploitation of humans and the exploitation of nature.[72] One can detect the influence of committee member Raphael Zon, the socialist forester who became Pinchot's good friend and ally.

William Greeley, who took over as chief in 1920, disagreed with the committee's recommendations and became the USFS's point man in defense of unregulated private forestry. He disagreed both on the matter of regulation, which he felt should be a last resort in the event that public and private interests diverged, and with the committee's foray into industrial relations, which he felt was a separate issue entirely. Despite the continued devastation of forests (which he readily admitted was occurring), he held that private owners could still be brought around to embrace "practical forestry" through cooperation, tax reform, and appropriate incentives.[73] Further, he argued that foresters should stick to matters of silviculture and not dilute their arguments with irrelevant dalliances into the wage-labor relationship. The NLMA and the WFCA mobilized behind Greeley's cooperative vision, unnerved at the prospect of public regulation. The lines, as Pinchot himself expressed it, had been drawn.[74]

Fire Suppression as Forestry? Greeley and Pinchot Agree to Disagree

Greeley and Pinchot aired their fundamental differences in an exchange of correspondence that followed Pinchot's receipt of a Forest Service circular sent to all state foresters in the summer of 1920. The circular asked state foresters (including Pinchot, as Pennsylvania's commissioner of forestry) to support a Forest Service proposal to provide federal money for fire protection in exchange for suitable state-level legislative measures for fire protection and to prevent the "devastation of commercial timberlands by destructive lumbering."[75] Pinchot refused to support the program on the grounds that state control was tantamount to no control at all. In a letter to Greeley, Pinchot asked,

> Do you imagine for a moment that Kansas and Nebraska, Pennsylvania and New York, will contribute their money through federal appropriations, and then sit calmly by and trust to the legislatures and State forces of Oregon and Louisiana for the enactment and application of measures which will assure to the farmers of the middle west and the workers of the industrial East the timber supplies they must have to earn their living? And do you imagine that their share of a million dollars [the minimum amount of the proposed federal subsidy] . . . distributed among 35 States, will be more powerful with the Legislatures of Washington and Oregon than the lumber lobbies which have dominated them for years?[76]

Significantly, this exchange also illustrates Pinchot's emerging recognition that the issue of fire protection was becoming cover for avoiding real action on forest devastation. A keen proponent of the "fire protection is forestry" school while he was chief forester, Pinchot struck a decidedly contrary note once he had moved on from the federal agency. In a remarkable passage, Pinchot charges that

> By emphasizing the importance of fire almost to the exclusion of forest devastation, your letter opens the gates, first for laxity in the enactment and enforcement of laws to prohibit devastation, and then for the side-tracking of such measures altogether. That is precisely what the lumbermen want. They have so far successfully kept fire in the forefront of the discussion. If they can overshadow the real issue by talking nothing but fire protection, they will succeed in escaping the compulsory practice of such simple forestry on commercial forest lands as will keep those lands reasonably productive.[77]

Greeley responded with a plea that while national control would indeed be superior, state control was the only constitutionally feasible route. By sticking to the demand for national control, Greeley argued, forestry advocates would "simply mark time and get nowhere for many years."[78] In addition, he maintained an emphasis on fire prevention above all else: "Accomplishment in timber production will, for a long time to come, be measured by the reduction in the yearly acreage of forest fires . . . It seems to me beyond question that our immediate efforts and the character of the legislation we seek should be bent toward reducing this fundamental cause of forest devastation."[79]

Pinchot flatly rejected Greeley's unidimensional understanding of forestry. "I do not believe," he replied, "that fire is in effect the whole problem . . . I would emphatically not say, for the next 10 or 20 years, forget everything else and concentrate all our energies upon that one thing of bringing our forest fire losses down." Pinchot argued that federal control of lumbering would in fact go a long way toward reducing fire losses, since fires often resulted from careless lumbering practices to begin with. He suggested that with federal control of lumbering, "conditions would . . . be kept favorable for forest perpetuation, and the lands made less susceptible to fire. When the lumbering was over, Federal control would cease, and the federal agents would move on. *There would be no Federal organization to fight fire.*"[80]

In the end, the two men's differences could not be overcome. Pinchot, deciding that little remained to be said, declared that "it remains for the public, through Congress, to consider and decide the matter."[81]

Capper and Snell

The struggle did indeed move into the congressional realm shortly thereafter with the introduction of two bills that became rallying points for the regulation and cooperation camps. In the end, though, Pinchot's assessment that "the public" would decide the matter (and his faith that his program would win out) proved overly optimistic. Rather, the issue was worked out through a coalition between Greeley and the organized timber industry.

The regulatory bill was the product of collaboration between Gifford Pinchot and Kansas senator Arthur Capper, after whom the bill was named. At its core was a provision for national control over private timber harvesting, holding to the idea that this and only this would produce real results in slowing or halting forest devastation. The Capper Bill failed to make it out of committee, largely because it was strongly opposed by Greeley's Forest Service together with organized industry under the leadership of the WFCA's Edward T. Allen, forest expert David T. Mason, and the NLMA's Wilson Compton. A 1922 Supreme Court ruling on an unrelated law declared that law enforcement by taxation was unconstitutional, presenting additional legal problems for the Capper Bill, which relied on taxation for its enforcement.[82] Greeley worked very closely with industry representatives in creating and shepherding an alternative to Capper—the Snell Bill (H.R. 15327).

The competing Snell Bill was—by the NLMA's own admission—essentially the work of Greeley in close cooperation with the National Forestry Program Committee (NFPC), a body struck by organized timber specifically in reaction to the threat of federal regulation.[83] The NFPC originated at a 1920 meeting attended by Greeley and representatives of the NLMA, the WFCA, the American

Pulp and Paper Association, the US Chamber of Commerce, the American Newspaper Publishers Association, the Association of Wood Using Industries, the National Wholesale Lumber Dealers Association, and the American Forestry Association.[84] Their goal was to establish common ground, both within the ranks of capital and between capital and the public foresters, on which a national forest policy could be founded.[85] This common ground became the key planks of the Snell Bill. Rather than propose federal regulation, the Snell Bill contained provisions for the federal government to provide money and technical assistance to states that developed policy for continuous forest production, with fire protection playing the lead role. Regulation would be left to the police power of the states rather than to the federal government.

At the hearings in January 1921, a mix of USFS personnel, state foresters, and industry representatives from the American Newspaper Publishers Association, the National Wholesale Lumber Dealers Association, the NFPC, the WFCA, the NLMA, and the Association of Wood Using Industries all testified in favor of the Snell Bill. The American Forestry Association's president, Charles L. Pack, also testified in favor (he was also a member of the NFPC). Pinchot testified against the bill. Just prior to the hearings, in early January, the lumbermen had gained assurances from President-Elect Warren Harding that he would side with the Snell proposals rather than with the Capper proponents' regulatory approach. A handwritten note from Allen to Kellogg reported that an NLMA delegation that met with Harding "followed my advice, giving the Snell bill as our gospel . . . Worked fine. Harding said [Pinchot] had been pestering him with crank theories, but *he would take his dope from people who really dealt with forests.*"[86] Thus the lumbermen were reasonably confident that Harding would eventually bring Secretary of Agriculture Wallace to heel and that the principle of cooperation would prevail. Between 1921 and 1923, drafts and revisions of the bill went back and forth between industry representatives and Greeley, with Allen dictating specific changes to Greeley whenever he thought the forester was straying too far from the principle of cooperation by giving discretionary power to the secretary of agriculture (who, at the time, they correctly viewed as Pinchot's ally).[87] Greeley advised the lumbermen on their proposed lineup of representatives who were to testify before the House Committee on Agriculture on the issue, as well as on the content of their testimony.[88]

However, even with the very cozy relationship between Greeley and the various timber organizations, tensions between industry's profit-driven requirements and the state's desire to adequately manage forests became evident. By February 1921, Greeley had revised the Snell Bill's text—likely under pressure from Wallace, who, according to Kellogg, was "anxious to do nothing to displease G.P. [Pinchot]"[89] The bill now included a provision for the "recommendation" of "essential requirements" for silviculture and fire protection by the secretary of agriculture.[90] Greeley's rewrites and his correspondence with Allen acknowledged that the public perceived a conflict of interest between private lumbering and forest perpetuation, which suggested the need for public control over forests.[91]

Greeley's industry allies were greatly displeased. Allen lamented to Kellogg that "it is certainly too bad that Greeley could not have at least tried to iron things out with us before shooting . . . How in the world advocates of the Snell bill principle can avoid attacking such a change in its spirit, if it comes to a showdown, I don't know."[92] Allen wrote to Greeley informing him that the revisions were certain to come at the expense of lumbermen's support for the bill and also of "the whole spirit of interest and constructive effort which hitherto you have done so much to arouse."[93] Allen fretted that the revisions would "be widely interpreted as almost complete abandonment of the co-operative principle, leaving it a strictly Governmental measure to be opposed by most states and forest owners."[94] He advised Greeley to remove any language that smacked of centralized control over regional forest practices and to stick to the central issue of cooperation in fire protection. Allen's goal had always been to keep federal dollars for fire protection free of regulatory strings. In a 1920 letter to Harris Reynolds of the Massachusetts Forestry Association, Allen wrote that the prospects for a national forest policy would be doomed by "an attempt to introduce regulatory features into legislation designed to bring about fire co-operation."[95] In addition, Allen argued, there was no basis in principle for attaching regulation to fire protective funding, since "an appropriation [for fire protection] from Congress is warranted because of the interest of the general consumer and taxpayer in forest perpetuation."[96] In other words, the organized timber industry suggested that while it had every right to cut timber on private lands as economics and accumulation dictated, the federal government should pay to ensure that this practice did not result in a future wood shortage. Doing so was in the public interest. This was the line put forward not only by Allen but also consistently by Wilson Compton and William Greeley, both as forester and later, when he headed the West Coast Lumbermen's Association. It became a staple of organized timber's public campaigns for fire money.

Partly as a result of the conditionality implied in the Snell Bill's provision for federal funding, organized timber capital's position on Snell began to fragment. Greeley's testimony before a Special Forestry Committee of the Senate in 1923 indicated that "some [lumbermen] favored it and some opposed it." The NLMA and the WFCA remained in support, but some regional associations and individual lumbermen saw the bill as a great threat to their rights as owners. "The latter," according to Greeley, "were moved not so much by objection to the cost of leaving some seed trees, etc., as by fear that it would be an entering wedge making for legislation inimical to property rights . . . They felt that taxation reform and adequate protection against fire should logically come first."[97] Greeley also reported to his staff that a number of members of Congress saw both Snell and Capper as threats to states' rights, failing to see the difference between the two bills.[98]

With support for the Capper Bill limited to a few "advocates of the extreme Pinchot doctrines"[99] and the momentum behind Snell faltering, Greeley took Allen's advice and suggested dropping even the thin regulatory content of the Snell Bill in favor of a bill focused almost exclusively on cooperation among the federal government, the states, and private owners for fire protection. As Steen reports, the US Senate created a Select Committee on Reforestation in 1923, chaired by Oregon senator Charles McNary, to try to pave the way for a national forest policy.[100] Hearings were held across the country, with strong representation from the timber industry, led prominently by the NLMA. The latter argued that reforestation was a public responsibility, too risky to be taken on by private capital and too important to the public to let slide. Compton, on the NLMA's behalf, reiterated that continuous production on commercial forestlands would develop only on the back of profitability and that the greatest obstacle to profit was the scourge of fire.[101] A unified chorus of lumbermen argued for fire cooperation with minimal or no regulation attached. Greeley ensured that the testimony was saturated with witnesses who pointed to fire as the greatest obstacle to reforestation,[102] focusing the committee fixedly on the lumbermen's line that fire protection was forestry and that private forestry would advance once the fire problem was dealt with—this despite a USFS staff revolt, led by Raphael Zon, against Greeley's optimistic assessment of private forestry's proven and potential progress. Many of his staff argued that the forester cleaved too strongly to the line that forestry is and ought to be governed by the dictates of the free market. They pointed out that progress in private forestry was minimal and should not be exaggerated. Greeley agreed with his staff that bad practices should be revealed for what they are but suggested that focusing on positive examples would encourage more progress.[103] His strategy in coordinating the testimony before the select committee hearings suggests that he saw federal fire protection as the only possible way forward for influencing private forestry.

The Select Committee on Reforestation summarized the 1,500 pages of testimony it had heard by repeating that forestry on private lands was thwarted by the risk of fire. The bills sent through the US Congress by Congressman John D. Clarke and Senator McNary stuck close to the committee's findings. Capper had reintroduced two versions of a regulatory bill, both of which threatened to charge lumbermen $4.95 per thousand board feet of timber for improper logging. Both versions were defeated in favor of McNary's bill. Steen's recounting of the process is worth quoting here, since it is very clear concerning what had been lost and what the focus of national forest policy became as a result: "In the Senate, McNary had felt that Snell asked for too much and had gone to Greeley to find out what could be eliminated from the bill. Everything but fire, the senator was told, and he drafted it accordingly." In recognition of Edward T. Allen's pivotal role—it was Allen, after all, who had patiently and diplomatically coached Greeley to ditch the regulatory content and stick to fire protection—McNary wired him directly after the bill was passed to inform him of the news. One item was deleted from the final version of McNary's bill: the restoration of presidential power to create new national forests from public lands.[104] National forest policy had been whittled down to national fire policy.

As this account demonstrates, the eventual legislation passed as the 1924 Clarke-McNary Act—the act that provided the basis for the Forest Service's role in national fire protection—was not the product of a powerful state agency pursuing its own autonomous agenda. Rather, it was a product of a state agency attempting to navigate the tension between what it saw as a looming economic crisis brought on by destructive private logging and the need to maintain profitability and the integrity of private property rights. Beginning with the Society of American Forester's 1919 assessment of what was needed to perpetuate the forests, with fire protection as just one item on a long list of recommendations, the Forest Service had been reduced just four years later to pushing for legislation that would enable it to pay states and private owners to establish fire protective systems—something private lumbermen had wanted since 1902.

Clarke-McNary played two important roles for the lumber industry: it codified the lumbermen's claim that protecting private commercial forests from fire was a public responsibility, and it deflected the threat of regulation. Clarke-McNary, according to Royal S. Kellogg, "definitely established the principle of federal cooperation with the states and timberland owners in the protection and perpetuation of our forest resources. After that the proponents of federal control of private operations—led by Pinchot—had no chance of success."[105] The *American Lumberman* reported that the bill's passage would provide "relief from radical threats," such as the Pinchot-Capper brand of regulation.[106] Greeley further soothed the lumbermen by commenting that with the passage of Clarke-McNary, he considered the matter of federal policy dealing with forestry "complete for many years to come."[107] The lumbermen, through their influence on Greeley, had successfully lured the capitalist state into sharing the costs for the "reproduction of the conditions of production" and dodged the threat of any enforceable reciprocal obligations.[108] In addition, since the Clarke-McNary Act tied the level of federal payments to the fire suppression efforts of states and private landholders, it established a national policy of fire suppression across ownerships.[109]

The outcome of the struggle between regulation and cooperation that culminated in Clarke-McNary was partly a result of Greeley's insistence on a cooperative approach but also largely of the organized power of timber capital, as exercised primarily through the WFCA, the NLMA, and the NFPC. While Greeley (and others) saw Clarke-McNary as his crowning achievement, its text is more heavily imprinted by Allen and Kellogg than by Greeley himself. The influence of the timber industry on the office of the forester is unmistakable in the close correspondence between Allen's written recommendations to Greeley and the final text of the legislation. A WFCA report written in 1948 that reviewed the application of Clarke-McNary in the western states credited Allen outright with writing the act and shepherding it through.[110] Providing further evidence of the power behind Clarke-McNary is a letter from Associate Forester Edward A. Sherman to Francis Cuttle, chair of the Tri-Counties Reforestation Committee in California. Cuttle had written to suggest a small amendment to Clarke-McNary. Sherman replied that Greeley was "entirely agreeable to the idea, but before going too far, I feel that we should first *make sure that we have the backing of the people who made the Clarke-McNary law possible* . . . I would be loath to take any action which might lead its supporters to fear that there was any danger of any considerable part of the benefits which they expected to receive from it being diverted to some other interests."[111]

During the hearings on the Snell Bill, Pinchot explained in frank and self-deprecating terms the industry's power over the office of the US forester, implicating himself no less than his successors in the Forest Service's accommodation to Big Timber. Having delivered a blistering attack on the Snell Bill's reliance on state control, highlighting the power of organized timber capital in the state legislatures of Washington, Oregon, and California, Pinchot was asked by a committee member: "If this bill is subject to the criticism that you have offered, how do you account for our Forestry Department being handled in such a way that they are supporting this measure?" Pinchot replied: "Perhaps, if [you] will let me dodge the question, I will answer it in this way: While I was the Forester, a certain number of lumbermen came to Washington, and, through their representatives, they sat up with me, they held my hand, and they told me how good and statesman-like I was. They finally persuaded me to come out in favor of a tariff on lumber as a means of protecting the forests of the United States."[112] Later that day, Pinchot wrote a letter to be included in the record to the effect that he never intended to impugn the "character or purpose of the men of the Forest Service."[113]

While Greeley's personal commitment to establish and maintain a cooperative relationship with timber capital did play some role, his correspondence with Pinchot, his remarks in service committee meetings, and his testimony before the US Congress suggest that he was moved more by a realization of the limits of the Forest Service's power to achieve regulation than he was by a belief that private owners would, on their own, move toward what today would be called "sustainable business practices." Both Pinchot and Greeley, as well as Henry Graves, recognized that the office of US forester existed at the pleasure of organized timber capital and that its role was to facilitate profitable forestry over the long haul. Pinchot, recall, became a crusader for federal control and a thorn in the side of organized timber capital only after his tenure as head of the USFS. During his tenure, he led the chorus of cooperation with gusto. Greeley, no less than the post–Forest Service Pinchot, believed the police power of the state would eventually have to be brought to bear on private cutting to avert timber famine. However, he also believed "the time had not yet come when either the States or the National government should go into it to any extent."[114] This was an admission that a regulatory approach would not, at that point, have gained the support of lumbermen and was thus a non-starter. Greeley's earnest desire to "get something started"[115] (that is, to attain any action whatsoever that would contribute to movement toward private forestry) led the Forest Service down the path of least resistance—a fork in the road of the organization's history that led its employees away from being foresters and toward becoming firefighters.

REGULATION REDUX

The battle over Snell and Capper, ending with the monocular Clarke-McNary Law, deprived the Forest Service of the means many foresters believed were necessary to deal with what both they and the USFS saw as an impending economic and environmental crisis. It also set the Forest Service firmly on the path toward institutional dependence in its firefighting role. While Clarke-McNary was the most significant instance of organized timber capital pushing the Forest Service away from meddling in private forest production and toward a singular focus on fire protection, it was not unique. For if, as Greeley and the timber industry hoped, the threat of regulation was dead, it had a remarkable recovery beginning in the early 1930s with Ferdinand Silcox's rise to the office of chief forester. While the story of Clark-McNary tells of a political partnership between Forest Service leaders and capital to avert regulation, what follows tells a tale of overt conflict between the USFS and the industry. In response to the continued devastation of US commercial forests, in the 1930s the Forest Service sought to enact regulatory controls and expand public ownership. Again, the forces of "progressive forestry" would be denied by the organized timber industry and set back to rolling the stone of fire suppression instead.

Even as early as 1926, organized timber was nervous about the longevity of Clarke-McNary and the cooperative principle it encoded. Two years after passing the legislation, the president, the director of the budget, and the US Congress were in a belt-tightening mood, and the increase in appropriations for Clarke-McNary that was necessary to bring more states into the program appeared not to be forthcoming. Edward T. Allen, again stepping up to defend the lumbermen's interests, coordinated with George Long and John W. Blodgett to send a delegation of lumbermen to meet with President Calvin Coolidge and impress upon him the need to fully fund both Clarke-McNary and the national forest fire suppression account. Allen's concern was that the lack of funding would "kill the Clarke-McNary law as a national policy standing for Federal cooperation instead of Federal police power."[116] The delegation was successful. Coolidge reportedly thanked the sixteen lumbermen "for bringing this matter of forest fire protection to my attention. You have my complete sympathy. I think we should perhaps raise our appropriation for this purpose."[117] Greeley wrote to Allen two months later to thank him: "Undoubtedly the presentation made to the President by the western delegation had very much to do with the favorable action which has been taken on these matters. I certainly appreciate it very greatly and your own part in bringing it about."[118]

Having averted an early funding crunch, organized timber enjoyed the fruits of Clarke-McNary for decades to follow. However, after Greeley left the Forest Service in 1928, the agency became more deeply dissatisfied with the progress of private forestry under the policy of improving fire protection, and it developed a renewed conviction that "cooperation" in the form of absorbing the costs of reproducing forests for private owners would not suffice to prevent forest devastation.

The issue resurfaced in a number of venues in the early 1930s, first in the *Journal of Forestry* in 1930. Gifford Pinchot, having taken up a renewed interest in forestry after being absorbed in Pennsylvania state politics, offered a $1,000 prize for the best essay on the state of the nation's forests and a proposed remedy for forest problems. The winning essay was submitted by Ward Shepard under the title "Cooperative Control." However, what Shepard was proposing was not Greeley-era "cooperation." Far from taking a conciliatory tone toward the progress of industrial forestry, Shepard began his essay with an unflinching critique of industrialism's sacrifice of the forests:

> The impact of modern industrialism, with its omnivorous appetite for raw materials, caught the forests of America unprepared either by public safeguards or by private traditions of forest culture, to withstand the onslaught made against them. Now, greatly reduced in extent and disastrously impaired in vitality by seventy-five years of big-scale lumbering, they face further and unprecedented inroads with wholly inadequate safeguards. The public forests and a partial system of forest fire control have somewhat restricted the field of destructive exploitation; but essentially in the great bulk of our forests, lumbering has remained unchanged except that mechanization and intensive utilization have made exploitation more severe.[119]

Shepard's first proposed remedy was the institutionalization of cooperation between industry and government, to be accomplished through national, regional, and county "Forestry Boards." These boards were to be established with the primary goal of getting the lumber industry's chronic problem of overproduction under control, thus increasing and stabilizing lumber prices. Coordination among producers to stabilize volume and prices was a long-sought-after goal of timber capitalists,[120] despite their publicly stated creed that forestry must be driven by the laws of the market, and Shepard was likely extending an olive branch with this suggestion. However, he went on to stress the inadequacy of federal encouragement of private forestry, making a case for the necessity and legality of direct public control of logging. He particularly picked on Greeley's notion that forestry should be governed by the logic of free-market economics: "Reliance on supply and demand for forest perpetuation is . . . a dangerous gamble on continental deforestation. It is not enough that government should merely encourage private forestry; it must, on the contrary, create definite safeguards against deforestation."[121]

Despite the flurry of controversy Shepard's essay provoked within the Society of American Foresters, no legislative action toward public regulation accompanied it. Rather, the federal government was busy putting its conservation eggs in the basket of President Herbert Hoover's Timber Conservation Board (TCB). The seed for the TCB was planted by a suggestion made to the president by the

NLMA's Wilson Compton, who was at the forefront of the struggle to stabilize a lumber industry buffeted by overproduction, the chaotic liquidation of standing timber—particularly in the Pacific Northwest—and depressed markets.[122] He believed the recommendations of a president-appointed conservation board would support his own views of what the industry needed: the withdrawal of publicly owned timber from sale, tax reform, and the loosening of antitrust laws that prevented mergers and industry coordination on production levels. *The American Lumberman* asserted that the establishment of such a scientific, fact-finding body as the TCB would ensure that "if any sort of control over production and manufacturing methods is to be exercised, it [would] be dictated by indisputable facts, not by exaggerated statements of the sort used by Gifford Pinchot."[123] However, not leaving the results to chance, Compton worked to ensure that the board was composed almost entirely of lumbermen or those sympathetic to their views.[124] Members of the thirteen-member TCB included former NLMA president John W. Blodgett, president of APPA and of Marathon Paper Mills David C. Everest, William M. Ritter of the W. M. Ritter Lumber Company, railroad executive Carl Raymond Gray, and former NLMA president John H. Kirby of the massive Kirby Lumber Company.

Unsurprisingly, the TCB, which heard testimony from such industry luminaries as William Greeley, David Mason, and Edward Allen, produced a report recommending two major initiatives. The first was encouragement for "sustained yield management" as a means to rein in overproduction. This was Mason's idea; it was embraced by the industry, rejected initially by USFS chief Robert Y. Stuart as anticompetitive, and later adopted by the Forest Service. The second was tax reform. This recommendation was in direct opposition to the findings of the chair of the TCB's subcommittee on taxation, Frederick Fairchild, who argued that taxation was not a significant barrier to forestry. In a letter to Compton, Fairchild argued that contrary to the timber industry's longstanding position, "as a result of the most thorough investigation it has become perfectly evident that there is no evidence to support the belief that taxation has by and large been responsible for the rapid cutting of the American forests or had any substantial effect upon the management of mature forests."[125] According to Robbins, the TCB's final report "differed only in length and minor detail from Wilson Compton's first proposals."[126]

Strong Diagnoses, Weak Prescriptions, and Soured Relations

The regulatory threat bubbled up again from the usual stew of discontented foresters and conservationists shortly thereafter. Aware that the TCB was an industry vehicle, they had been stirred by the publication of *A National Plan for American Forestry,* otherwise known as the Copeland Report. In 1932 Senator Royal Copeland introduced a resolution for the Forest Service to undertake a "State of the Forests" assessment, including recommendations to ensure "all of the economic and social benefits which can and should be derived from productive forests."[127] The Forest Service replied in March 1933 with the 1,600-plus-page Copeland Report, in which it presented a dismal view of the nation's progress in forestry and laid the blame squarely at the feet of private commercial lumbermen. According to Secretary Wallace in his transmission of the report to the president, one of the inquiry's main findings was that "practically all of the major problems of American forestry center in, or have grown out of, private ownership."[128] The report stressed "that reliance upon private ownership of forest land has clearly failed to assure forest welfare and social and economic stability."[129]

The Copeland Report thus amounted to a direct assault on the assumptions of the Clarke-McNary Law, in essential agreement with the arguments Pinchot had been making for over a decade about the inadequacy of "cooperation." Just prior to the release of the Copeland Report, in fact, Pinchot had written to Roosevelt, anticipating the report's findings and recommendations. "In the past," Pinchot wrote, "the official assumption in Washington, codified by the Clarke-McNary Act, has been that private altruism, plus a government subsidy in the form of aid in fire protection, plus patting the lumberman on the back would result in the general practice of forestry on private lands. Experience has proven this assumption to be absolutely wrong... Voluntary forestry has failed the world over. There is no reason to assume that it will succeed in the United States."[130]

Rather than regulation of private cutting, the report recommended a massive program of public forest acquisition, intensification of management on the national forests, and, predictably, expanded and intensified fire protection for private lands.[131] The most radical recommendation was for the nationalization of forestlands; interestingly, it was largely supported by organized timber as part of its drive to curtail production and raise prices. The scale of the suggested public acquisition was massive. A memo from Chief Stuart to Secretary Wallace stated that "if the economic and social values of the forest lands now privately owned are to be safeguarded and conserved, public ownership of approximately 224 million acres of such lands eventually will be inevitable." While Stuart admitted to the "theoretical" nature of this estimate, it was, according to the Forest Service's research, "evident that public ownership of forest lands must in time triple or quadruple in area."[132] This estimate was tantamount to the nationalization of about half of the lumber industry's timber stands.[133]

Pinchot, who had been asked by Roosevelt to draw up a plan for a national forestry program, had—again anticipating the Copeland recommendations—moved away from his longstanding commitment to federal regulation and toward support for nationalizing forestlands on a grand scale. His views on the matter had apparently been transformed by a conversation with Robert Marshall, director of forestry in the Office of Indian Affairs. Marshall had also contributed to the preparation of the Copeland Report. He had impressed upon Pinchot that "the two things we should stress were public ownership and forestry through unemployment work." Marshall also claimed to have "argued him [Pinchot] out of regulation with surprising ease."[134] In his letter to Roosevelt, Pinchot explained that he had abandoned regulation on the grounds that it "would be difficult to apply when the majority of timber land owners are bankrupt, or verging upon it. If they ever became rich and powerful again, it would be equally difficult to keep them from controlling the agency which regulates them."[135] Only the nationalization of most US forestlands would halt their continued devastation and deterioration, Pinchot argued. He continued: "Private forestry in America, as a solution to the problem, is no longer even a hope. Neither the crutch of subsidy nor the whip of regulation can restore it. The solution of the private forest problem lies chiefly in the large scale public acquisition of private forest lands."[136]

Not everyone was convinced that regulation was unfeasible and that public ownership was the best solution. Some foresters believed the recommendations in the Copeland Report were out of synch with its findings. Zon wrote to Pinchot: "It should be obvious to anyone who has read carefully the evidence marshaled in the Copeland Report that the logical conclusion is, first of all: stop forest devastation of the remaining merchantable timber. Yet, the conclusions given in the report dodge this fundamental issue."[137] In addition to Zon, Ward Shepard was critical of the Copeland Report and active in renewing the push for regulation. In a letter to Chief Stuart, he argued that by rejecting regulation in favor of public acquisition, "the Forest Service is committing a strategic and moral blunder of the first magnitude." He protested that without regulation, "our best forests will be condemned to annihilation while the public painfully buys up the devastated crumbs."[138]

Both Shepard and Zon saw a powerful opportunity to achieve public control over forest practices as part of the developing National Industrial Recovery Act (NIRA, 1933). Through the NIRA, the government was agreeing to industry's longstanding wish for price and production controls, and both Zon and Shepard believed that, in return, the government could and should force a quid pro quo of regulation of private cutting strong enough to halt forest devastation. In a memorandum forwarded to President Theodore Roosevelt, Shepard suggested that "the Industrial Recovery Act gives a brilliant opportunity to end the regime of destructive logging that is rapidly devastating our remaining privately owned virgin forests, destroying them as productive organisms, and destroying the great industry itself whose permanence depends on making these forests permanently productive." He proposed a plan "to couple control of lumber production with control of forest devastation, in order to protect the public against the further needless destruction of our forests as living organisms."[139]

Meanwhile, Zon badgered Pinchot to reconsider his position on regulation. He criticized the Copeland Report for falling short of recommending public control and expressed his hope that the lumber industry's inclusion in the NIRA opened the door for regulation of forest practices: "To permit the lumber industry to control prices and production and eliminate the small operator, without insisting on controlling the cut, would mean throwing away the greatest opportunity we have to bring the management of private lands under public control."[140] Zon suspected that any legislation authorizing increased acquisition would remain "a mere gesture" for want of adequate funding and, further, that any money spent would simply go "into the pockets of the lumbermen and other large holders of cut-over land," thus failing to provide the economic impetus available from other kinds of government spending.[141] In an effort to stir Pinchot into action on the regulatory front, Zon claimed that "the foresters feel that they are again on the move. In such a mood, they naturally look to you for the command to march and for clarification of the destination for which they are bound . . . I am sorry that you have given up your position on public control over private lands just at a time when it has the greatest chance of being accepted."[142] This was a major shift for Zon, who four years earlier, just prior to the stock market crash, had been despondent regarding the prospects for federal regulation. "The forestry problem cannot be separated from the general political and economic life when big business, large corporations sway the thought and politics of the country," he wrote. "The National Lumber Manufacturers Association is riding on top of the economic wave . . . It looks to me as if we are to go through the devastation process and then start on the slow march of reclamation. The people, of course, will have to pay through their noses."[143] The fact that by 1933 Zon had come to see such promise for the regulatory project testifies to the lumber industry's desperation for federal assistance in its stabilization efforts. To his way of thinking, the lumber industry's economic crisis opened the door to adequate management of the environmental crisis it was creating.

The president did eventually insist on the inclusion of an article on conservation in the Lumber Code of Fair Competition—the code agreed to by the industry and the National Recovery Administration that set the rules for the lumber industry's supervised self-government. The Lumber Code was written by the industry between May and August 1933 under the guidance of the NLMA, and it met its demise in 1935 at the hands of the Supreme Court in the Schechter decision, which hamstrung the NIRA. Prior to that, however, the code had already proven to be ineffective because of a debilitating lack of enforcement, particularly with regard to price controls. Article X of the code committed the lumber industry to participate in a conference with relevant public agencies, with the goals of establishing "a program of industry action to establish sound forestry practice in the operation of private forests" and "a program of public action to remove unreasonable economic obstacles and in other ways to make practicable the practice of forestry on private lands."[144] The conference that followed in 1934 only committed the industry to practice selective logging and sustained yield management "where practicable" (assumedly as governed by the requirements of profitability) and to "recognize their responsibility for fire protection in their logging operations," a commitment the industry argued it had already been meeting. The state, for its part, promised a program of land acquisition; enlarged cooperation on fire protection for private lands; an extension program, including inspection and enforcement of the code; tax reform for timberlands; loans and credit for owners; and an expanded research program (which for the most part acted as a subsidy for the timber industries to develop new markets, new wood products, and new processes to minimize waste).[145] An "Omnibus Bill" to put all of these commitments into effect was in the works but failed to pass prior to the collapse of the NIRA.[146] The private commitments of Article X (which was also written by the industry and agreed upon by the president) on the conservation front were very weak, and language that made conservation measures necessary only "where practicable" excused forest owners from action.

Article X, like Clarke-McNary, was an instance of the industry working to stave off government regulation by showing its good progress toward implementing forestry. Having reviewed an early draft of the code, Shepard commented that it contributed nothing to the basic problem of conservation and argued that it should be overhauled entirely to commit lumbermen to a program of sustained yield management. The Society of American Foresters gave its full support to the Shepard proposal and expressed as much to the president.[147] According to Colonel George Ahern—a staunch ally of Pinchot's, signatory to the 1919 SAF Committee's letter to foresters, author of the conservation polemic

Deforested America, and the man responsible for setting up the Philippine Forest Administration under Roosevelt—Article X constituted "the same old platitudes of the past forty years but [there is] still not a tooth in the whole darned thing."[148]

Following the collapse of the NIRA and the Lumber Code along with it, the joint committee established by the Lumber Code conference strove to keep Article X's work going on a voluntary basis. A 1937 encore of the conference rehashed the same private commitments and urged public action to remove "obstacles" to private forestry, emphasizing fire protection. Again, however, action was aimed at heading off a new impetus for federal regulation, this time coming directly from the office of the chief forester.

In 1933, following the mysterious death of Robert Stuart, Ferdinand Silcox was appointed chief. In his initial address to the Forest Service after taking office, Silcox laid out a broad vision of how forestry fit with US society—urging his staff to see forestry "in its social relation to industrial life."[149] He connected forest devastation with unemployment and community deterioration and showed an understanding of the profit-based nexus between the exploitation of humans and the exploitation of nature.[150] Addressing the Society of American Foresters two years into his tenure, Silcox laid out his first principle of forestry's "new frontier": "The primary objective of forestry is to keep forest land continuously productive. This must take precedence over private profit. Forest devastation is no longer excusable anywhere."[151] He suggested that forests must shift from being a source of profit for privileged individuals, with the attendant social and economic wreckage that involved, toward being a continuously productive and stable source of livelihood for forest communities. His message was unambiguous regarding the pressing need and public support for federal regulation of private lands. He hearkened back to the 1919 SAF Committee for the Application of Forestry, from which the struggle among foresters over the regulation of private lands emerged. "After 30 years of preaching by foresters," Silcox pointed out, "forest devastation has not stopped." What lay ahead was a determined push by the Forest Service to gain the means to manage private forests. In the unlikely event that the lumbermen were missing the message, Silcox boiled it down: "The issue, in a nutshell, is selfish private interest against social stability."[152] The lines were again drawn, as they had been in the earlier Pinchot-Greeley divide. Conflict between the timber industry and the Forest Service began to increase under Silcox and continued to do so under his successors Earle Clapp and Lyle Watts. The long struggle over public control over forests that extended from the mid-1930s to 1952 is an important piece of the test case for the claim of Forest Service autonomy.

Silcox was unconvinced that fire protection alone would solve the problem of forestry on private lands. He proposed a three-pronged approach to managing forest devastation: large-scale acquisition of forests, increased public cooperation with private owners, and public regulation. The latter was to be tried first by the states, with the federal government seen as a regulator of last resort. In an effort to bring some stability and employment to forest communities, Silcox proposed that the public, either federal or state, "undertake the logging and if necessary the milling of their own timber where this is desirable for the maintenance of existing communities [or] the creation of permanent employment."[153] Silcox's proposals were a response to the president's request for recommendations for a "broad Federal conservation policy."[154]

The lumber industry was greatly upset with these plans. George Jewett, a leading timber capitalist and secretary of the North Idaho Forestry Association, wrote the president to register his dismay at Silcox's "distinctly socialistic" proposals. In a handwritten note to Edward Allen, Jewett claimed he "hit the roof when he read Silcox's speech. I was not the only one."[155] Indeed, he was not. At a special meeting of the Joint Committee of Conservation (the body set up to administer Article X of the Lumber Code), Chair David Mason reported that "considerable alarm and concern has been stirred up in the industry by the speech made by Chief Forester Silcox . . . Many sharp complaints have come to the executive offices of the Lumber Code Authority, and it is evident that some of our most temperate elements are greatly alarmed."[156] Relations between the industry and the Forest Service were souring to an unprecedented degree, and the industry turned to its familiar line that what was necessary was cooperation from the federal government rather than competition in the form of public logging and milling and regulation of private cutting. Assistant Forester Earl W. Tinker tried to smooth the industry's ruffled feathers at a conference in 1937 by contending that the word "regulation" had stirred up unfounded fears over the Forest Service's designs. The industry representatives present, however, pressed him at length on what specific form of regulation the USFS had in mind. Tinker was unable to provide many specifics, other than to reiterate Silcox's line that cutting practices should be developed at as local a level as possible. John Woods, an NLMA forester—in a remarkable moment of transparency—described the industry's view to Tinker: "I think we are going to have to admit we are going to have devastation as you are going to have to scramble some eggs to make the omelet." Rather than spend so much time fighting over control of forest cutting practices to prevent devastation, which was bound to occur in the transition from old growth to managed second growth, Woods argued, the industry and the Forest Service could both agree on the necessity of "keeping the fires out."[157] Efforts should remain focused on dousing fires.

Despite Tinker's efforts, the industry remained suspicious of the Forest Service's regulatory intentions. At a conference with Silcox in 1938, Jewett accused the chief forester of betrayal, declaring outrage at Silcox's "willingness to throw overboard the mutual confidence which has been developed between industry and the Forest Service by years of cooperative effort."[158] Silcox replied flatly that he believed regulation was necessary to deal with both the environmental and the human devastation wrought by private lumbering to date and that the industry has been "too insistent upon receiving cooperative funds and not willing enough to put its house in order."[159] The conference ended with no fences mended.

"A Splendid Opportunity": The Joint Congressional Committee on Forestry

As relations spiraled downward, with the Forest Service leadership maintaining its position on the absolute necessity of regulation, the president asked the US Congress to again inquire into the facts regarding the nation's forest situation and to make policy recommendations—essentially to decide on the issue of federal regulation. A Joint Congressional Committee on Forestry (JCF) was convened, and it began to conduct nationwide hearings. Industry, for its part, was greatly relieved to have this "splendid opportunity" to once again put its case for cooperation and private enterprise before the US Congress rather than to be fighting off a regulatory bill, as it had feared might be the case.[160] As long as it could present its case to a committee of "well-balanced individuals," the industry was confident that it could prove that regulation was not an appropriate solution to forest management problems.[161] Concerned that "it will make quite a difference who is on this committee," Jewett made a number of inquiries to other members of the organized lumber network as to how a lumber-friendly committee might be ensured, speculating on whether Wilson Compton might pull strings with Secretary Wallace.[162] In the end, lumber capital's organized forces were highly satisfied with the JCF's composition, harboring doubts about only two of the ten members.[163]

Despite conflicts within the timber capital network over how it should frame its testimony before the JCF, the group eventually presented a nearly united front. At issue was whether the industry ought to attack specific Forest Service personnel outright (prior to Silcox's death in December 1939, he was the suggested target; after Silcox's death, Earle Clapp took on that position) and make an ideological pitch against the spreading influence of socialism or whether it should stick to technical matters of forest management. Compton and Greeley argued heavily in favor of the latter approach, with Compton advising that the testimony should focus on the development of private forestry through cooperation and "avoid any attack on them [Forest Service personnel] as 'socialistic,' 'destructive of the American system,' etc."[164] He made this argument despite the fact that, as I. N. Tate of Weyerhaeuser admitted, the record of private forestry's development in the United States was extremely weak. "What I am afraid of," Tate confessed to Woods, "is that our story is not good enough; that there is too long a record of clean cutting behind us and not enough examples even now of constructive forest handling to convince any commission that private cutting can be safely left to private owners without government regulation. Of course, we must get together all the facts we can and make as good a showing as possible."[165] This belief was little different from John Woods's own thoughts on the matter, which he had expressed to David Mason two years earlier. Woods predicted that the cooperative, private approach embodied in the Article X joint committee was "headed for the rocks, principally because certain elements of the industry are no longer interested [in forestry], and they are no longer interested because they think the danger of public regulation has past [*sic*]."[166] Woods's comment sheds a great deal of light on much of the industry's attitude toward forestry, specifically that forestry measures were primarily a sideshow with the principal objective of heading off direct federal control. In the end, however, despite these misgivings and as a result of the NLMA's enormous efforts at coordination, industry representatives presented a unified face that stuck largely to Compton's strategy. Even George Jewett—a rabid defender of private property rights and proponent of the virtues of free enterprise, with a tendency to see a communist or a fascist under every rock—put forward only a moderate anti-socialist screed and stuck mostly to forestry issues.[167]

Throughout the hearings, the constant theme from both industry representatives and state (not federal) foresters was the evil of flames. Industry testimony focused on the need for expanded and intensified fire protection on private lands. C. S. Chapman, speaking for the West Coast Lumbermen's Association and the Pacific Northwest Loggers Association, told the committee that while priorities might vary on a number of the elements of the industry's preferred policy program, "on one matter . . . you will all have been impressed. Unqualifiedly, industry feels that protection against destruction of both young and old forests, through fire, is a prerequisite to forest growing or profitable forest ownership."[168] To effect such protection, the industry program recommended an increase in the

Clarke-McNary appropriation to $9 million (from $2.5 million). On the issue of regulation, Compton, on behalf of the NLMA, argued that the surest road to sound forestry was to work through state laws, with the federal government facilitating this through expanded funding for fire, insect, and disease protection under Clarke-McNary. "More support for forest fire protection is the greatest single help to American forestry on private lands which the Federal Government can give," Compton argued.[169] The industry did not consider publicly funded fire suppression and prevention on private timber stands a subsidy but instead "the cost of administering one of the major protective functions of Government."[170] If regulation must be put in place, as Compton agreed it occasionally must, it should be locally appropriate and administered under state, not federal, law. The federal role should be, as it was, limited to offering the carrot of Clarke-McNary funds in exchange for progress in forestry by private landholders. If the government wanted to hand out a larger amount to subsidize employment on private lands and in the mills, so much the better, but the idea that the federal government should become an active, direct producer of lumber through logging and milling, as Silcox had suggested, was completely unacceptable.[171]

Industry analysis of the hearings process suggested that capital faced tough sledding in selling this message wholesale to the committee. The NLMA's analyst, Wellington Burt, who followed the JCF across the country to attend all the hearings, suspected that committee members were tending toward Silcox and Clapp's quid pro quo argument: that the federal government should see better behavior from private lumbermen for its cooperative dollar. However, Burt's summaries of the hearings show a consistent line put forward by both state foresters and forest owners: the problem is fire. Private forestry is proceeding apace, although it still faces obstacles, primarily in the form of fire and taxation. State regulation would be acceptable if private forestry falters, but what the federal government needs to do above all is put fire at bay with a more generous allocation to the states and private owners.[172]

Following its cross-country journey, the Joint Congressional Committee on Forestry released its report in 1941, after several delays. It laid out the grim facts of the "forest situation," stressing that it would take concerted effort and a national program of significant scope to get the nation's forests back into productive shape.[173] Like the Copeland Report, it claimed that private lands were the crux of the problem and that "various measures [were required] to restore and maintain them in satisfactory producing condition."[174] Primary among these measures, the committee believed, and primary among its final recommendations was the "extensification and intensification of cooperative protection against fire

on private and state-owned forests lands." To accomplish this, the JCF recommended quadrupling the Clarke-McNary authorization to $10 million in three
$2.5 million annual increments. The states, as under the original Clarke-McNary
Act, would be charged with developing and enforcing adequate fire control measures, with funds withheld if they failed to do so.[175] *The Timberman* editorial-
ized that "with their feet braced for something of a shock or at least a suggestion
for federal regulation, the forest industries awaited the report with considerable
anxiety." However, its analysis of the report suggested a "keynote . . . of federal cooperation rather than federal domination."[176] Senator John H. Bankhead, chair of
the JCF, introduced a bill to enact the recommendations, but it failed as a result
of weak support from the industry and a lack of support from the Forest Service,
which was still holding out for federal regulation. Both the NLMA and the
Western Pine Association supported the JCF report, with the former claiming
that the committee had undertaken its duties "in an atmosphere friendly to the
lumber industry."[177] However, their support was not unqualified, and a number
of regional associations were lukewarm toward the bill because of its suggestion
of the possibility of state regulation.

In December 1941, building on Bankhead's bill, Secretary of Agriculture
Claude R. Wickard again attempted to broker a bill for federal regulation but
with the president's request that it include no subsidies to timber owners, that
it be entirely federal, and that it include no "matching funds" provisions. The
Forest Service and Secretary Wickard's staff eventually proposed such legislation,
including complete federal control over private cutting, an increase in Clarke-
McNary funds to $9 million, a return to the early Forest Service practice of doling
out technical advice to private forest owners, and a number of smaller items. The
Bureau of the Budget recommended presidential approval of expanding fire protection but advised against approving federal regulation. The bureau suggested
that "forest industrial interests would . . . fight vigorously this regulatory proposal"
and noted that while "the views of foresters and other qualified persons . . . as to
the necessity for and desirability of public regulation of forest practices are widely
divergent," both the AFA and the SAF tended to be more supportive of state-level
regulation.[178] The budget director—despite the JCF's findings—argued that private forestry was proceeding nicely on its own, that the danger of timber famine
was fading, and that the cooperative approach would bring about timber growth
sufficient to meet national demands. The bureau dismissed the prospect of wood
shortages and scotched the Forest Service's efforts to obtain regulatory authority
a second time in December 1942, when the USFS attempted to go through the
War Production Board to obtain regulatory power.[179] Further, in his memo to

President Franklin Delano Roosevelt, the director warned that "the introduction of legislation providing for federal regulation in this field will certainly arouse a major controversy and would be particularly untimely now [during the war] when unity of effort is so essential."[180] Roosevelt's "OK," penciled in the margins next to the director's recommendation, indicated his desire not to inflame the timber industry over regulation, particularly since wartime lumber production was so urgent. The recommended increase in fire protection was approved, even with Roosevelt's austere wartime mood. Through its highly organized intervention in the scope, composition, and activities of the JCF, the industry had managed to turn the agenda away from authorizing public oversight of private logging, channeling the Forest Service back into its commercially supportive, comfortable, and widely praised role of chasing fire from the woods.

The regulatory battles continued, however, through World War II and on into the early 1950s under the leadership of Clapp and Watts. Watts, appointed to the top post in the Forest Service in January 1943, gave a speech in September of that year that started off a new round of sparring between the industry and the USFS on the topic of regulation. His Milwaukee address to a chapter of the SAF unveiled his belief that "comprehensive forest legislation, including but not limited to regulation of cutting practices[,] is now more urgently needed than ever before . . . I have seen much more destructive cutting than good forestry. I want to say with all the force I have that nation-wide regulation of cutting practices on private forest land under strong federal leadership is absolutely essential."[181] The emphasis on federal, rather than exclusively state-based, regulation was seen as pivotal for the prevention of forest devastation. As Steen reports, state regulations were scattered and weak, with only five states having passed any such regulation prior to World War II. Seven more had joined by 1945.[182] All of these regulations were focused almost exclusively on fire protection, with minor incentives to encourage regeneration. In Washington, Oregon, and California, as Pinchot had predicted would be the case with state legislation, the timber industry had written the regulations and lobbied for their passage.

Watts also took exception to the industry's efforts at public education on forestry matters. Responding to an ongoing public relations campaign by the industry, carried out by the NLMA's newly launched American Forest Products Industries (AFPI) to promote an image of advancing private forestry, Watts claimed: "I cannot let the misleading publicity of the forest industries to remain unchallenged . . . I cannot escape the conclusion that the real object of this campaign is to ward off public regulation which was recommended in one form by the Department of Agriculture in 1940, brought before Congress in several forms since then and proposed for legislation in fourteen states during the last winter."[183] Watts based his justification for federal intervention on a broad claim of public interest in the state of the nation's forests and on the federal government's substantial contribution to private forestry through fire protection, forest credit programs, insurance, and research.

Predictably, the industry fired back. It appealed to the need for unity in a time of war and for the latitude to do whatever it took to produce the lumber required for the war effort. "We are harvesting extra trees because we need them now," claimed Compton, who became the front man for the industry in the battle with Watts. "After the war, they can be replaced."[184] On the whole, however, Compton portrayed the Forest Service's warnings of an impending national timber shortage as "gloomy" and discredited. Inasmuch as there were going to be regional and local shortages, Compton suggested that the problem was a lack of demand for wood, causing low prices and pressure to liquidate to meet carrying costs. His appeal was for "education, economic inducement, and . . . cooperation" to stimulate the private enterprise of forestry. Interestingly, in closing his rebuttal, Compton admitted that federal regulation would "force action more quickly" on forest devastation, with the result, however, of producing the unthinkable: "its consequence would be the substitution of public for private forest ownership."[185]

A year earlier, the American Forestry Association had called for setting aside the debate on regulation to promote "greater unity of workers in the forest field in the interest of meeting military needs for forest products." The AFA, according to pro-regulation forces inside the Forest Service, had over time come to be a mouthpiece for the industry. Pinchot had long before criticized the AFA for its weak posture with the lumbermen, an opinion later adopted by both Clapp and Watts.[186] Earlier, Raphael Zon had made similar observations about the Society of American Foresters.[187] Zon's view was vindicated most obviously when the SAF council refused to accept a resolution sanctioning the AFPI for its rosy and misleading "public information" campaign about the forest industry, opting eventually to send a letter to the AFPI "expressing concern over false optimism."[188] Indications are that the two major civil society and professional organizations concerned with forestry had come under heavy industrial influence, as Representative William E. Humphrey had charged regarding the AFA in 1913.

The AFA executive secretary's annual report for 1942 claims that "the Directors recognized, at the outset of the war, that the controversy over federal regulation of private timber owners, insisted upon by the Forest Service, had reached a point which if continued would divide and weaken the war effort."[189]

The Forest Service, as demonstrated by Watts's continued efforts, refused to abide by the AFA's suggestion, much to the consternation of the timber industry. Stuart Moir, forester for the Western Pine Association, wrote Watts a typically angry letter rife with accusations of betrayal: "For some reason, probably based on your previous remarks, I have been living under the assurance that for the duration [of the war] at least the bugaboo of Federal regulation threats would not arise to detract time and energy of the forest industries from the war effort." Moir contended that given that "government control is abhorrent to industry" and that the forest products industries were "a ranking leader among the nation's great industries" and thus wielded considerable political clout, "a drive by the Forest Service at this time for Federal regulation will not facilitate the war effort nor accomplish anything beneficial for forestry."[190] In short, Moir was confident in the industry's ability to beat back the regulatory push and found it more of an irritant than a threat. His confidence was eventually shown to be justified.

As the Forest Service continued to publicly pronounce the need for federal legislation, the industry—again crying "socialism" and fearing for the sanctity of property and free enterprise—fought back. It mobilized its propaganda wing (the AFPI, headed by William Greeley) and its direct lobbying wing, the newly formed Forest Industries Council (FIC)—a body composed of representatives from the NLMA, the APPI, and the American Pulpwood Association (APA) charged with establishing relations with key congressional committee members. Its policy development wing (the NLMA) was, as usual, also at the heart of the struggle. The NLMA swore to wage a no-holds-barred struggle that would proceed "full blast against any and all attempts to promote federal regulation."[191] The Forest Service's regulatory program was eventually introduced by Senator Clinton Anderson in 1949, and it sparked an outraged but highly sophisticated and well-orchestrated response from organized timber. Harold Steen's account is worth quoting at length here because it shows clearly how advanced the lumber industry's policy machinery had become after the war, relative to its fairly straightforward association activities early on:

> The industry prepared for an all-out battle, believing that after decades of threats, the Forest Service was ready to go all the way. By late 1949 the lumber industry had organized its forces against federal domination. AFPI led the way. Materials flowed to newspapers, professional and trade journals, and popular magazines. The frontal assault on Forest Service propaganda blanketed the nation. Emphasized were two "facts": the industry was doing a good job, and private enterprise was more efficient than the federal government.[192]

This two-pronged attack has since become a staple of industry opposition to environmental regulation. However, while the industry and the Forest Service put considerable effort into shaping public opinion, they realized that the real targets were the members of the US Congress. Steen continued: "Every congressional district was to have an industrial contact [a network already established under the guidance of the FIC]. Each man [*sic*] was to be fully instructed in the industrial position and the best methods of approaching congressmen and senators with this information. Witnesses at hearings needed careful grooming to assure optimum presentation. Little was left to chance."[193]

The lumbermen worked to enlist the support of all other segments of the forest industries ("some 40 or 50 associations" by their count), the natural resource industries, state foresters who felt threatened by federal oversight, and sympathetic Forest Service employees.[194] The WFCA assembled talking points for industry spokespersons, which included instruction on the limits of legitimate government intervention in forestry. A telling example states: "The government does have a rightful place in cooperation with the forest land owners and the States, in cooperative fire protection, forest research, and education . . . Such cooperative efforts can be conducted within the framework of private forest ownership and business incentive. This is preferable to starting along the road toward nationalization of our forest resources."[195]

Early in the fight, well-placed industrial forest owners assessed the strength of the enemy, and it appeared to be substantial. According to NLMA executive vice president Richard Colgan, the Forest Service has had "publicity favorable to their position in practically all newspapers and magazines and through special pamphlets made readily available to women's clubs, garden clubs, leagues of women voters and many other organizations of like character. They have had the further advantage of use of government facilities . . . together with almost unlimited finances. There can be little doubt that there is widespread public sentiment in favor of public regulation of our industry."[196] Civic associations were behind the Forest Service and were committing considerable resources to the fight. Despite all this, effective industrial opposition ensured that the Anderson Bill never made it out of committee.

One last gasp on regulation was heard from the Forest Service when Assistant Forester Edward Crafts gave a speech at Yale University in 1951, in which he declared the continuing need for federal control of private logging and accused the lumbermen of opposing such control not on technical grounds but instead on the basis of emotion and an irrational, misplaced phobia regarding totalitarian socialism. Far from the thin edge of the wedge for nationalization and socialism,

Crafts portrayed regulation as the step required to stave off socialism by making private forestry continuously productive. Chief Watts endorsed the speech, raising industry hackles and prompting a flurry of intra-industry correspondence on the resurgent socialist menace.[197] Richard McArdle was then appointed chief just prior to the 1952 presidential election that swept Dwight D. Eisenhower into the White House. Eisenhower had campaigned on a "wise use" election platform that emphasized minimizing government control over land use, and many suspected that unless he toed the White House line, McArdle would be replaced. The forest products industries met with the new secretary of agriculture, Ezra Taft Benson, to ensure that his staff in the Forest Service would hold to Eisenhower's policy, and the matter of federal regulation of cutting was snuffed out, never to be rekindled. McArdle's view was that the endless struggle for regulation had cost the Forest Service critical support for more important issues. Principal among them was fire protection.[198]

CHAPTER FIVE

OUT OF THE FRYING PAN

Catastrophic Fire as a "Crisis of Crisis Management"

> The development of civilization and industry in general has always shown
> itself so active in the destruction of forests that everything that has been
> done for their conservation and production is completely insignificant in
> comparison.
>
> *Karl Marx, Capital, vol. 2 (New York: Vintage, 1979), 322*

The thirty-three-year struggle for federal regulation, which began in 1919
with Forest Service employees and allied conservationists working through the
Society of American Foresters (SAF) under Gifford Pinchot's leadership, ended
in defeat. The USFS leadership's role had swung from one side of the issue to the
other, eventually letting the struggle drop. Pinchot, Henry Graves, and William
Greeley—in particular the latter—had been pivotal in entrenching the principle
of cooperation, through which they hoped to induce private owners to adopt
practices of sound forestry as they understood it. Pinchot was the first to aban-
don this hope, and he did so with a conviction that saw him butt heads time and
time again with the organization he had helped launch. Greeley, on the other
hand, remained convinced about the promise of free-enterprise forestry throughout his career, growing more anti-regulation as he moved from the Forest Service
to the West Coast Lumbermen's Association to the American Forest Products
Industries (AFPI). With Ferdinand Silcox's ascent to its helm, the USFS swung
decisively toward a belief that the end of forest devastation required strong federal

action—including police action—and the subordination of individual private gain to social benefit. Earle Clapp and Lyle Watts carried that torch until the early 1950s.

Throughout all this, the Forest Service's essential mission remained constant: perpetuation of nature's contribution to capitalist production in the form of timber. The agency's relations with the timber industry and its proposed means of accomplishing its mission fluctuated from cozy and cooperative to antagonistic and regulatory with the leadership. Regardless of the character of the relationship and the proposed management strategy of various Forest Service administrations, however, the cooperative principle encoded in Clarke-McNary remained the law. Thirty-three years of effort to install some form of (generally weak and highly qualified) federal regulation of forestry broke constantly against the walls of organized timber capital. Each time it did so, those charged with managing the nation's forests fell back on the established ground of "cooperation." The latter, although it encompassed research and replanting to some extent, boiled down largely to an agreement by the federal government to assist in putting out fires nationwide and to induce the states to help with that effort. In return, federal foresters continually hoped for improved private forestry as the obstacle of risk on investment (and thus pressure to liquidate "assets" in the form of forests) was reduced. Contrary to the industry's relentless public relations efforts, which never stopped claiming that private forestry was steaming forward toward sustainable forestry and would accelerate once the risk of fire was subdued, every assessment the Forest Service carried out showed that its hopes were in vain, thus renewing and strengthening its conviction that federal regulation was needed. After the last big push in the late 1940s, the USFS abandoned the project and focused on meeting national timber needs not by ensuring that private lands remained productive but instead by throwing open the doors of the publicly owned national forests and inviting in the lumberjacks.

The lumber industry had been relentless in its calls for the extension and intensification of fire protection on public and private lands. Organized lumbermen hammered repeatedly at the federal government and the states to live up to their obligations for fire protection as established under Clarke-McNary, to maximize the authorizations and appropriations for fire protection, and to extend the "cooperative principle" into other areas of forest protection, such as the fight against disease and insects.[1] In agreeing to support state foresters in their successful push to maximize the 1939 Clarke-McNary appropriation, Wilson Compton wrote, "As you know, we have been battling for more liberal provision for this work for many years, in fact ever since the authorization was first established."[2] Organized timber called on the federal government to pick up an increased share of the burden of fire protection at every opportunity, making use of trade journals, print and broadcast media, and direct lobbying.[3] In cooperation with the American Forestry Association, in 1939 the National Lumber Manufacturers Association (NLMA) worked to "make forest fire prevention its Public Campaign No. 1," with the goal of increasing the Clarke-McNary authorization to $9 million.[4] First on every association's list of "what is to be done" was: keep fire out of the forests. The WFCA called for "protection of the forests from fire . . . on a scale where even abnormally bad fire seasons will no longer threaten the security of mature timber and reforesting lands."[5] From the original Clarke-McNary authorization of $2.5 million in 1924, "cooperative" assistance from the federal government to the states rose—with enthusiastic capitalist support—to $20 million in 1955, an eightfold increase over a thirty-year period.[6] While these figures are stated in nominal terms, the increase is indicative of priorities, since during that period the entire Forest Service budget increased from just over $10 million to $47 million.[7] By 1947, despite Clarke-McNary's original intention that protection would be funded 50 percent by the public and 50 percent by private owners, private owners' share of actual protection expenditures was 11 percent.[8]

Only in one instance did the industry as a whole oppose the Forest Service's budget requests for fire protective purposes, in the 1949 Granger Act. Granger proposed substantially increasing the authorization for fire protection under Clarke-McNary, as well as authorizing $6 million for the Forest Service to provide free forestry consultations for forest owners. The industry suspected that this was an attempt to "load up the Clarke-McNary Act with benefits to private owners so that later they can add regulation of forest landowners to the Act on the excuse that for all such benefits landowners would agree to take a certain amount of regulation. This is Silcox's 'Quid pro quo.'"[9] The Granger Bill was introduced just prior to Senator Anderson's bill, discussed in chapter 4, which called for direct regulation of forest industry operations. In a letter appealing to consulting foresters to oppose Granger and Anderson, the NLMA charged that the two bills were the first and second steps toward the socialization of forestry in the United States. George Fuller, vice president of the NLMA, urged all consulting foresters to contact key Senate Agriculture Committee members "protesting this vicious and socialistic legislation."[10] Richard Colgan, president of the NLMA, issued a press release in opposition to Granger and Anderson, claiming they will "take the United States another long and dangerous step down the road toward statism."[11] Clyde Martin of the Weyerhaeuser Timber Company and forest engineer for the Western Pine Association counseled the NLMA that it was through modifications to Clarke-McNary that "the Forest Service really expects to secure its regulatory controls."[12] The industry was determined to keep fire protection funds completely separate from all other federal programs and assistance.[13]

As a result of their suspicions about Clarke-McNary, their fiscal conservatism, and their generalized fear of Silcox's vision of social forestry, the lumber associations came out in unanimous opposition to the fire protective funding increases in the Granger Bill. While holding to its public support for cooperative and universal fire protection, the industry claimed it was time to consider the larger picture of federal fiscal responsibility and question whether the federal government should be shouldering fully half of the burden of fire protection.[14] However, by the mid-1950s—with a more cooperative administration in place in the Forest Service and relations between the industry and the USFS on the mend[15]—the industry had returned to its support for maintaining and increasing cooperative fire protection, even while calling in some cases for cuts in other elements of Forest Service budgets.[16]

While foresters both inside and outside the USFS struggled to attain the authority they thought was necessary to adequately manage industrial logging's devastation of US forests, the industry repeatedly assured the US Congress and the public that if the scourge of fire could be brought to heel, lumber industry representatives would manage forest devastation themselves on the combined basis of self-interest and noblesse oblige. The Forest Service, for its part, took on the fire protective role enthusiastically. As debates within the USFS flared over the appropriate role of fire and how the nation would relate to fire in the woods, a much larger debate over who would control the woods and for what purposes was having a much stronger effect on policy. The cooperative principle of Clarke-McNary hinged on maintaining the belief that fire was forestry's enemy. The Forest Service saw its expertise in fire suppression, sharpened during the 1910 fires, as a unique capacity—one it could offer to private lumbermen in exchange for their modification of cutting practices. If the USFS could develop that capacity to its fullest and demonstrate it on the national forests, the agency could have some small measure of power over the way private lands were managed. Having attempted to gain more direct control and failed, the agency fell back on its established expertise and on the role that continually earned it budgetary allocations—largely as a result of the industry's unflagging support. In this way, Stephen Pyne's argument that the fire suppression policy grew up around the structure of the budget is totally accurate. However, budget allocations were not controlled or shaped entirely or even primarily by the Forest Service or the Department of Agriculture. Money went to fire-related programs because the industry asked for it, just as money was allocated for timber sales in the early 1950s because the industry asked for it. The agency did, indeed, "do what it was paid to do, which was fire suppression," as Pyne contends.[17] But it did not write its own job description. If it had, it would certainly have included management of much greater acreages of forestland and direct control over forest management on private lands.

Inasmuch as, over the past century, the policy of fire suppression has contributed to the current forest health crisis and created the conditions for catastrophic fires, authors, activists, and politicians seeking to assign blame have pinned it squarely on the Forest Service and, to a lesser degree, on the USFS's partner land management agencies. Since the Forest Service is the primary agent and most public advocate of fire suppression, it seems reasonable to point to the USFS's internal organizational dynamics as the motor of fire suppression. However, the Forest Service has not had its way with many of its policy goals, which have often been shaped in both coordination and conflict with outside groups—most notably industry associations. To fully understand the challenges land management agencies and environmental activists face today, we need to understand the policy environment in which the Forest Service operates. In addition to looking at the USFS's historical acts, recounted in chapter 2, we need to examine the context in which those acts were undertaken. We need to understand the Forest Service's position relative to the structures of politics and economy that channel, encourage, and constrain the actions and decisions of public managers. Sociological theory has a great deal to offer in this vein.

FIRE EXCLUSION AS METABOLIC RIFT

Clearly, the history of forestry in the United States is one of crisis management. These crises have been both economic and ecological and have had enormous repercussions for workers, communities, and the ecological integrity of forests. The primary role of the Forest Service has been to attempt to manage these crises—to stabilize lumber markets, provide a supply of raw materials during times of scarcity, provide employment and community stability in forest regions, and—above all—to oversee the reproduction of the conditions of production in the form of readily exploitable nature. However, as we have seen, the Forest Service has not been free to pursue its management objectives in whatever way it sees as most effective. In the eyes of many conservationists, foresters, and leading administrators, regulation was the most vital "tool in the box" for appropriate management of the environmental and economic crises resulting from commercial lumbering.

The agency was repeatedly denied that regulation on the basis of its threat to both private property and the profitability of commercial timber companies. Instead, the USFS was granted the increasing authority and capacity to remove the "obstacle" of fire.

The Forest Service exercised this authority with enthusiasm, effectiveness, and a strong sense of righteous heroism. However, in doing so, the USFS served as the stagehand for what is now discussed openly as a forest health crisis. Thus I argue that the history of forest and fire management in the United States is best understood as an upstream attempt to manage one crisis and, in the attempt, the downstream creation of a second crisis. I have already discussed the first crisis. This is the crisis of forest devastation I characterized in terms of James O'Connor's "second contradiction of capitalism." The major fear the Forest Service expressed relates to the economic moment of crisis. Up until the mid-1950s, the USFS was preoccupied with the threat of shortage, spectacularly referred to as "timber famine." This was a logical outgrowth of both the Forest Service's original mission to ensure a continuous supply of wood to the nation (and a continuous opportunity for the profitable exploitation of nature) and its view of forests as stands of increasing value, to be realized following the swing of the ax.

However, the second crisis is not well captured by O'Connor's theory of capitalist environmental crisis. O'Connor's second contradiction of capitalism becomes a crisis only when the underproduction of the conditions of production registers in the realm of prices. Only when shortages or unsuitable arrangements of nature, labor power, and infrastructure work their way through to firms' cost structures does a crisis manifest itself. In O'Connor's scheme, ecological ruptures and degradation that fail to show up immediately as shortages, bottlenecks, or increased input costs or that are not immediately problematic for continued capitalist production are not crises. However, the cogs between ecological decline and prices are, at the very least, missing a few teeth. Prices and supply shortages are far from accurate signifiers of ecological processes and scarcities.

A crisis in environmental health will not translate immediately into information conveyed by price, if indeed it ever does so. One prominent example documented by economist Michael Perelman is the extinction of the passenger pigeon.[18] While relative prices are presumed to adjust to conserve scarce resources, Perelman notes that passenger pigeons were hunted to extinction (from a population of staggering numbers) between about 1840 and 1900 without so much as a blip in their price. The reason for this "anomaly" was that passenger pigeons were easy to hunt, even as their numbers dwindled, and were seen as a substitute for chickens—or, more accurately, chicken (it is the meat rather than the bird that is relevant here)—which was still in plentiful supply. For the market, there was no crisis. For the passenger pigeon, however, there certainly was—one that turned out to be terminal.

The forest health crisis is not restricted to, or even primarily focused on, the economic moment. Certainly, it represents a manifestation of "fiscal crisis" for the state,[19] since much of the restorative work that could be done to reduce the threat of catastrophic fire and to restore fire as a natural ecological process is risibly beyond the Forest Service's fiscal capacity. As the state has taken on the burdens of both fire suppression and now the project of "fuels management" (the alteration of a landscape's vegetative structure to produce a certain distribution of fuel and thereby reduce the risk of high-intensity fire)—the former in response to the demands of timber capital, the latter in response to its previous managerial interventions—it has finally run aground on the hard shores of budgeting. Cost estimates for "thinning" by mechanical means range between $500 and $1,500 per acre. Estimates for the more cost-efficient process of thinning by prescribed fire run from about $50 to $500 per acre.[20] Given that the Forest Service estimates that up to 650 million acres of public and private land would benefit from fuel treatment[21] and (unrealistically) taking the low range of the cost estimates for mechanical thinning, the cost would be $325 billion just to start the process. Even if the Forest Service could do a prescribed burn on every acre it determines is in need—a scenario precluded by terrain, real-estate proximity, recreational infrastructure, and the career-ending prospect of a fire getting "out of prescription" (for example, a fire getting out of control and torching a substantial part of Los Alamos)—the cost would be $32.5 billion.

Taking these expectations down a notch, merely treating the land within the National Forest System that requires it (the estimated 51.1 million acres of Fire Regime Condition Class three land),[22] the cost would be $25.75 billion to thin mechanically and $2.6 billion to carry out prescription burns. The entire Forest Service budget enacted for FY 2008 (including emergency and supplemental appropriations) was $5.8 billion. The budget for FY 2009 was $4.55 billion, so even at the lowest of the low end of cost estimates for prescribed burning, the Forest Service would have to dedicate well over half of its total budget to fuels treatment.

There is, of course, the possibility that this could be carried out over the long term, and research by Mark Finney and his colleagues suggests that treating just a small portion of high-risk forests per year can break the fuel structure sufficiently to disrupt the growth of large fires.[23] So annually, a smaller number of acres could be burned or mechanically thinned to reduce the risk of catastrophic fire. Nonetheless, such treatments must continue on an annual basis to offset new growth. Fire managers interviewed for this study confirmed the hopelessness of efforts to return forests to their historical condition class through fuels treatment projects, given current funding levels. I asked Brett[24] what he thought about the prospects of restoring the land to a condition in which fire could be reintroduced into its ecological role. His response was typical of most, highlighting a mix of public resistance to prescribed burning on a massive scale and funding constraints:

> It's not going to happen. We're so far behind with where the forests are at that in today's budgets . . . the political realities of doing that much fuels treatment every year [are] not realistic. We don't have the people, we don't have the funding, and I'm not sure the public would be tolerant of us lighting off, like we need to do, about 80,000–100,000 acres a year just to keep up ecologically, and we're doing about 20,000–25,000 and we're a big unit. We're doing the most of any forest by far, but we aren't keeping up. So, you know, no. The only way we'd have a chance is for the public to be willing to accept more fire use on the landscape. That's the only way. Because we're not going to do it with prescribed fire. We'd need so many more people and so much more money. So, no.

Another manager, Ian, told me that while he and his workers were doing "a lot" of prescribed burning in their fuels reduction program, it was less than half what they would need to do—about 40,000 acres per year—to move the forest toward its historical fire regime. The ecological consequence of the severe underfunding of fuels treatment relative to the acreage and increasing complexity of the work is a mounting risk of catastrophic fire. According to Frank, a fire manager from eastern Oregon:

> Well, [the consequence of the funding shortfall] is a continued accumulation of biomass, which is reflected in fire behavior. On a typical summer day, it results in uncharacteristic wildfire effects and greater risks to people and communities and less willingness for us to aggressively engage when a fire's behaving that way. Because you take all that and lay on top of it the South Canyon/30 Mile/Cramer stuff [fires in which there were firefighter fatalities] and liability and firefighting that doesn't put people at risk, which is the right thing to do, but put all that together and you're in a situation where you're just going to continue to have large fires . . . You're always going to get your top priorities done if you're given any resources. And then you just work your way down. But is it far enough down to have any effect? I don't know.

Some of the funding crunch was alleviated in 2009–2010, as for the second time in its history the Forest Service was a major beneficiary of an economic crisis. While in the 1930s public funds paid public workers to lay much of the basic infrastructure for fire suppression and to actually put out fires, the financial meltdown that began in 2008 has yielded a similar windfall for the USFS. The 2009 American Recovery and Reinvestment Act (ARRA), designed to provide a Keynesian fiscal stimulus to an economy entering what many predicted would be a deep and prolonged crisis, included $500 million in funding for wildland fire management. Half of this amount was dedicated to hazardous fuels reduction, forest health protection, hazard mitigation, and rehabilitation on federal land; the other half was slated for similar activities on state and private land. The Department of the Interior received another $15 million under the ARRA. Given the massive numbers discussed earlier, however, and the long-term financial commitment required, it remains in serious doubt whether the concerns expressed by managers such as Brett, Frank, and Ian will be alleviated in any significant way. However, while the budgetary shortcomings—to which I return in greater depth in chapter 6—do make clear the state's inability to undertake its managerial ambitions, the forest health crisis, unlike the earlier crisis of timber famine, is an ecological crisis that has yet to register in the sphere of production. It has not manifested as any kind of spike or even a blip on capital's financial seismometers. There is no cost squeeze resulting from the declining state of US forests. The economic costs of past management practices are being contained within the state and managed by shuffling money from, or cutting back on, other areas of government provisioning.

A second element of the forest health crisis that distinguishes it from crises arising from the second contradiction of capitalism is that the latter are conceptualized as a direct product of dynamics internal to capitalism. The forest health crisis, on the other hand, is immediately caused by previous policies enacted by the state as a manager of crisis. In examining the case of forest and fire management in the United States, we are forced to investigate how the relationship between capitalist production and nature is mediated through the state.

The contemporary forest health crisis, along with other crises that threaten the healthy functioning of ecosystem processes—crises for nature rather than for capitalists—requires an explanatory theory that gives equal attention to both sides of the dialectical relationship between humans and nature. In addition, it requires a theoretical framework that allows for the inclusion of the state as a mediator of human-nature interactions. Such a theory is available through the concept of metabolic rift first put forward by Marx and expanded and developed by contemporary ecological Marxists such as John Foster, Brett Clark, Richard York, Becky Clausen, Jason Moore, and others.[25] Essentially, metabolic rift refers to a rupture in the cycles of exchange within natural systems, including material and energetic exchanges between humans and nature. Marx and ecological Marxists have argued that the key sphere in which this exchange takes place is that of production, in which humans—as part of the labor process—transform nature (including themselves) in the pursuit of needs satisfaction. The labor process—and the social relations that condition it—thus becomes the central area of human endeavor through which our relationship with the environment is determined. Marx's initial example of a rift in the metabolic relationship between humans and nature was the town-country divide that emerged as a result of the separation of the English peasantry from the land and their concentration in towns as wage laborers. The result was that the fertility of the land, embodied in food and fiber, was separated from the land through exchange and consumption, becoming a concentrated sea of pollution in the towns rather than being returned as a nutrient to the soil from which it came. As intensifying agricultural production bled the soil of its fertility under these conditions, capital and the state scrambled to manage the burgeoning crisis by importing fertility from elsewhere in the form of guano, bones, and crops.[26]

The rift was then theorized at the world-systems level by Foster and Clark[27] and by Moore.[28] Moore takes the notion of metabolic rift and integrates it with Wallerstein's world-systems approach to suggest that "the rupture in nutrient cycling between the country and the city in historical capitalism" can be examined on a world scale, exploring the relations between core and periphery:[29]

> With the transition to capitalism, a new division of labor between town and country took shape—on a world scale and between regions . . . Nutrients were pumped out of one ecosystem in the periphery and transferred to another in the core. In essence, the land was progressively mined until its relative exhaustion fettered profitability. At this point, economic contraction forced capital to seek out and develop new ways of exploiting territories hitherto beyond the reach of the law of value.[30]

More recently, scholars have used the theory of metabolic rift to explain how capitalist dynamics have contributed to global climate change[31] and the crisis of marine ecology.[32] These more recent contributions have moved away from the spatial analysis that was characteristic of Marx's metabolic rift (in which rifts opened in part because of the intensification of the exploitation of nature—soil in particular—and in part because of the social and geographic separation of workers from the soil) and highlight instead how rifts *within* natural ecological systems open in response to capitalist interventions. Technological and managerial transformations in processes of production motivated by the dictates of profitability (and in some cases, such as aquaculture, in response to previous manifestations of rift)[33] result in "disruption or interruption of natural processes and cycles, the accumulation of waste, and environmental degradation."[34] The emphasis increasingly is less on how humans are physically separated from the land and more on how the specifics of the labor process—the process of transforming nature for human use—as shaped by the social relations of capitalism result in the opening of rifts within natural systems. The rift concept allows us to grasp and illustrate how human interventions in natural systems for the production of either use value or exchange value shape landscapes and ecosystems. As the state comes to bear a heavier burden for the mediation and conditioning of human relationships to nature and to regulate the labor process in the hopes of staving off "second contradiction"–style crises, scholars are obliged to account for its actions in the formation of metabolic rifts.

One of the most dramatic and effective human interventions in nature, in a wide variety of places, landscapes, and ecosystems, is the manipulation of fire. Prior to industrialization, large-scale transformations of nature by human populations took place almost exclusively through the use of fire. Land clearing, and in some cases the precise manipulation of ecosystems in the service of encouraging and discouraging certain flora and fauna, was and is carried out by use of the torch. Fire has unquestionably been a pivotal element in multiple anthropogenic transformations of the western United States, from the arrival of Native Americans onward. In the case of industrial-era interventions in western landscapes, one of the most significant ecological transformations has been the large-scale suppression of open flame. This massive change in the purposes for, and ways in which, human societies have sought to transform nature (from a situation in which Native tribes used fire to influence the ecosystem for the production of a wide array of use values to one in which European Americans sought to suppress fire to intensify the production of a single commodity for exchange value) has had tremendous consequences for the structure of certain forest ecosystems and had at least some impact on the likelihood of catastrophic fire resulting from fuels buildup. Fire is a fundamental part of the process of metabolism between humans and nature. Its application and removal have had significant effects on metabolic processes within natural systems.

More than a half century of highly effective fire suppression in the western United States has been central to the creation of a metabolic rift the Forest Service now characterizes as a "forest health crisis." Along with the incursion of invasive species, unmanaged recreational impacts, and the loss of open spaces, the USFS describes severe fire as the major contributing factor in this crisis. Since many forest ecosystems in the West evolved in tandem with a specific pattern of fire—a variable but bounded fire-return interval and a certain intensity of burning—its removal has disrupted vital processes of nutrient cycling, species selection, and regeneration. The banishment of flame and the USFS's continued battle to keep it out of the woods have created an instance of metabolic rift similar to those described as having taken place in the ocean[35] and in the world's climate cycle.[36] Metabolic rift is produced not only by the initial removal of fire (that is, through pre-suppression and suppression efforts)[37] but also through post-fire managerial interventions, such as salvage operations (in which commercial logging firms remove timber within a burn perimeter). Advocates defend post-fire logging on the basis of its economic benefits, combined with an alleged reduction of the threat of re-burns and contribution to forest regeneration. This premise is controversial, however. Some studies suggest that post-fire logging can actually increase the amount of downed fuels in a burned area and that it disrupts many ecological processes integral to healthy forest regeneration.[38] Another argues that forests regenerate equally well in the absence of post-fire interventions.[39] However, scientists take pains to point out that there remains a dearth of solid experimental evidence on post-fire logging's effects, adding further uncertainty to the political questions of how to manage the forests and for what ends. Post-fire (and now post-disturbance more broadly, including disease and insect infestation) logging has recently become a flash point for conflict between environmentalists on the one hand and the Forest Service and commercial timber harvesters on the other. Its significance is huge because post-disturbance logging opens up new, previously off-limits sources of commercially valuable timber from the national forests. "Salvage" logging accounted for about one-third of the total timber volume offered by the Forest Service in 2004.[40]

The view of catastrophic fire and the deterioration of forest health as manifestations of metabolic rift helps us understand these phenomena as products of a particular set of social relations that determines how humans see and interact with forests. At the same time, it keeps us focused on a definition of crisis that recognizes ecological destruction independent of its consequences for capitalist production.

In addition, the theory of metabolic rift's emphasis on the labor process directs our gaze to the state as a manager of human-nature relationships in the sphere of production. We have seen that in the case of forests the creation of rift has been profoundly affected by the managerial goals and methods of the USFS, the Bureau of Land Management, and, to a lesser degree, other federal and state land management agencies. These goals and methods themselves are not products of the state as an autonomous actor but instead are the result of the state's contradictory roles in capitalism as both a facilitator of accumulation and the agency responsible for the adequate reproduction and arrangement of "nature" as an industrial input. The genesis of the forest health crisis is found in the state's initial efforts to manage a previous economic and ecological crisis produced by the poor fit between industrial capitalist and ecological modes of production. Catastrophic fire and the forest health crisis are, in short, "crises of crisis management."[41]

CONTRADICTIONS OF THE ENVIRONMENTAL STATE

Claus Offe's concept of "crises of crisis management" was introduced in a collection of essays first published in English in 1984. This concept is the most useful and powerful for understanding the failures of fire management in the United States. Offe's concept is similar in some ways to the concept of "iatrogenesis," a term with roots in medical terminology. In the world of medicine, iatrogenesis refers to illness produced through medical examination or treatment. Ivan Illich[42] and John McKnight[43] extended this concept to refer to pathologies and dependencies that arose from a variety of "service interventions," including medical intervention but also including social services, educational systems, and criminal justice systems. More recently, Dean Bavington has taken up Illich's and McKnight's ideas and applied them to environmental management, arguing persuasively that our efforts to manage the environment have consistently produced disastrous and unforeseen results.[44] Indeed, Bavington's work challenges the very idea of environmental management on the basis that interventions based on the "managerial paradigm" inevitably produce iatrogenic effects. Iatrogenesis leads one logically to question the entire project of management (since it suggests that management of one pathology is virtually guaranteed to produce another, more virulent or debilitating pathology).

Offe's work, however, suggests that it is not management per se that is the problem; rather, it is the managerial efforts of a heterogeneous state with frequently contradictory goals working within a capitalist context that produce managerial failure. While his concern was primarily with the failures of the *welfare state*—that is, a state that had to be simultaneously concerned with the contradictory goals of supporting commodification and "decommodification" (reducing certain groups' reliance on the sale of labor power to meet their subsistence needs)[45]—my concern is with the profound difficulties the *environmental state* faces within capitalism—that is, the difficulties implied in the contradictory roles of protecting and facilitating accumulation on the one hand and reproducing nature in sufficient quantities and qualities so it is available both as a basic condition of life and as a condition of production.

The state is viewed by the public, and is presented in environmental histories, as the institution in which responsibility for environmental protection is primarily lodged. While neo-liberalism attempts to shift more of this responsibility to the free market (primarily through the development of alternative technologies, "green" consumerism, and the spurring of economic growth), the state has indeed been the central institution over the past century through which the public desire for environmental protection has been channeled. As a result, it is widely argued that any progress that has been made in the preservation and conservation of nature can be attributed to the power of the state.[46]

The United States Forest Service features prominently as an embodiment of the idea of the environmental state, particularly prior to the mid-1950s. The agency fought for a conservationist vision of human relations with nature—a battle that at times brought it into bitter conflict with extractive capital over access to resources, the prerogatives of private property in relation to social welfare, and the legitimacy of the state's intervention in the sphere of production. Prior to the 1950s and its accommodation with the timber industry to maximize the harvest from public lands, the Forest Service was not infrequently at odds with capital as it struggled to ensure the long-term availability of forest resources for exploitation.

This history fits nicely with environmental and institutional accounts that identify the US federal government as a champion of environmental protection.[47] Indeed, as Fred H. Buttel points out, this scholarship presents a strong case that "a society's ability to make possible environmental protection is essentially a function of the nation-state's capacity to enact and implement regulations of private behaviors."[48] Buttel argues that the state is uniquely positioned among social institutions to take on the role of environmental protection: "The government or political system can be distinguished from other social institutions in that the government or state is the only institution with the ability, and thus ultimately responsibility, to make possible what might be called the rationalization of society"; thus, "responsibility for ensuring environmental protection ... is inherent in the state's role in a societal division of labor."[49] He and other historians[50] point to the 1970s as the "golden age" of US state-based environmentalism; on the basis of the relatively substantial amount of environmentally focused legislation and regulation that emerged during that period, Buttel concludes that "there can be little doubt that the environmental regulatory state in the United States has contributed richly to environmental protection in America."[51] Even more strongly, he accurately points out that the consensus within recent histories of environmentalism is that "environmental protection can go only so far as there is capacity of government resource management and environmental agencies to implement an environmental regulatory and control agenda."[52]

However, just as the history of the Forest Service belies its image as a simple tool of the timber industry, so it demonstrates the profound and irreconcilable contradictions of the environmental state in capitalism. The USFS struggled, not without success, to conserve the remaining US forestlands from the depredations of industrial logging. It was a flagship organization of the conservation movement and was held in high esteem by the public for its scientific, professionalized approach to forest management. When they felt it necessary, some USFS leaders stood against private interests in the defense of what they saw as the public good, sometimes in the face of public vilification as "fascists" or "totalitarians." In the long term, however, the location of the state within a capitalist context constrained the agency's capacity to implement an effective "environmental regulatory and control agenda." Not only was the agency denied the power to regulate private forestry and the objective of nationalizing the remaining US forestlands—both of which were seen as essential elements of a control regime to halt forest devastation and stave off timber famine—but it was eventually forced to develop a close cooperative relationship with timber capital that made public forests abundantly available for harvest. All of these actions were conducted on the explicit grounds that the role of the state was *not* to infringe upon the exclusive sphere of capitalist control—that of production—but rather to facilitate accumulation through "cooperative" action. In Offe's terms, the environmental state was subject to a process of "positive subordination" to the economy.[53] Offe defines this as the development of a "relationship between the economy and the . . . political-administrative system in which the latter [is] structured in such a way that [it] positively contribute[s] to, and create[s] the preconditions for, the functioning of the dominant organizational principle [exchange] and the sphere of the economy determined by it."[54] In this case, the Forest Service was charged with removing perceived obstacles to profitable forestry—fire primary among them—and with managing the crisis of forest devastation and the threat of timber famine.

However, despite the refusal of capital and its representatives and allies in the US Congress to allow the Forest Service access to key tools that would have greatly increased its institutional capacity for management—tools that would also have violated owners' exclusive control over disposing of their property as they see fit—the *responsibility* for management remained. Both capital and civil society demanded that the Forest Service continue to ensure the future of US forests, initially almost exclusively as a condition of production but also—increasingly in the 1960s with the emergence of wilderness-focused environmental movements—as a condition of life. The agency's legitimacy was crucially dependent on the perception that it was acting to protect forests. Lacking the ability to protect the forests from destructive logging practices, the agency managed by turning increasingly to "protecting" forests from fire.

Fire protection shored up legitimacy in two ways. First, the public relations aspect of the fire prevention and suppression programs, particularly the incredible success of the Smokey Bear campaign, went a long way to maintaining the public's image of the Forest Service as a legitimate steward of the nation's public forests. The paramilitary aura of firefighting, the romantic and heroic image of the USFS standing in the path of roaring destruction, saturated with machismo and coated in ash, clearly resonated with the public. Second, capital viewed fire protection as a productive and legitimate expenditure of state revenues, as evidenced by the organized push to obtain state-subsidized fire control in the early 1900s and the almost universal support for increased Clarke-McNary funds. We now understand that the legitimacy gained through fire suppression was purchased at a high cost to the healthy functioning of many forest ecosystems. The USFS's hobbled efforts to manage the threat of timber famine gave way to a reliance on fire suppression for legitimacy, funding, and minimal leverage over private logging practices. This reliance, in turn, has contributed to the emergence of a new crisis—a crisis characterized by a metabolic rift in the ecological processes of fire-adapted forest ecosystems. This raises the question, how is the state responding to the threat of catastrophic fire? Is there any sign that the state has more recently been able to resolve or transcend its contradictory location through a process of ecological modernization, or does it remain a perpetual crisis manager?

CHAPTER SIX

THE WEIGHT OF PAST WEAKNESS

Prospects for Ecological Modernization in Fire Management

> I think it's also dangerous to let it go to the ideal situation of wildland fire use, minimal suppression, all that sort of stuff, because of the damage we've done already. I mean, it's been so significant to have suppressed fires for so long. The number of acres that have been disassociated from that process is huge, and for us to just step away and say, go ahead [and burn], you wouldn't have any trees left.
>
> *"Suzanne," USFS fire manager*

The idea that the state in a capitalist society or world system can be a contributor to a process of "greening" has been held out as one institutional plank in the larger fields comprised by ecological modernization theory (EMT) and as a pivot in the discourse of sustainable development. EMT advances the proposition that, in the era of ecological modernization, radical environmental change is independent of radical social change. Arthur Mol and Gert Spaargaren suggest that "within principally the same modern institutional layout (a market economy, an industrial system, modern science and technology, a system of welfare states, etc.) we can thus look for—and design—radical environmental reforms."[1]

However, theoretical work on EMT and empirical research into indicators of ecological modernization, such as the Environmental Kuznets Curve, emphasize the critical contribution of the state to the postulated processes of change.[2] The central role given to the state in this research supports Fred H. Buttel's assertion that "a full-blown theory of ecological modernization must ultimately be a theory of politics and the state," since "the most sophisticated versions of ecological modernization revolve around the notion that political processes and practices are particularly critical" in making ecology central to the process of modernization.[3] As such, it is crucial that scholars grapple seriously with the question of whether the state is capable, within the current social relations of production, of transcending its role as a manager of crises to become a proactive force in defense of the environment. If the state is bound by the structural requirements imposed on it by capitalism—that is, if it lacks any real autonomy in determining its own goals and is critically hindered in developing its capacities, as the history outlined in chapter 4 suggests it has been—then the process of ecological modernization becomes doubtful.

To evaluate the extent to which the state is promoting a broad process of ecological modernization, including a restructuring of its own managerial goals and methods, one must assess its current behavior as well as its history. While the history of the Forest Service suggests that the agency has been "positively subordinate" to the timber industry from its inception, a strong discourse within the USFS currently casts its history as the "Bad Old Days." This reference is generally to the post–World War II period, during which timber harvesting dominated the Forest Service's agenda. The fire managers I interviewed were uniformly adamant that their agency has turned a corner from timber- to ecosystem-based management and a focus on forest health. When I asked Brett whether he thought there was any merit to environmentalists' claim that the Healthy Forests Restoration Act (2003) was a "timber grab" by the agency, he responded:

> No. No merit. I can see how they got there. Twenty years ago, the culture of the Forest Service [FS] was to cut trees, to provide the public with lumber and fiber, and that was what the agency did. Well, yeah, they cut a lot of freaking trees down and probably too many. So the environmental groups got active and said "wait a minute," and in a lot of cases they were right. But now it's like there's no trust. The FS got the message that we aren't a timber company, but we need to cut some trees at times for the health of the forest. But the environmental groups don't trust us. So I don't think that in today's agency there's any truth [to the claim]. Even hard-core foresters that we work for, they're not there to sell a bunch of trees. They're there for forest health.

Matthew, a district ranger, gave a slightly more ambiguous view, referring to the residual culture of the "old days" when he discussed his return to the Forest Service after an absence:

When I left the FS, when I worked there in the 70s and 80s and left in [the 1980s], the main thrust in those times, although it was changing, . . . was more of an output emphasis . . . When I came back, the focus was more on . . . ecosystem management, and we basically manage the uses on the national forest such as grazing to achieve ecosystem health. Or we would have a grazing output, a forage output, if we could do that in an ecologically sound manner. So there was a different philosophical approach to how the forests were managed and used. Although there is still this underlying culture in the agency of past practices and past approaches.

While statements of this kind should not be taken as hard evidence of change, the budgets seem to agree with the assessments. Research on Forest Service resource allocations to timber and non-timber activities does show a pronounced shift in the focus in the late 1980s.[4] Most striking, harvest levels from public forests have declined steeply since their peak in 1987 (following a steep increase in the first half of the 1980s). In 1987 the Forest Service administered a harvest of over 12 billion board feet (bbf) of timber. That figure had declined to 5.9 bbf by 1993[5] and to 1.9 bbf in 2009.[6] While Timothy Farnham and Paul Mohai point out that the fluctuation of timber output between 1981 and 1993 reflects swings in the US economy in general, the level has remained low since the initial decline in 1988.[7] In addition, allocations to non-timber activities during the 1981–1993 period show an increase in non-timber budget lines, such as wildlife and fish habitat management and recreation.[8]

The budget numbers support the idea that non-commodity management has come to occupy a more significant role for the Forest Service than it did historically, although this does not mean the forest products aspect of USFS activities is vanishing. As table 6.1 indicates, despite increases in the percentage of the Forest Service's budget allocated to wildlife and recreation since 1983, timber continues to outweigh both areas by a considerable margin.

Total USFS funding for the timber sale program remained relatively stable during the first decade of the twenty-first century ($378 million in 2004 and $381 million in both 2006 and 2008), so the increasing percentage from 2004 to 2006 reflects a decline in total discretionary appropriations. Heather, the highest-ranking member of the agency I interviewed, emphasized the continuing importance of timber, even in the context of the national furor over fuels and fire:

For my mind, from a managing standpoint the National Fire Plan was the biggest blip on the screen and [the] most immediate because with it came a lot of resources, a lot of targets, a lot of direction, and a lot of accountability in terms

TABLE 6.1. Forest Service priorities, National Forest System budget

	Budget Item (as % of USFS total discretionary funding)		
Year	Recreation, wilderness, and heritage	Wildlife and fish management	Timber sale
1983	4.60	1.60	7.50
1992	6.90	3.60	8.50
2004	5.16	2.75	7.66
2005	5.38	2.82	7.86
2006	6.33	3.07	9.26
2007	5.50	2.80	8.14
2008	5.21	2.63	7.56
2009	5.77	2.86	7.86

Note: Timber sale figures are the totals of the NFS forest products, salvage sales, timber sales pipeline restoration fund, road construction/reconstruction for timber sales, and stewardship contracting categories.

Sources: 1983 and 1992: Timothy J. Farnham, "Forest Service Budget Requests and Appropriations: What Do Analyses of Trends Reveal?" *Policy Studies Journal* 23(2) (1995): 253–267; author's calculations. 2004–2006: USDA Forest Service, "Fiscal Year 2006 President's Budget: Budget Justification Overview," 2006, B-2. Available at http://www.fs.fed.us/; accessed May 15, 2009. 2007–2009: "Fiscal Year 2011 President's Budget: Budget Justification," 2011, D-22011. Available at http://www.fs.fed.us/; accessed April 3, 2011; author's calculations (2009 figures are budgeted).

of working fire into the ecosystem, so it really opened the door to making fire management [a] top priority. And then HFI [the Healthy Forests Initiative] and HFRA [Healthy Forests Restoration Act] so quickly, so since 2000 all our major legislation is around fire. So that's a huge change. Does it replace timber? I don't think so [laughs emphatically]. I don't think so at all.

WILDLAND FIRE MANAGEMENT: ECOLOGICAL MODERNIZATION IN ACTION?

Reflecting the change in budgeting priorities over the last two decades, USFS memoranda are replete with references to ecosystem-based management and the importance of non-timber values. As part of the agency's recasting of its identity as an ecosystem manager concerned with forest health rather than a timber farmer, there has been a great deal of introspection on the topic of fire management. This introspection has grown more pressing as fire has recaptured political and media attention with high-profile blazes (Yellowstone, Los Alamos, Biscuit, Hayman, Rodeo-Chediski), firefighter fatalities, and increasing expenditures on suppression. Policy pronouncements containing rejections of the total suppression fire management paradigm have been piling up at an accelerating pace for well over a decade.[9] The shift away from the doctrine of full suppression, which began its slow progress in the 1960s with the Leopold Report on Wildlife Management in the National Parks (1963) and the Wilderness Act (1964) and made its way into official USFS policy in 1978, has slowly increased in momentum—particularly since 1995—to the point where the vast majority of the fire managers interviewed for this study agreed that a full-suppression policy makes neither economic nor ecological sense. According to Matthew:

> My perspective from what I see in the ranger's chair since I came back is that yes, we have an ecosystem "bent" or orientation, we're trying to manage for healthy ecosystems, that is our goal. That is our mission. What's getting in the way of that has been our many years of having a different philosophy and a different approach, particularly to fire, which has created an unhealthy ecosystem . . . [In the 1980s] we were still in that mode of using full suppression, and our eyes were just starting to be opened [to the reality] that we had created a situation where we would have large fires. We were having large fires in Yellowstone, in Northern California, in southern Oregon in the late 1980s, and so I think that's when our sensitivity was starting to be piqued. And as we went into the 90s and had some more not only large fires but also deadly fires . . . I think the situation began to be taken more seriously. That this fuels imbalance that we've allowed to happen, this fuel loading that we've created by our fire policy of full suppression has resulted in such overstocked stands that now . . . when we have fires, they're so severe that we can't really stop them. We catch them when they slow down, but we can't stop them. So we realize that we've got to reverse our practices, but we're faced with this situation that was created over decades.

Many participants expressed a wish that they could reintroduce fire, even if it meant dealing with negative fallout from forest users or local communities. According to Suzanne:

> I think we shouldn't be so scared of doing burning and prescribed natural fires [wildland fire uses] because we think the public won't accept it. Like people don't want to see brown or orange trees in their view-shed. But I would rather do the burning and deal with the public when they [come] in screaming about what the hell are we doing burning that piece of forest. I would rather explain to them all the good we are doing for the forest after we've done the burning.
>
> The organization has committed to a new managerial approach to fire emphasizing a plurality of options ranging from wildland fire use [letting a naturally ignited fire burn within prescribed boundaries and conditions]

TABLE 6.2. Wildland fire management budget

Year	Total Forest Service Budget (in billions)	WFM Budget (in billions)	WFM (% of total)
2004	$4.941	$2.347	47.5
2005	$4.786	$2.128	44.5
2006	$5.048	$2.095	41.5
2007	$5.419	$2.194	40.5
2008	$5.807	$2.480	42.7
2009	$4.552	$1.977	43.4

Note: Total Forest Service budget includes both mandatory and discretionary appropriations. The 2004–2008 figures were enacted; those for 2009 are budgeted. WFM figures for 2004–2008 include emergency and supplemental funding. Figures for 2006 were adjusted to maintain hazardous fuels funding in the WFM budget line for consistency and comparability.
Sources: 2004–2006: USDA Forest Service, "Fiscal Year 2006 President's Budget: Budget Justification Overview," 2006, B-2. Available at http://www.fs.fed.us/; accessed May 15, 2009. 2007–2009: "Fiscal Year 2011 President's Budget: Budget Justification," 2011, D-22011. Available at http://www.fs.fed.us/; accessed April 3, 2011; author's calculations (2009 figures are budgeted).

to full suppression, with an underlying mandate to allow fire to play to the maximum extent possible its natural role in the ecology of fire-adapted forests. However, quite apart from the public pronouncements of the Forest Service, a shift in priorities is best evaluated from the evidence provided by [its] spending patterns and by actual work on the ground.

Budgetary Indicators

Perhaps the most telling indicator of a shift in managerial approach is the budget. Dollars spent on various activities are generally a better reflection of an organization's priorities than are pronouncements from its employees or its public relations department. At the very least, they can corroborate public relations materials and interview data or call them into question. The Forest Service and its critics in the environmental community recognize that suppression is environmentally problematic on a number of fronts (including the direct ecological costs of suppression activities, as well as long-term metabolic rift effects) and that intensifying the firefighting effort is not a viable strategy for dealing with the threat of catastrophic wildfire. Therefore, if the Forest Service were a reflexive, ecologically modernizing agency, we would expect to see a reallocation of funding from suppression toward restoring fire to the forests. The budget numbers, however, show no decline in suppression spending; in fact, they show the reverse. Nine of the ten most expensive fire seasons (adjusted for inflation) have occurred

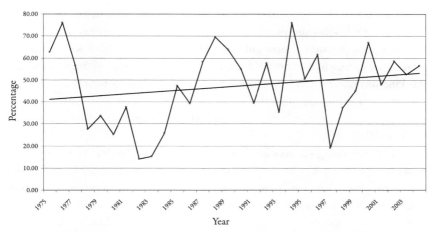

FIGURE 6.1. Suppression costs as a percentage of total fire budget, 1975–2006. The jagged line represents actual costs; the dashed line represents the historical trend (expected values). Sources: House Committee on Appropriations, Subcommittee on the Department of Interior and Related Agencies, 1975–2006; United States Forest Service Central Accounting Data Inquiry, 1975–2000; Foundation Financial Information System, 2000–2002, courtesy Krista M. Gebert, USFS economist; author's calculations.

since 1987, and suppression costs broke the billion-dollar mark in 2000, 2002, 2003, 2004, 2005, 2007, 2008, and 2009.[10] While suppression costs fluctuate sharply from year to year, the data show a clear upward trend since the 1970s.[11]

The same is true for the costs of suppression as a proportion of the total allocation for fire management. The wildland fire management (WFM) budget now makes up over 40 percent of the total USFS budget and almost half of the Forest Service's discretionary budget. Table 6.2 shows the figures for the years 2004–2009.

Of the total WFM budget, suppression operations accounted for 56 percent in 2003 and 53 percent in 2004, including supplemental and emergency funding. These numbers are by no means historically unprecedented. From 1975 onward, the proportion of the budget eventually spent on suppression has fluctuated dramatically, as shown in figure 6.1.

In the midst of this fluctuation, the trend line shows an upward drift from 40 percent to 53 percent, indicating that the Forest Service is making little headway in its effort to shift away from suppression. The problem with these indicators, however, is that suppression costs are often heavily driven by a small number of large fires.[12] As blazes increase in intensity and size as a result of climatic changes and the buildup of fuels from previous suppression, the Forest Service spends more money on suppression almost automatically. Even if the USFS were attacking fewer fires, opting in more cases for wildland fire use instead of suppression and working to restore forests to something resembling their historical fire regimes, the suppression budget might still rise as a result of the increased costs of fighting catastrophic fires and the increased complexity and consequences of fighting fire in the wildland urban interface (WUI).

What the rising suppression budget does accurately reflect is the organization's feeling that the public expects it to continue to fight these large fires, no matter the cost or how small the probability that human intervention will significantly affect the trajectory of a wildfire in full bloom. In fact, public expectation, which in interviews fire managers tended to equate with "politics," was the most widely and vociferously cited reason for continuing what amounts to—in terms of the near-universal attack response to fire—a full-suppression policy.

Haunting Successes of Propaganda: Public Resistance to Fire

In discussing the difficulties of reintroducing fire in his management area, Brett commented:

> Local communities have a huge influence. If someone disagrees with how we're treating fire, maybe we're smoking them out, all they have to do is call their congressman [sic], and we have a congressional inquiry that we have to answer, and that gets the attention of management, and the governors have their agenda, and the president has his. It's all that stuff . . . Now, if the public is content [in the event of a large fire] . . . for us to stand back and order a couple of helicopters and kind of control one edge and protect a couple of homes, we can do that and it's going to be less expensive, but they want to see stuff in the air, and they want to see us being aggressive, and that's the political climate. I guess my point is . . . you can't have cheap megafires, and the public expects us to go after those full bore. That's the way it is.

Ian expressed a similar sentiment about the communities around his national forest, which is in an area that is much more rural and impoverished than Brett's: "To me the big factor is that social-political consideration. The government says we can let fire play a more natural role. To save money, we'll let [fires] get bigger . . . But socially and politically, I don't think that's accepted nationally because what people see is our natural resources or playground going up in smoke."

134

Jason, the sole frank advocate for full suppression I interviewed, suggested that the public generally supports his position and the way it translates into practice on the national forests: "I think our fire plan is very well supported because it is a hit-hard suppression strategy. There is certainly a big tension between the Forest Service's new philosophical approach to dealing with fire and people's fear of fire, intolerance for smoke, etcetera."

If the high degree of autonomy attributed to the Forest Service—its image among journalists, scholars, activists, and timber companies alike as "Forester Kings"—indeed reflected reality, this expressed powerlessness would be surprising. If the Forest Service had the kind of autonomy the dominant narrative of fire in the United States attributes to it, we would not expect it to be so subordinate to the public's or the US Congress's unrealistic expectations about fire. However, as we have seen, the agency's inability to accomplish what its employees and leaders see as necessary for forest health is nothing new. The agency's lack of autonomy explains much more about its relationship to fire than do its mythical independence, insularity, or bullying tendencies. Of course, given that early white settlers in the West and the Native Americans they displaced saw fire as an inevitable part of the landscape, we can understand modern expectations to some extent as a creation of the agency itself. Rather than view public expectations as some exogenous or extra-organizational force, they must be understood as a product of the Forest Service's own proselytizing about the evils of fire and its optimistic assessments about its long-term ability to manage nature. In this sense, state-centric theories are correct in stressing that the state matters in and of itself. The Forest Service proved a highly reliable and effective transmitter of the anti-fire policy that arose in the early 1900s, and it now seems trapped by a public expectation of its own making. Brett was well aware of this dynamic.

> **Brett:** I think the bottom line is that it has to do with the political arena. What is the public willing to accept? It's like driving in a car, and the seat belt is uncomfortable, and do you take it off? You play the odds. You know, your house out there is just one house. You play the odds, you'll probably be OK. But . . . we have to change the perception of the population, particularly in the West, because that's where fire is part of who we are. It's like managing a river. We're always concerned about water rights and scenic rivers and navigating. It's the same. Fire is just as much a part of the ecosystem as rivers and lakes are. And so is the public willing to let fire play its natural role, or are they willing to say, no, I'm going to play the odds, my house is probably going to be OK, and I don't want to see these big fires, I don't want to be smoked out, I don't want to see the hill I look at with some burned trees and stuff. I don't think

we're going to change anything until the public really appreciates and understands and accepts the role of wildland fire in the west. And then if they do, that translates into the political arena in Washington, and we get more laws to make fire management easier. In my mind that's the bottom line. I mean, we're just hanging on. We're successful, but we're hanging on.

MH: Well, is that part of the problem? Is part of the public perception of "my house is going to be OK" a product of how successful the FS and the BLM [Bureau of Land Management] have been at putting out fires?

Brett: Yes. Exactly. People have a lot of trust in our success.

However, one could certainly *not* claim—referring back to Gregory Hooks's characteristics of state-centered theory in chapter 3—that the policy agenda necessitating a propaganda campaign to demonize fire in the forest itself was defined solely or even principally by the state. The state's desired policy agenda for much of the early twentieth century was geared at holding back forest devastation and, in some cases, supporting community stability and employment through federal regulation of logging or nationalization of forestlands. The agency's defeat on these fronts created the context in which it became organizationally defined by its fire protective role. This shored up the USFS's legitimacy in the eyes of the public and, in combination with its post–World War II emphasis on timber harvesting, in the eyes of capital. As we saw in chapter 4, capital not only pushed the state into socializing the costs of fire protection and creating a national fire policy, but it contributed actively and substantially to funding and complementing the Forest Service's public relations campaign to equate fire with carelessness, bad morals, traitorousness, and ungodliness.

Sparking Tinder in the Rain: Fire Reintroduction in the Pacific Northwest

Within the context of this widespread public antipathy for its new mission of reintroducing fire, how has the Forest Service fared to date? Early evaluations of the agency's progress make for dismal reading, as was briefly mentioned in chapter 2. David Parsons was unflinching in summarizing the land management agencies' efforts:

> Despite clear legislative and policy direction to preserve natural conditions in wilderness, the maintenance of fire as a natural process has proven to be a significant challenge to federal land managers. As of 1998, only eighty-eight of the 596 designated wilderness areas in the United States, excluding Alaska, had approved fire plans that allow some natural ignitions to burn; and even

those areas with active natural fire programs continue to suppress many natural ignitions. As a result, none of the four federal wilderness management agencies have been able to restore fire to a level that even approaches pre-settlement fire regimes.[13]

Nationally, an estimated 98 percent of ignitions are still immediately subject to aggressive suppression.[14] In Region 6 (the Pacific Northwest), where I conducted my interviews and where much of the forest east of the Cascade Mountains is fire-adapted, only two forests (of a possible nineteen) had wildland fire use plans for wilderness areas in place as of 2005.[15] At least one wildland fire use plan in place prior to 2005 had been rescinded because a fire "slopped over" onto adjacent lands. While the Forest Service allowed its first lightning-ignited fire to burn in the Selway-Bitterroot Wilderness of Montana in 1971 (three years after the National Park Service changed its policy to allow wilderness fire to burn), wildland fire use came to a shuddering halt after the 1988 fire season—during which 3.7 million acres of land burned in the western United States, including in Yellowstone National Park. A moratorium was placed on wilderness fire use pending a review of federal fire policy. While this and subsequent reviews have affirmed the practice of wildland fire use, by 1998 Parsons reported that the area burned by natural fire on federal land had yet to regain even pre-1988 levels.[16] Since 1998, when the Forest Service began cooperating with the National Interagency Fire Center to collect wildland fire use and prescribed fire statistics, there has been little growth in the numbers of fires the agency allows to burn in wilderness, although two recent years show relatively large acreages burned (figure 6.2).

Over the twelve-year period following the 1995 review of the Federal Wildland Fire Management Policy that reaffirmed the goal of reintroducing fire to the maximum extent possible as a natural ecosystem process, some, but not nearly enough, progress has been made. Suppression, even in the limited lands represented by designated wilderness, remains by far the dominant management strategy. A fair assessment of whether the agency is engaging in a process of ecological modernization—bringing environmental considerations to the center of its decision-making framework for fire—however, should look not only at the extent to which fire has already been reintroduced in the form of wildland fire use but also to the extent to which the ground is being prepared for its reintroduction.

After a century of suppression, there has indeed been a major modification to the fuel structure of many fire-adapted forests, as represented by the Fire Regime

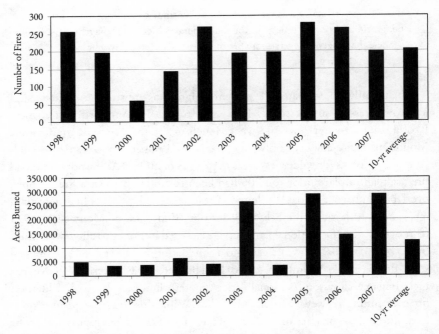

FIGURE 6.2. USFS wildland fire use: number of fires and acreage burned, 1998–2007. Source: National Interagency Coordination Center, http://www.nifc.gov/stats/; accessed December 20, 2006; February 16, 2009.

Condition Class map in chapter 2 (figure 2.3). Allowing fire to run in these altered forests would likely result in fires that are uncharacteristically large and intense. Forests that are adapted to lighter, more frequent burns are at risk of what the Forest Service calls "stand replacement," in which even larger fire-resistant trees burn, and the intensity of the heat damages the soil. To minimize this risk, the Forest Service has a program of fuels treatment, some of which is mechanical (cutting the smaller-diameter trees out of dense stands and cutting out ladder fuels that allow fire to climb into the canopy) and some of which involves prescribed burning. Has the amount of prescribed burning and other forms of fuels treatment increased as a result? Figure 6.3 illustrates the trend since 1998.

National forest managers have indeed been doing more prescribed burning since 1998, rebuilding the program after a dramatic drop in prescribed burns in 2000 (the year of the prescribed National Park Service burn at Cerro Grande, which got out of control and threatened Los Alamos). In 2004 the Forest Service lit 4,859 fires that burned over 1.5 million acres of land, up from 2,954 fires

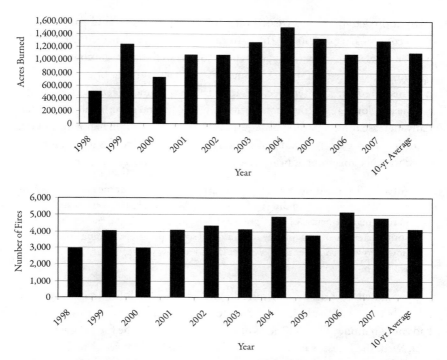

FIGURE 6.3. USFS prescribed burning: number of fires and acres burned, 1998–2007. Source: National Interagency Coordination Center, http://www.nifc.gov/fire_info/; accessed March 26, 2009.

and 728,000 acres in 2000. Acreage burned peaked in 2004, although 2006 saw slightly more prescribed ignitions than the previous year. Therefore, there does seem to be some progress on this front. However, fire managers like Ian and Brett attest to the fact that the scale of the prescribed burn program is nowhere near sufficient in relation to the need for fuels treatment in the national forests. While these managers are treating 10,000 to 25,000 acres of land per year with prescribed burning, with the higher number representing a relatively aggressive program of prescribed burning, they know that to make a real difference ecologically and in terms of prepping the ground for a return of natural fire, they need to be doing at least four times that amount just to "break even."

The picture is no rosier with respect to mechanical treatments. In his testimony on the HFI and HFRA before the US Congress, Chief Dale Bosworth reported that the Forest Service, using all authorities available to land managers and allocations for both hazardous fuels reduction and other "landscape restoration activities," had treated only 8.5 million acres of land from 2003 to the second quarter of 2006.[17] This is in the context of an identified need for 190 million acres of treatment. Managers point out as well that in the context of continuing fire suppression, fuels treatment is a perpetual game of catch-up, since treatments require maintenance. So rather than a onetime injection of funding to get the job done, an ongoing commitment by the federal government to substantially increase funding would be required. The reverse has been happening of late, according to Brett, with funding for fuels treatment falling off as money is reallocated to other government priorities, such as the wars in Afghanistan and Iraq:

> After 2000, for two-three years [following the introduction of the National Fire Plan] we had the funding that we needed. We had large increases also in fuels management. What we've seen now with the deficit and the war and stuff, there isn't enough money to go around so our budgets are going down, down, down . . . So essentially, we're at the point now where we don't have enough money to run our program.

Frank, who works on a historically fire-adapted, high fire-frequency forest, similarly lamented the lack of funding for land treatment: "In terms of fuel, we had enough money for 8,500 acres of fuel treatment with the fuels program every year. Well, the forest is more than a million acres. You can see that that puts us way behind the curve. We've got those other programs that contribute to it as well, but we're still not . . . [trails off]."

Funds attached to the American Recovery and Reinvestment Act, mentioned in chapter 5, will help. If the economic downturn continues, however, we can confidently anticipate budget reductions in the near future. While the prospect exists for some mechanical thinning to be paid for by allowing contractors doing the thinning to sell the material removed, the economics of this plan are highly problematic at the moment. While large-diameter timber is the most valuable "fuel" in the forest, it is also the most fire-resistant. Taking it out to pay for hazardous fuels reduction (as George W. Bush's administration suggested would be done under the HFI) amounts to a transparent grab for timber that even the Republican-dominated Congress knew would not fly. Thinning to reduce the risk of severe fire requires leaving the large-diameter timber standing and removing small-diameter timber and ladder fuels, for which few markets exist. Apart from niche markets for chips and "pee-wee logs," with narrow margins of profit that can be wiped out even by transport costs, it is difficult to pay for thinning lower-diameter material with the revenue generated by selling it. For now, the vast majority of mechanical thinning has to be paid for out of pocket, and the size of the bill to clean up from the results of the past policy of full suppression is more than the state is willing to absorb. It seems that, in this case, the reversal of past ecological transformations implicit in the idea of ecological modernization might come at a price that is too high to bear.

Most fire managers placed the blame for their inability to increase the prescribed burn program on this combination of budgetary shortfalls and a lack of public acceptance of prescribed burning. While maintaining a strong line that, as public servants, their job is to do the best they can with the funds Congress allocates (most people I interviewed believed these allocations are a reflection of the public will), they simultaneously argued that those funds are totally insufficient to adequately treat lands in the context of continued suppression. Public resistance to both wildland fire use and prescribed burning, according to those interviewed, is rooted primarily in the fear that burns will get out of prescription and destroy private property and in objections to diminished air quality from smoke. The consequences of a fire getting out of prescription, or escaping the boundaries defined by the management plan, can be severe for Forest Service employees. Gary described the career and personal risks for Forest Service employees who used wildland fire in wilderness areas or who pushed for more aggressive prescribed burning. He identified not just the general public but also the state forestry department, county commissioners, and the timber industry as strongly opposed to wildland fire use:

> The timber companies still hate WFU [wildland fire use]. They say, "That's a Forest Service thing. As long as it stays on national forestland, fine, but don't let it come onto private land." Meanwhile, the county commissioners are saying, "You can do your WFU thing, let the greenies have it in the wilderness, but *do not* let it get out of the wilderness." It's a veiled threat. If I let it out of the wilderness, they'll be there with the lynch mob. We *cannot* have failures, but there will be one, maybe on this forest even. Then we'll see how deep the support goes . . . The ODF [Oregon Department of Forestry] is also not onboard with WFU. The customers of ODF are the timber industry and private landowners. They do not want the WFUs to get out the door. This is understandable, given that their mission is different than ours and how they're funded [through the timber industry] . . . A Forest Service supervisor was hung in effigy in [name of town] after a fire got away in 1994. I was told that I was going to be given the same treatment if [I ever let the same thing happen].

In some timber-dependent communities, managers reported public resistance to burning on the grounds that the wood being torched would better serve the community by being fed into the mills. A fire manager in a forest that provides timber for three mills in a low-income rural setting said: "The economy, of course, is very dependent on the timber industry, and they [residents] see that losing of natural resources in fires as just burying the economy, throwing away money. So the local constituency understands fire, but they don't like it. They'd rather be out harvesting the material, thinning and getting that resource into the mill, supporting the economy."

Another possible economic factor in local managers' cautious approach in moving away from full suppression is local communities' dependence on fire suppression as a source of income. However, only one manager interviewed explicitly mentioned a local need for firefighting jobs and contracts as a source of pressure, although many commented to the effect that "small towns love fire crews" because they mean an infusion of dollars into the community. Since suppression is still by far the dominant response, it makes sense that the private contractors who increasingly provide the hand crews, engines, and air support for fire suppression have yet to feel threatened by the Forest Service's policy to reintroduce fire as an ecosystem process. The industry trade association, the National Wildfire Suppression Association, has taken no public stance on the issue of suppression policy, focusing instead on safety and industry-wide standardization of training and certification. In addition, there is some scope for local community employment by contracting out fuels treatment work, whether prescribed burning or mechanical thinning, which could replace suppression dollars. It is doubtful, however, that allocations for fuels treatment (which are granted in a non-emergency context, in the absence of telegenic flames lapping at ranch homes) would ever be as free-flowing as dollars for emergency suppression have been. So, while there is clearly an existing incentive for rural communities and private contractors to support continued suppression because of the infusion of public dollars they receive, few managers reported it as a significant obstacle to the reintroduction of fire.

While managers believed the Forest Service would support them personally as long as they managed a fire use or a prescription burn according to a sound plan, some suggested that a skewed incentive system within the organization dissuades managers from taking any risks (and there is always, no matter how well-laid the plan, a degree of risk, as every manager acknowledged—fire is inherently uncontrollable, despite the enormous advances in the science of fire behavior). According to Peter, a retired Forest Service fire manager:

> The rangers and the forest supervisors, their basic rebuttal to [critiques that practice did not conform to the new policy on fire management] was, "I still

have no incentive to change the way I do fire. And even though I've got ponderosa pine, sugar pine out there, big trees that I know will survive and even
thrive if I let that fire back through, I'm going to throw everything at it. I'm
going to spend a couple million dollars of the taxpayers' money putting out a
fire that really doesn't need to be put out." So until the line officers, and this
is a very hierarchical paramilitary organization in which the line officers have
tremendous power, until they were "incentivized" somehow to let fire burn, to
aggressively pursue that idea that we now know that fire's not the enemy, we
now know that it's part of the deal, they're not going to do it.

The specter of a potential career-ending event hangs over the shoulder of
every manager who makes the call about whether to follow the usual routine
of full suppression or take a chance on a wildland fire use or even a prescribed
burn. Peter reflected on his experience with Forest Service employees who had to
decide whether to suppress or do a managed burn:

> A Forest Service line officer can maintain an absolute jungle, mess, fucked-up
> ecosystem that's incredibly flammable and going to be incredibly destruc-
> tive when it does burn, and nobody'll say a word. The same manager lights a
> prescribed underburn, say a forty-acre underburn, and gets a little extra wind
> and it burns five acres that [he or she] didn't plan on. Didn't burn any houses,
> just five acres. It's in all the papers. It's a career problem for him or her. And if
> it goes a thousand acres out, it's a career-ending event . . . Generally, the line
> officer . . . has a great deal of influence over that decision [about whether to
> fully suppress]. And in most of the situations with which I'm familiar, he or
> she—although it's usually a he—says "put the fuckin' thing out." So to the
> extent that the district ranger or the forest supervisor can influence the out-
> come, they're almost always going to go full suppression because it's the best
> way to avoid a career-ending event. People aren't stupid, you know.

Joseph's comments corroborate this testimony about the organizational and
career risks that face managers who contemplate letting fire out of the bottle and
back into the woods:

> Could we do more [fire use]? Sure. Because what it is is how much risk is
> that decision official willing to take because the risk to do nothing or let [a
> fire] burn where it's reasonable [to do so] is a ton of risk. Because what hap-
> pens if that 1-acre fire becomes 100,000 acres and then goes on to take out
> San Diego? So, that's exactly what happened on the Cedar fire; a fire that was
> on public land, lightning-ignited, went to 1,000 acres, then 3,000 acres, and
> twenty-one hours later it was 220,000 acres. Who's going to stand up and say
> "well, that person made a good decision?" It was inside three roads, and we

can catch it when it comes out on the road, was what their strategy was, and it was indirect, it made sense, but then when it came to the road the Santa Anna winds came up, forty-seven-mph winds, and in three one-hour periods it burned 30,000 acres an hour. So we don't hold that decision in high esteem, but that's one of the consequences of something that's as dynamic and risky as fire, to say OK, we'll just let it hunker in the woods. It's what happened at Biscuit. And yet we get complaints that we didn't have firefighters behind every tree, and we didn't put it out when it [was] small.

Managers must also consider the community response to their actions, since they live and work in communities that might be threatened by wildland fire use or prescribed fire. Frank related the pressures managers feel as members of communities next to the national forests:

We had an OIG [Office of the Inspector General] group come out just to try to learn what we do on large fires, so I spent a lot of time talking to them about that, and one of the things they asked was, "you're spending a million dollars a day on this fire, and it's just burning up there in the national forest. Why are you doing that? We know that fire's important for the health of that system, why are we putting a million dollars a day into it?" What I said was "can you imagine being the district ranger that was responsible for making a decision about whether to let this be a wildland fire use fire, losing any time at all making that call even if you decided not to, but losing the time making the decision, and then losing 105 houses the next day?" There's not a hanging tree big enough in town to hang everybody on the district that was involved in that decision. So you can talk about wildfire use and how it's good for the health of the system and we ought to be doing it, but when it comes to a practical matter of applying it, how are you going to do that? In small communities where the district ranger and his staff have to live in that community, every time they have to make a decision about a wildland fire use, if that decision goes bad everybody's going to "what if" him. You know, if only you would have hit this when it was a small one, you could have put it out with a shovel, and you could have been done, and instead you burned my house. How can you make that kind of decision?

A final and highly constraining issue for the return of fire—one that intertwines with issues of cost, public fear of fire, and managerial risk—is the new geography of human settlement in the West. More and more people are moving to the fringes of the West's remaining forested land, resulting in an explosion of land designated as WUI and rural intermix. In both of these areas, forested land abuts or is mixed in with residential housing, increasing the risk of loss of life and property in the event of a wildfire. Fire managers see the growth of the WUI, the incursion of new and increasingly dense real-estate developments into forested areas, as a significant obstacle to bringing fire back to the forests. This is particularly the case when that real estate is expensive, high-value housing. Fire managers are under intense scrutiny in their decisions about whether and how to fight fire, and loss of property comes second only to loss of life in prioritizing where to allocate firefighting resources.

Real-estate development in much of the West would be a much more risky proposition were it not for the willingness and ability of the Forest Service and its partners to suppress fires. In the absence of that willingness, developing a subdivision in or near some towns in central or eastern Oregon would be tantamount to setting up on a floodplain with no prospect of Army Corps of Engineers–funded levees or federal flood insurance. The Forest Service, in this respect, is providing a significant subsidy to western real-estate developers and homeowners. Fire managers I interviewed often expressed intense frustration with developers' and homeowners' lack of concern about the risk of wildland fire. According to Joseph:

> I was there when [Hurricane] Ivan came in. People were putting houses right back where they got washed off, and you go "gosh, wouldn't you try to get out of the floodplain?" No. They're right back where they were. Fire goes through that, right there [pointing at Sisters, Oregon, on the map, a town threatened by the B&B fire complex (label given to the Booth and Bear Butte fires when they merged) in 2003], three months later they'll have permits and are putting houses right back where they burned. Look at what Colorado did after the Hayman fire. I bet that 90-plus percent of the houses that got burned down are built right back in the same place. And now they say "gosh, I've got a better view." The density in Malibu, when it last burned, was six times what it was sixteen years previous. It killed 2 people, burned 340 homes, and sixteen years later it kills 13 people, burns 2,232 homes, so if that's possible, sixteen years from now 100 people will get killed and 12,000 homes will go up. Because conditions will come back. The brush will come back. And are we going to say we're going to let fire burn there? No.

Because of the need for huge buffer zones between fires and private property that abuts or is mixed in with forested lands, the only place the Forest Service can even consider the possibility of wildland fire use is in large wilderness areas. The inherent unpredictability and uncontrollability of fire mean fires cannot necessarily be stopped at a pre-selected boundary line. National forests that lack large wilderness areas present a serious problem for fire managers striving to reintroduce fire. Topography can also be a limiting factor when residential developments sit uphill from wilderness areas that might otherwise be candidates for wildland fire use. The result is that the Forest Service is heavily constrained in accomplishing the objective of allowing fire to burn in a way that resembles its historical ecological role as a natural process vital for forest regeneration and health.

The stream of paper that has flowed from the Forest Service's Washington, DC, office over the past thirty years indicates that ecological considerations have become more central to the agency's approach to managing fire. However, change needs to proceed beyond the level of discourse and rhetoric for it to make a difference ecologically. The process of ecological modernization that appears so vibrant on the pages of USFS policy proclamations stumbles at the threshold of the office door. On the ground, fires are still suppressed. The effort to replace natural fire with prescribed burning is woefully insufficient. While most fire managers recognize the need to let fire back onto the land and profess a strong desire to do so, they lack both the autonomy to let natural fire burn and the capacity to significantly treat the land through prescribed burning.

Fire is now largely a prisoner of history. Having been funneled onto the path of full fire suppression by a lack of other avenues for managing "forest devastation," the Forest Service now finds that the way back is, if not fully closed, beset by obstacles created by its own passing. Despite Gary Machlis and his colleagues' research findings that the public is gaining a more accurate understanding of fire,[18] state actors express a grounded sense that, for the most part, the public fears fire. As Matthew put it, "When things blow up, people get excited." They demand action, and their elected representatives frequently seize the opportunity to take the spotlight in the protector's role, adamantly demanding the same. In July 2008 *The Los Angeles Times* highlighted the phenomenon of "CNN drops,"[19] a colloquial term for the deployment of air tankers and helicopters that—while having little or no impact on actually controlling a fire—reassure people and politicians that action is being taken, that control is actively being established. Having presented the public with an ideology that, with will and organization, humanity can control nature, the Forest Service has encouraged the new geography of settlement in the West. Few residents, especially new ones, understand the historical role of fire in the ecosystems they inhabit. As Joseph pointed out bluntly:

> Ninety-plus percent of people in the West are afraid of fire. So when they see that one tree on fire, they may call in that the whole woods are burning, and [in reality] it could be put out with a cup of water. What is interesting is how people get imprinted when the fire scares them. "I moved out here to be safe and get away from the city and everything, the rat race," so it's a real interesting phenomenon. And that's why when we say we want to put fire out there and

make it our friend, between you and me, that's bullshit. There's 2 percent of the people that believe that and really understand that.

The new geography of settlement, combined with the expectation that the Forest Service will continue to fight to protect life and property, prevents the return of fire on an ecologically relevant landscape scale. Most managers suggest that successful human management of the forest health crisis is unlikely given the public's commitment, both in terms of inconvenience and funding. Rather than a "soft landing" from the forest health crisis accomplished through timely and effective fuel treatments on a scale sufficient to make a difference, some managers suggest that large, high-intensity wildfires will likely be the ultimate mechanism of hazardous fuels reduction. In addition to the likely destruction of previously fire-adapted ecosystems, communities unlucky enough to be lower on the priority list for managed fuels reduction will suffer the consequences. As Ian, who lives and works in an economically marginal rural community, put it: "Nationally, we run from $20 an acre to do prescribed burning to $1,000 an acre to do mechanical treatment. Is investing $1,000 an acre a good investment? Maybe it is if you're doing it around Bend [Oregon], near some resort or where you've got million-dollar homes lined up in a row, but probably it isn't if you're out in this country [where he works]."

Ian's comment speaks to the reality that in this case at least, ecological modernization involves significant costs—costs that come from a public purse whose volume is dependent on the ongoing struggle over how society's economic surplus is concentrated and allocated. The relevant state agency in this case—the USFS—has behaved highly reflexively. It is well aware of the damaging ecological consequences of its actions, in terms of both the immediate environmental costs of suppressing fire (e.g., dropping chemical retardant, bringing heavy machinery into fragile and vulnerable ecosystems, soil erosion resulting from digging fire lines) and the long-term increase in ecosystems' vulnerability to stand-replacement fires. The Forest Service also understands the ecologically appropriate course of action: to allow fire to return to its normal historical role in fire-adapted ecosystems. It has gone through a three-decade process of policy revision, described in chapter 2's section on détente, and confirmed its organizational commitment to this course, even in the face of widespread resistance from politicians and the public. Internally, with only two exceptions out of fifteen, those who were interviewed for this project were ideologically committed to that policy.

Undoubtedly, the agency still faces a number of internal organizational constraints to the reintroduction of fire. Performance assessment measures used to evaluate managers reward successful suppression efforts but do little to encourage the reintroduction of fire. The risk assumed by those who allow fire to burn, rather than suppressing it immediately with all available resources, remains high, and managers lack a strong sense that the agency would support them unfailingly if a fire were to get out of control—even if fire use plans were being followed to the letter. These, however, are not the barriers managers emphasize when they talk about changing people's relationship to fire in the West. In attempting to mend the metabolic rift generated by the removal of fire, managers are running up against hard barriers created at the turn of the twentieth century by the agency's weakness relative to other social forces.

CONCLUSION

The Chronic Parolee

The landscape and ecology of the western United States, no less than smoke and ash, are products of fire. Humans have busily applied the torch and just as busily mobilized an arsenal of extinguishers. Our application and withdrawal of fire have been powerful elements in labor's transformation of nature, and our choices about whether to burn or to douse have been shaped by the imperatives of production. Over the last century, the pattern of fire has been a rebellious reflection of the drive to profitably exploit forests—for timber, yes, but, more important, for profit. Fire—a complex process with enormous ecological significance—became a threat to the maximization of timber production and a menace to investment. As both capital and the state mobilized to minimize threats to continual accumulation, fire was chased from the forests with amazing success. While there is truth to the critique that the Forest Service throws money at big fires until the rain comes, there is no doubt that the habitat of open flame has dwindled since the US empire's western advance. Only very recently have many of those who work with fire and forests come to see that the removal of fire has created a rift in the natural processes of forest ecology and in some places created the very conditions for the conflagration it sought to subdue.

The United States Forest Service is taking the rap. Charges leveled at the USFS include mismanagement, flawed policy, addiction to fire funding, disregard for research, and—most important—an arrogant belief in its own ability to control nature. The Forest Service's insularity and autonomy—its lack of accountability to civil society—have been most frequently cited as the underlying problems. A missionary ideology of conservation, although perhaps well-intended, blinded the Forest Service leadership to the ecological effects of suppression as it piled fuel on the bonfires-to-be that now make up the nation's Fire Regime Condition Class 3 zones. That mission deafened USFS leaders to the voices of forest users, frontier folk, and maverick fire ecologists. The ideological commitment to scientific management and the reductionist lens it placed over the Forest Service's eyes have resulted in forests that are not just combustible but actually explosive.

The argument presented in the preceding chapters of this book does not set out to prove this narrative false (at least not all of it). The ideology of control did exist. The Great Fires of 1910 made a profound impression on key members of the Forest Service, stoking their drive to demonstrate the fledgling agency's managerial competency. The Forest Service was dogged in its smoke chasing, not only amassing a formidable capacity to put out fire once it started but also enlisting the entire US public in its demonizing campaign. However, the argument presented does suggest that much of the tumult—many of the riffles, waves, and eddies of debate over fire policy—has formed on the surface of a more profound current of history: the entrenchment of class-based access to, and control over, nature and the struggles of an impossibly placed state to manage the resulting environmental devastation.

To blame scientific management as an isolated ideology for the forest health crisis and for catastrophic fire is to ignore the conditions in which the ideology took hold. There is no question about the emphasis both the Forest Service and private lumbermen placed on fire protection in addressing the "forest problem" in the United States in an effort to develop what Jenks Cameron has described as "a perfect forest order."[1] Every USFS chief, lumber spokesperson, and government commission report identified fire as "the problem of problems" in US forestry.[2] The questions that remain unanswered as scholars have plumbed the history of fire policy are, what is "the forest problem" and, in a capitalist context, what represents a perfect forest order? The answers are found, if we care to look, in the early mission of the Forest Service, which focused almost entirely on gaining acceptance of what it termed "practical forestry." What was "practical" about this had nothing to do with ecology but instead revolved entirely around the economics of accumulation. This was partly a result of US forestry's roots in the science of colonial exploitation and administration—a science that took as its starting point the creation of ordered, legible, exclusive, maximizing systems that could be made available to colonizers. It was also partly a result of the social location of US forestry's founder. Gifford Pinchot was the son of an elite family, a member of the capitalist class, and—early in his career—a believer that on US soil, forestry must pay or perish. In addition, "practical forestry's" focus on the economics of accumulation resulted in part because the state lacked the will and the capacity to force less profitable forestry practices on private landholders.

Thus from the very beginning, forestry in the United States was constrained by profitability. The perfect forest order was not a functioning ecosystem. The forest problem was not a problem of maintaining ecological processes vital to the perpetuation of real forests. The forest problem was how to grow timber and make a profit from doing so. Forestry's perfection was the creation of an environment conducive to efficient industrial production that—above all—returned a profit. A characterization of scientific management as an abstract ideological commitment to efficiency and to state-based, scientific control over nature misses the point of scientific management entirely as it developed in tandem with the rise of capitalism. Scientific management in the United States in particular (as well as in England) has always been in the service of industrial profitability.

With this political geology forming the bottom and the banks on which the history of fire flows, it is obvious that those charged with keeping the lumber mills supplied were in a difficult spot from the beginning. Faced with the sight of rapidly vanishing forests and the shadow of "timber famine" looming ever larger, the state mobilized to manage the crisis. Scratching around for what it believed would be adequate tools, it found the most important of them beyond reach. Regulation and nationalization were withheld. The Pulaski and, eventually, the air tanker were proffered in their place.

The USFS leadership's response to this reality was varied. Some, like William Greeley, accepted the limitations and worked closely with industry to keep "radical" regulatory proposals from gaining ground. The Clarke-McNary Law Greeley worked so hard to usher in was explicitly intended as a bulwark against regulation. During these periods, the state worked as a willing partner to industry, shoring up the barriers against threats to private property and profitability in hopes of sweetening the rewards of good forestry rather than prohibiting the industry standard of "forest devastation." Others—like Gus Silcox, Earle Clapp, and Lyle Watts— pushed hard against the dominance of private property, struggling to redefine the role of forestry in relation to society and to grasp the levers of power that had been withheld to that point. Relations ran from intimate to hostile as new chief foresters took office. Despite this, the Forest Service's mission remained constant: to ensure the continuous flow of timber from public and private lands and to do so in a way that provided ongoing opportunities for the profitable exploitation of nature. In addition, even when the Forest Service was at its most oppositional relative to capital, it was unable to effectively pursue what it thought was necessary for the success of its mission. This suggests that the agency's structural location and its role in the context of the industrial-capitalist exploitation of forests, rather than the individuals who led or administered it, provide the most powerful explanation for past USFS policy and practice. The keystones of federal regulation of private logging, national ownership, or both, of much more forestland proved impossible to attain in the face of organized capital's opposition. Fire suppression as a national policy was encouraged and seemed the only hope for coaxing private loggers to practice forestry.

Thus while the Forest Service did indeed push hard for fire protection, and while it moved mountains and worked cunningly to accrue the resources required to effectively suppress fire, these were not the actions of a bullying, autonomous state. Far from suppressing fire in opposition to lumbermen, the USFS was seriously encouraged on this front by organized timber capital and ferociously discouraged on all others. The Forest Service was not even the instigator of state-funded fire protection. The push for publicly socialized fire protection was initiated by timber capital in the Pacific Northwest and eventually won through organized, class-based struggles in that region's state legislatures. The Forest Service's historical devotion to fire suppression is an indicator of its weakness in the face of organized timber capital rather than an indicator of its strength.

The Forest Service thus attempted to manage what it perceived to be an impending supply-side crisis by suppressing fire and eventually by making the timber companies welcome to the national forests. The result has been the manufacture of a new crisis—a "crisis of crisis management." This latter crisis is rooted in the ecological consequences of removing fire from forests that have evolved in tandem with particular patterns of burning, creating a metabolic rift. The crisis manifests itself occasionally, weather permitting, as an uncharacteristically large and destructive fire. I have argued here that given the weakness of the state in the United States relative to the power of a well-organized capitalist class, the state is likely to remain in a cycle of crisis management. The prospects for the emergence of a US "environmental state" appear, on the basis of history, dim at best. Even with a sustained, decades-long push by an allegedly strong state agency with a highly professionalized staff and backed by well-established civil society organizations, the state was unable to win the regulatory tools required to halt the widespread destruction of forests. In wielding the one managerial tool it was granted, the state has unwittingly manufactured a new and perhaps equally intractable problem. It is now struggling, just as it struggled to confine and reverse the problem of "forest devastation" prior to the 1950s, to come up with a strategy for confronting the threat of catastrophic fire. Again, the prospects appear less than promising.

In grappling with this problem, the Forest Service faces two management challenges. The first is rooted in the crisis management pattern: how do we keep catastrophic fires from killing people and torching property? That is, how can we alter the landscape to reduce the risk of an uncontrollable fire? The answer lies in the program of hazardous fuels reduction, which means either prescribed burning or mechanical thinning. While former president George W. Bush initially attempted to tie this program to increasing harvest levels by allowing contractors to remove fire-resistant, large-diameter trees to fund the removal of some of the smaller material, his versions of the Healthy Forests Initiative and the Healthy Forests Restoration Act were considerably modified by the US Congress; as a result, funding seems to be going mostly to projects that will actually reduce fuel loading. Funds may not be going to projects that have the highest priority in terms of community safety or to projects in places that make the most sense ecologically.[3] However, it also seems that funding is not going to many of what one Forest Service employee described as "TSIDs"—Timber Sales in Drag. The major problem is that funding levels for these hazardous fuels reduction projects are miniscule compared with the funding that would be required to make a true ecological impact in the woods, based on the Forest Service's assessment of the damage that has been done. While the vast majority of fire managers I interviewed for this project were pushing as hard as possible to treat the land, the budget—even given increases in recent years—is orders of magnitude too small to have any effective impact on the landscape.

The second problem is how to restore fire to its historical ecological role in the forests to the greatest extent possible. To deal with this problem adequately, the Forest Service would have to move away from the cycle of environmental crisis management and put ecological considerations at the heart of its decision-making. However, a combination of factors is blocking significant progress on this front. These obstacles are themselves, at least in part, a legacy of the policy of fire exclusion. In the absence of low-intensity, frequent fires in some forests, fuels have accumulated to the extent that simply letting fire back into the woods would indeed be catastrophic—both ecologically and also potentially for communities. The public has been taught to fear fire in the woods and to understand it as a destructive menace. With open flame chased from the landscape, new opportunities for real-estate development opened up, and the spread of human settlement into what is now called the wildland urban interface accelerated. US national forests are islands in the midst of mixed land ownership, and wilderness areas are even smaller islands within forests crisscrossed by logging roads and dotted with recreational infrastructure. In Oregon, a taboo on letting free-burning fire (or even "managed fire") out of these wilderness zones is enforced by timber companies, the state forest department, and, in some cases, local communities. As a result, while the Forest Service's policy statements indicate that a radically new approach to fire is on the march, the USFS's efforts to keep fire off the landscape are as intensive as they have ever been.

Both of these problems suggest that the process of ecological modernization, held out as a golden promise for environmental redemption—a mending of the metabolic relationship between humans and nature—is not nearly so simple as changing the way we think about nature or even as simple as owning up to past policy mistakes and altering those policies appropriately. The Forest Service has been well aware of the ecological and economic madness that is fire exclusion for more than thirty years; even before that, federal scientists were pointing out that some forests *needed* fire. The policy did eventually change, but the practice remains unaltered. In the case of fire management, the path of ecological degradation appears a difficult one on which to turn back. At the beginning of the twentieth century the Forest Service conducted a genuine drive to conserve US forests. It did so with an unquestionably reductionist vision of the value of forests. The focus was ever on maintaining the flow of timber rather than on maintaining healthy, ecologically resilient forests. This approach worked within the parameters of power that were set by capital. The USFS's management of the ecological crisis of forest devastation thus came to focus more and more on the misguided exclusion of fire from the forests. In turn, this created a "crisis of crisis management" characterized by metabolic rift that has taken the place of "timber famine" as the great threat to the nation's forests. Here we see the slow, tragic co-production of a disaster. Again, however, the agency finds itself without the power or the funding necessary to do what it knows is needed to adequately manage its creation.

If the state is to be the vanguard institution of ecological modernization, as Fred Buttel suggests it must be,[4] its lack of autonomy to carry out the ecologically informed policies it develops is troubling. As environmental degradation begins to threaten capital, James O'Connor suggests that a fissure begins to open for the democratic management of capital's transformations of nature.[5] The state—a potentially democratic institution in the presence of organized, anti-capitalist forces—is called upon to clean up the messes that inevitably result when ecological processes with their own modes of time and space are forced into the constraints of capitalist economic production. Whether the crisis is one of the "underproduction of the conditions of production," as in the Forest Service's understanding of chronic looming timber shortages, or one of metabolic rift, as in the new "forest health crisis," the state is expected—even required—to manage it. It is here that the potential for autonomy exists. As Karl Marx expressed, in times of crisis, capital realizes that it must "be condemned along with the other classes to like political nullity; that in order to save its purse it must forfeit the crown, and the sword that is to safeguard it must at the same time be hung over its own head as a sword of Damocles."[6]

However, as the struggle over regulation and nationalization suggests, capital arms its protector only with those weapons least likely to be turned back on it, no matter the protests of the guardian-state. Any powers that threaten the ultimate prerogatives of private property or that might be used to reduce capital's long-run freedom to exploit nature and labor remain locked safely away. While foresters such as Gifford Pinchot, Robert Marshall, and Raphael Zon shouted at both the state and at capital that regulation was the fundamental requirement for managing crisis, it was withheld. Even when individuals charged with managing the crisis from leadership positions within the state—men like Silcox, Clapp, and Watts—became convinced that "cooperation" was an insufficient mechanism for managing crisis, the Forest Service—despite another twenty years of struggle— was unable to gain the power of regulation.

The history of forest management in the United States is one in which when the state was called upon to put environmental considerations at the fore (even if historically those considerations were reduced to ensuring the perpetuation of an exploitable resource), it was allowed to do so only up to the point at which those considerations threatened to collide with the cornerstones of capitalism: private property, the freedom of capital to dispose of that property without interference, and ready access to exploitable labor and nature. The history of fire management suggests that the state does act with some autonomy at a surface level. After all, the Forest Service controls both the material resources to suppress and manage fire, as well as the vast majority of the existing knowledge and expertise about fire behavior.[7] Under the surface of this veneer of autonomy, however, the history of the Forest Service's struggle to contest the power of organized timber capital suggests that the state's "autonomy" is granted at the convenience and to the advantage of capital. The autonomy is limited, and the limits are set though the organized mobilization of class power. It might better be described as "managed autonomy" or perhaps as a condition of "chronic parole."

This is only one case, and, as such, it cannot be extended to a generalized claim about the ultimate limits of state-led environmental management under capitalism. It does, however, suggest a new hypothesis for exploration. In the case of forest and fire management, environmental considerations have failed to drive policy or practice, depending on the historical period. This begs the question of under what conditions, if any, the health of the environment is or can be made the paramount criterion for decision-making in the realms of production and legislation. It is, after all, the heart of the thesis of ecological modernization that this will occur at some point within the existing institutional arrangement of liberal capitalism, if indeed it has not already occurred in isolated cases.

One avenue for further research would be to evaluate the generality of this case through comparative research. As others have pointed out, much empirical research into the allegedly ongoing process of ecological modernization suffers from the same limits that this book does—it has been based on single case studies.[8] One possibility is to look at the environmental management practices (for example on the issue of climate change or on the production and disposal of hazardous wastes) of the most ecologically forward industrialized capitalist nations and determine the degree to which their environmental management strategies are (1) adequate responses to major environmental challenges as currently perceived (say, by scientific organizations such as the International Panel on Climate Change or by the community of toxicologists and epidemiologists working on the effects of persistent pollutants) and (2) threatening in any way to the political, legal, economic, or cultural prerequisites of capitalism. Identifying cases in which both (1) and (2) hold true would suggest that there is at least some hope for state-led ecological modernization. It would also help scholars identify the key conditions under which both (1) and (2) can hold. One such potential condition worth investigating is the existence of organized forces from within civil society acting in opposition to capital—particularly from within the ranks of the working class. In the case of fire management, the working class was notable in its absence. Rather, the state drew primarily on allies from the conservationist community in its push for regulation and nationalization rather than connecting this struggle to workers' interests and organized power.

The critical question for scholars interested in the long-term (or perhaps now medium-term) prospects for human survival on this planet ought not to be whether states, corporations, supra-national organizations, or citizens groups are introducing environmental criteria into their decision-making or whether states are establishing more parks and setting up state environmental agencies. All of that is marvelous. However, in the face of continuing degradation of natural systems and the global economy's stubborn refusal to "de-materialize," it does not answer the fundamental question of whether and under what conditions we might overcome the profound contradictions between the perpetuation of functional, resilient, healthy ecosystems on the one hand and the accumulative and exploitative logic of capitalism on the other. The answer to this question is inextricably connected to the question of how the organized power of capital can be effectively countered by those with an interest in nature as "the conditions of life" rather than exclusively as the "conditions of production."[9]

Notes

CHAPTER 1: INTRODUCTION

1. Douglas Gantenbein, *A Season of Fire: Four Months on the Firelines in the American West* (New York: Jeremy P. Tarcher/Penguin, 2003) 4; Quadrennial Fire and Fuels Review Integration Panel, "Quadrennial Fire and Fuel Review Report" (2005), 13. Available at www.nifc.gov/nimo/backgrnd/qffr_report.pdf; accessed February 16, 2006.

2. Strategic Issues Panel on Fire Management, "Large Fire Suppression Costs: Strategies for Cost Management." Report to the Wildland Fire Leadership Council (2004), 7. Available at http://www.fireplan.gov/reports/2004/costmanagement.pdf; accessed December 3, 2005.

3. By "state-financed" I mean funded publicly through both federal and state governments. The term "state," unless used in direct and obvious contrast to "federal," should be understood to mean the institutions of government rather than a specific level of government. Similarly, "state agency" refers to an agency of government, such as the USFS, rather than specifically to an agency of a state government, such as CalFire or the Oregon Department of Forestry.

4. National Interagency Fire Center (NIFC), "2008 Year-to-Date Report on Fires and Acres Burned by State" (2009). Available at http://www.nifc.gov/fire_info/ytd_state_2008.htm; accessed April 3, 2009.

5. Stephen F. Arno and Steven Allison-Bunnell, *Flames in Our Forest: Disaster or Renewal?* (Washington, DC: Island, 2002), 6–7; David Carle, *Burning Questions: America's Fight with Nature's Fire* (Westport, CT: Praeger, 2002); Dominick A. DellaSala, Jack E. Williams, Cindy Deacon Williams, and Jerry R. Franklin, "Beyond Smoke and Mirrors:

A Synthesis of Forest Policy and Science," *Conservation Biology* 18(4) (2004): 977; Gantenbein, *Season of Fire*; Nancy Langston, *Forest Dreams, Forest Nightmares: The Paradox of Old Growth in the Inland West* (Seattle: University of Washington Press, 1995); Robert H. Nelson, *A Burning Issue: A Case for Abolishing the U.S. Forest Service* (Lanham, MD: Rowman and Littlefield, 2000); President of the United States, *Healthy Forests: An Initiative for Wildfire Prevention and Stronger Communities* (2002), 1. Available at http://www. whitehouse.gov/infocus/healthyforests/Healthy_Forests_v2.pdf; accessed February 15, 2006; Stephen J. Pyne, *America's Fires: Management on Wildlands and Forests* (Durham, NC: Forest History Society, 1997), 15–22; Pyne, "Pyromancy: Reading Stories in the Flames," *Conservation Biology* 18(4) (August 2004): 874; Pyne, *Tending Fire: Coping with America's Wildland Fires* (Washington, DC: Island, 2004), 49.

6. Jewett, letter to Earle H. Clapp, acting chief, United States Forest Service, April 20, 1940. Box 63, Archive of the National Forest Products Association, Forest History Society, Durham, NC [hereafter Forest History Society.].

7. A. J. Glassow, Remarks of A. J. Glassow, president, NLMA, May 12, 1949, Shoreham Hotel, Washington, DC. Box 46, Forest History Society.

8. George F. Jewett, Statement to the Joint Congressional Committee on Forestry, January 16, 1940, Washington, DC. Box 91, Forest History Society.

9. George A. Gonzalez, *Corporate Power and the Environment: The Political Economy of U.S. Environmental Policy* (Lanham, MD: Rowman and Littlefield, 2001).

10. Richard W. Behan, *Plundered Promise: Capitalism, Politics, and the Fate of the Federal Lands* (Washington, DC: Island, 2001), 10–11.

11. See, for example, Mark Brunson and Bruce Shindler, "Geographic Variation in Social Acceptability of Wildland Fuels Management in the Western United States," *Society and Natural Resources* 17(8) (2004): 661–678; Greg Winter and Jeremy Fried, "Homeowner Perspectives on Fire Hazard, Responsibility, and Management Strategies at the Wildland-Urban Interface," *Society and Natural Resources* 13(1) (2000): 33–49.

12. Stephen J. Pyne, *Year of the Fires: The Story of the Great Fires of 1910* (New York: Viking Penguin, 2001).

13. Gantenbein, *Season of Fire,* 212–213; Nelson, *Burning Issue,* 33–39.

14. Claus Offe, *Contradictions of the Welfare State* (London: Hutchinson, 1984).

15. James O'Connor, *Natural Causes: Essays in Ecological Marxism* (New York: Guilford, 1998), 152–155.

CHAPTER 2: THE SOCIAL DIMENSIONS OF WILDFIRE

1. Ted Steinberg, *Acts of God: The Unnatural History of Natural Disaster in America* (Oxford: Oxford University Press, 2000).

2. Ibid.

3. The amount is more likely in the billions: between 1990 and 2000 alone, public service advertising featuring Smokey Bear was valued at $481 million. The Smokey program has been running since 1944 (Ad Council, National Association of State Foresters,

United States Forest Service, "Only You Can Prevent Forest Fires," press release, April 23, 2001).

4. Carle, *Burning Questions*; Ashley L. Schiff, *Fire and Water: Scientific Heresy in the Forest Service* (Cambridge: Harvard University Press, 1962).

5. http://www.naturalhazards.org/hazards/thunderstorm/index.html; accessed April 4, 2011.

6. Steinberg, *Acts of God,* 97–115.

7. Karl Marx, *The German Ideology* (Moscow: Progress, 1976), 34.

8. Noel Castree, "Marxism and the Production of Nature," *Capital and Class* 72 (Autumn): 20; Neil Smith, *Uneven Development* (Oxford: Blackwell, 1984).

9. Stephen J. Pyne, *Fire in America: A Cultural History of Wildland and Rural Fire* (Seattle: University of Washington Press, 1982), 78.

10. Langston, *Forest Dreams, Forest Nightmares,* 46–48.

11. William G. Robbins, "The Good Fight: Forest Fire Protection in the Pacific Northwest," *Oregon Historical Quarterly* 102(3) (Fall 2001): 272–273.

12. Ibid., 273.

13. Pyne, *Fire in America,* 80.

14. James Agee, *Fire Ecology of the Pacific Northwest Forests* (Washington, DC: Island, 1993).

15. Pyne, *Fire in America.*

16. Langston, *Forest Dreams, Forest Nightmares,* 249.

17. Quoted in Pyne, *Year of the Fires,* 6.

18. William G. Morris, "Forest Fires in Western Oregon and Washington," *Oregon Historical Quarterly* 35 (December 1934): 313–339.

19. Pyne, *Fires in America,* 100.

20. Pyne, *Year of the Fires,* 45.

21. Paul Trachtman, "Fire Fight," *Smithsonian* 34(5) (August 2003): 43.

22. Cited in George Wuerthner, "Out of the Ashes," *National Parks* 76(7-8) (September-October 2002). Retrieved from Academic Search Elite database, April 17, 2005.

23. National Interagency Fire Center (NIFC), "Wildland Fire Historical Statistics, Total Fires and Acres, 1960–2005" (2005). Available at http://www.nifc.gov/stats/wildlandfirestats.html; accessed March 16, 2006.

24. Pyne, *America's Fires,* 25, table 6(b).

25. USDA Forest Service, *The Use of the National Forest Reserves: Regulations and Instructions* (1905), 63. Available at http://www.lib.duke.edu/forest/Research/usfscoll/publications/1905_Use_Book/1905_use_book.pdf; accessed March 24, 2006.

26. Ibid., 65.

27. Ibid., 68. A backfire is lit to burn out all the fuel between a defensible line (e.g., a river, road, clearing) and an approaching fire. It represents a sacrifice of standing timber to deprive advancing flames of combustibles.

28. Quoted in Pyne, *Fires in America,* 262.

29. NIFC, "2005 End of Season Report Charts and Tables" (2005). Available at http://www.nifc.gov/nicc/predictive/intelligence/2005_statssumm/2005Stats&Summ. html; accessed March 16, 2006.

30. United States Department of Agriculture and United States Department of the Interior (USDA and USDI), *FY 2002 Performance Report: National Fire Plan* (Washington, DC: USDA and USDI, 2002); Timothy Ingalsbee, "Begging the Question: Appropriate Management Response as a Toolbox vs. Tautology: Integrating Safety, Ethical, and Ecological Sideboards into AMR." Paper presented at Fire in the Southwest: Integrating Fire Management into Changing Ecosystems, Association for Fire Ecology, Tucson AZ, January 30, 2008.

31. Carle, *Burning Questions*; Pyne, *Fire in America* and *Year of the Fires*; William G. Robbins, *American Forestry: A History of National, State, and Private Cooperation* (Lincoln: University of Nebraska Press, 1985); Harold K. Steen, *The U.S. Forest Service: A History* (centennial edition) (Durham, NC, and Seattle: Forest History Society and University of Washington Press, 2004).

32. William G. Robbins, *Lumberjacks and Legislators: Political Economy of the U.S. Lumber Industry, 1890–1941* (College Station: Texas A&M University Press, 1982), 16.

33. Pyne, *Fire in America,* 182.

34. Robert Wiebe, *The Search for Order, 1877–1920* (New York: Hill and Wang, 1967), 185.

35. Samuel P. Hays, *Conservation and the Gospel of Efficiency: The Progressive Conservation Movement, 1890–1920* (New York: Atheneum, 1969); Robbins, *Lumberjacks and Legislators.*

36. Robbins, *Lumberjacks and Legislators.*

37. W. N. Sparhawk, "The History of Forestry in America," *Yearbook of Agriculture* (Washington, DC: Government Printing Office, 1949), 702–714; Samuel Trask Dana and Sally Fairfax, *Forest and Range Policy: Its Development in the United States,* 2nd ed. (New York: McGraw-Hill, 1980).

38. Dana and Fairfax, *Forest and Range Policy,* 42.

39. Ibid., 50.

40. Congressional Record 1914, 4623, 4622.

41. Raphael Zon, letter to F. E. Olmsted, May 24, 1919. Box 3, Zon Papers, Archives of the Minnesota Historical Society, St. Paul.

42. Andrew Denny Rodgers III, *Bernhard Eduard Fernow: A Story of North American Forestry* (New York: Hafner, 1968), 167.

43. Ibid.

44. Quoted in Sparhawk, "History of Forestry in America," 705.

45. "First Things First" (editorial), *American Forests* 44 (July 1938): 313.

46. Steen, *U.S. Forest Service,* 26–27n13.

47. Hays, *Conservation and the Gospel of Efficiency,* 37.

48. Ibid., 39–44.

49. Christopher McGrory Klyza, "A Window of Autonomy: State Autonomy and the Forest Service in the Early 1900s," *Polity* 25(2) (Winter 1992): 181–182.

50. Randall O'Toole, "Memo to President Clinton: The Forest Service Has Already Been Reinvented" (n.d.). Available at http://www.ti.org/history.html; accessed July 19, 2006.

51. Klyza, "Window of Autonomy," 182.

52. Pyne, *Fire in America,* 102–103.

53. Henry S. Graves, "Protection of Forests from Fire," USDA Forest Service Bulletin 32 (Washington, DC: Government Printing Office, 1910), 7.

54. William B. Greeley, *Forests and Men* (Garden City, NY: Doubleday, 1951), 24; Greeley, "Man-Made Fires," *Perkins Glue Line* 33 (September 1954): 1. Box 40, Forest History Society.

55. Quoted in Pyne, *Fire in America,* 260.

56. Gifford Pinchot, *The Fight for Conservation* (New York: Doubleday Page, 1910), 45.

57. Wilson Compton, "Organized Lumber Business of the United States: Through the National Lumber Manufacturers Association, This Great Industry Functions for the Public Good," *The Washington Post,* March 4, 1925.

58. George H. Weyerhaeuser Jr., "The Three Impediments: Time, Fire and Taxes," in *Forest Policy for Private Forestry: Global and Regional Challenges,* ed. Lawrence Teeter, Ben Cashore, and Daowei Zhang (New York: CABI, 2003), 64.

59. Ralph Hidy, Frank Ernest Hill, and Allen Nevins, *Timber and Men: The Weyerhaeuser Story* (New York: Macmillan, 1963), 382.

60. Robbins, *American Forestry.*

61. Carle, *Burning Questions;* Schiff, *Fire and Water.*

62. DuBois, *Systematic Fire Protection,* 42.

63. Ibid.

64. Standardization Committee, Proceedings of the Standardization Committee, Western Forestry and Conservation Association, Portland, OR, April 24–25, 1919, 32.

65. Ibid., 35.

66. D. S. Jeffers, letter to H. H. Chapman, October 15, 1934. Box 50, Forest History Society; USDA Forest Service, *Report of the Chief of the Forest Service* (Washington, DC: Government Printing Office, 1936), 35.

67. USDA Forest Service, *Report of the Chief of the Forest Service* (1936), 35.

68. USDA Forest Service, *Report of the Chief of the Forest Service* (Washington, DC: Government Printing Office, 1934), 4.

69. USDA Forest Service, *Report of the Chief of the Forest Service* (1936), 10.

70. Page S. Bunker, letter to the regional forester, USFS, Atlanta, GA, November 23, 1938. Box 144, Record Group 95, CCC Cooperation Agreements, SCS 1939, National Archives, Washington, DC.

71. USDA Office of Information, "Fire Toll in National Forests Held to Low Level This Year," press release, October 5, 1933. File 144, Record Group 95, ECW Information, National Archives, Washington, DC.

72. Pyne, *Fire in America,* 288–289.

73. Ibid., 288.

74. Pyne, *Tending Fire*, 57.

75. Carle, *Burning Questions,* 81–87.

76. *American Forests,* quoted in ibid., 85–86.

77. George Vitas, *Forest and Flame in the Bible.* A program aid of the Cooperative Forest Fire Prevention Campaign sponsored by the Ad Council, State Foresters, and the USDA Forest Service (Washington, DC: Government Printing Office, 1937; reprinted 1961).

78. This reach, in addition to standard print, radio, and television advertising, included numerous "live appearances" and the production of licensed Smokey flashlights, innumerable stuffed Smokey Bears, coloring books, toy helicopters, ranger stations, fire engines, fire starter cones, action figures, hand puppets, board games, piggy banks, model train cars, T-shirts, painting easels, coffee mugs, souvenir baseballs, cookie jars, and a Macy's Thanksgiving Parade balloon sponsored by General Electric.

79. John Beale, "Cooperative Forest Fire Protection: Report to the 38th Annual Meeting of the National Association of State Foresters, September 13–15, 1960." Box 216, Records of the National Association of State Foresters, Denver Public Library, Denver, CO.

80. William Folkman, "Butte County, California Residents: Their Knowledge and Attitudes about Forest Fires Reassessed." Research Note PSW-297 (Berkeley, CA: USDA Forest Service, Pacific Southwest Research Station, 1973).

81. Gary E. Machlis, Amanda B. Kaplan, Seth P. Tuler, Kathleen A. Bagby, and Jean E. McKendry, *Burning Questions: A Social Science Research Plan for Federal Wildland Fire Management.* Contribution 943, Idaho Forest, Wildlife, and Range Experiment Station (Moscow: College of Natural Resources, University of Idaho, 2002), 95.

82. Ibid., 96.

83. Pyne, *Fire in America,* 294.

84. This policy adoption has a fascinating history of its own, well documented in Hal K. Rothman, *A Test of Adversity and Strength: Wildland Fire in the National Park System* (Washington, DC: Department of the Interior, n.d.). Rothman attributes the early adoption of fire use as a management tool to the strong influence of the Leopold Report on wildlife in the park system, the Robbins Report on research in the park system, and the increasing preponderance of wildlife biologists relative to foresters employed by the National Park Service—a key difference from the USFS.

85. Ibid.

86. USDA/USDI, *Federal Wildland Fire Management Policy and Program Review Report,* 1995. Available at http://www.fs.fed.us/land/wdfirex.htm; accessed December 21, 2004.

87. David J. Parsons, "The Challenge of Restoring Natural Fire to Wilderness," USDA Forest Service Proceedings RMRS-P-15, vol. 5 (2000): 281.

88. J. Boone Kauffman, "Death Rides the Forest: Perceptions of Fire, Land Use, and Ecological Restoration of Western Forests," *Conservation Biology* 18(4) (August 2004): 880.

89. Wildland Fire Leadership Council, *Guidance for Implementation of Federal Wildland Fire Management Policy*, 2009. Available at http://www.fusee.org; accessed March 31, 2009.

90. Personal communication with Deb Schweizer, Sequoia/Kings Canyon fire education and information specialist, and David Bartlett, Sequoia/Kings Canyon fire management officer, April 3, 2009.

91. James Agee's *Fire Ecology of the Pacific Northwest Forests* provides the classic account of fire's impact on Pacific Northwestern forests. Stephen Arno and Steven Allison-Bunnell's *Flames in Our Forest: Disaster or Renewal* presents an excellent overview of the interaction of fire and forests in the West.

92. Arno and Allison-Bunnell, *Flames in Our Forest,* 5.

93. Ibid., 60.

94. This benchmark is highly problematic. The state of western forests when the European settlers arrived has been set as the target for restoration efforts on public lands. Essentially, a snapshot of a landscape significantly transformed through the labor of indigenous populations for their specific productive needs has been defined as "natural." Without going too deeply into the obvious underlying racism of this definition, it also begs the question of whether this "natural" landscape either can or should be statically maintained and, if so, to what end.

95. USDA Forest Service, "Fire and Fuels," 2004. Available at http://www.fs.fed.us/projects/four-threats/documents/firefuels-fs.pdf; accessed April 7, 2006.

96. David E. Calkin, Krista M. Gebert, J. Greg Jones, and Ronald P. Neilson, "Forest Service Large Area Burned Suppression Expenditure Trends, 1970–2002," *Journal of Forestry* 103(4) (June 2005): 179.

97. United States General Accounting Office (GAO), "Forest Service: A Framework for Improving Accountability," 1999. Report to the Subcommittee on Interior and Related Agencies, Committee on Appropriations, House of Representatives, GAO/RCED/AIMD–00–2. Available at http://www.gao.gov/new.items/r100002.pdf; accessed November 23, 2005.

98. Strategic Issues Panel on Fire Management, "Large Fire Suppression Costs."

99. Calkin et al., "Forest Service."

100. See, for example, DellaSala et al., "Beyond Smoke and Mirrors," 976–986; Gantenbein, *Season of Fire,* 4; Timothy Ingalsbee, "Wildfire Paradoxes," *Oregon Quarterly* 82(2) (Winter 2002): 18–23; Kauffman, "Death Rides the Forest," 879; Nelson, *Burning Issue,* 6–7; President of the United States, *Healthy Forests;* Quadrennial Fire and Fuels Review Integration Panel, "Quadrennial Fire and Fuel Review Report," 13; Gerald W. Williams, "Wildland Fire Management in the 20th Century," *Fire Management Today* 60(4) (Fall 2000): 15–20.

101. President of the United States, *Healthy Forests,* 1.

102. Commission on Presidential Debates, "Debate Transcripts, the Second Bush-Kerry Debate (October 8, 2004), Washington University, St. Louis, Missouri." Available at http://www.debates.org/pages/trans2004c.html; accessed December 12, 2006.

103. Nelson, *Burning Issue.*

104. DellaSala et al., "Beyond Smoke and Mirrors"; Kauffman, "Death Rides the Forest."

105. Jacqueline Vaughn and Hanna J. Cortner, *George W. Bush's Healthy Forests: Reframing the Environmental Debate* (Boulder: University Press of Colorado, 2005).

106. American Forests and Paper Association (AF&PA), "AF&PA Hails Passage of Healthy Forests Restoration Act," press release, November 23, 2003. Available at http://www.afandpa.org/Template.cfm?Section=Press_Releases1&template=/PressRelease/PressReleaseDisplay.cfm&PressReleaseID=251&PressReleaseCategoryID=10&Show Archives=0; accessed November 5, 2005; AF&PA, "AF&PA Praises Forest Emergency Recovery and Research Act: Bipartisan Legislation Seen as Vital to Long Term Forest Health," press release, November 3, 2005. Available at http://www.afandpa.org/Template.cfm?Section=Press_Releases1&template=/PressRelease/PressReleaseDisplay.cfm&PressReleaseID=757&PressReleaseCategoryID=10&ShowArchives=0; accessed November 3, 2005.

107. Sean Paige, "Uncle Sam Gets Burned Out West," *Insight Magazine* (June 2000). Available at http://www.cei.org/gencon/019,03091.cfm; accessed March 30, 2006.

108. Sierra Club, *Forest Fires: Beyond the Heat and Hype* (Washington, DC: Sierra Club, n.d.). Available at http://www.sierraclub.org/forests/report01/ecl01_forestfires.pdf; accessed March 30, 2006; American Lands Alliance, *After the Fires: Do No Harm in America's Forests,* 2005. Available at http://www.americanlands.org/documents/1130 855803_AftertheFiresFinalEmail.pdf; accessed January 23, 2006.

109. Wilderness Society, *Forest Fires: Beyond the Heat and Hype* (Washington, DC: Wilderness Society, n.d.).

110. President of the United States, "President Thanks Work Crews and Firefighters," Office of the Press Secretary, August 22, 2002. Available at http://www.whitehouse.gov/news/releases/2002/08/20020822-2.html; accessed March 31, 2006.

111. Vaughn and Cortner, *George W. Bush's Healthy Forests.*

112. United States General Accounting Office (GAO), *Forest Service: Information on Appeals and Litigation Involving Fuels Reduction Activities* (Washington, DC: GAO, 2003).

113. Vaughn and Cortner, *George W. Bush's Healthy Forests,* 202.

114. Quoted in Margaret Kriz, "Fighting Fire with Logging," *National Journal* 34(28) (2002): 2093.

115. Chad Hanson, "The Big Lie: Logging and Forest Fires," *Earth Island Journal* 15(1) (Spring 2000): 12–13; Sierra Club, *Forest Fires,* 5.

116. Daniel C. Donato, J. B. Fontaine, John L. Campbell, W. Douglas Robinson, J. Boone Kauffman, and Beverly E. Law, "Post-Wildfire Logging Hinders Regenerations and Increases Fire Risk," *Science Express* (January 5, 2006): 1. Available at http://www.sciencexpress.org.; accessed February 12, 2007; Robert L. Beschta, Jonathan J. Rhodes, J. Boone Kaufmann, Robert E. Gresswell, G. Wayne Minshall, James R. Karr, David A. Perry, F. Richard Hauer, and Christopher A. Frissell, "Postfire Management on Forested

Public Lands of the Western United States," *Conservation Biology* 18(4) (August 2005): 957–967; James D. McIver and Lynn Starr, "Environmental Effects of Postfire Logging: Literature Review and Annotated Bibliography," 2000. Gen. Tech. Report PNW-GTR-486. USDA Forest Service, PNW Research Station, Portland, OR, 23–25.

117. Randi Spivak, "The Politics of FERRA." Paper presented at the Public Interest Environmental Law Conference, University of Oregon School of Law, Eugene, March 4, 2006.

CHAPTER 3: FORESTER-KINGS? FIRE
SUPPRESSION AND THE STATE

1. Langston, *Forest Dreams, Forest Nightmares*; Gantenbein, *Season of Fire*; President of the United States, *Healthy Forests*.

2. Pyne, *Fire in America*; Pyne, *Year of the Fires*.

3. Carle, *Burning Questions*; Schiff, *Fire and Water*.

4. Nelson, *Burning Issue*.

5. Eric A. Nordlinger, *On the Autonomy of the Democratic State* (Cambridge, MA: Harvard University Press, 1981), 1.

6. Edwin Amenta, "State-Centered and Political Institutional Theory: Retrospect and Prospect," in *The Handbook of Political Sociology*, ed. T. Janoski, Robert Alford, Alexander Hicks, and Mildred Schartz (New York: Cambridge University Press, 2005), 96.

7. Theda Skocpol, "Bringing the State Back In: Strategies of Analysis in Current Research," in *Bringing the State Back In*, ed. Peter B. Evans, Dietrich Rueschemeyer, and Theda Skocpol (New York: Cambridge University Press, 1985), 4–37.

8. Ibid., 6.

9. Max Weber, *Economy and Society: An Outline of Interpretive Sociology*, ed. Guenther Roth and Claus Wittich (New York: Bedminster, 1968), vol. 2, 901–902; Alfred Stepan, *The State and Society: Peru in Comparative Perspective* (Princeton: Princeton University Press, 1978), xii.

10. Weber, *Economy and Society,* vol. 3, 991.

11. Ibid., 991–992.

12. Ibid., 991.

13. Ibid., 989–990.

14. See, for example, Theda Skocpol, *Protecting Soldiers and Mothers: Political Origins of Social Policy in the United States* (Cambridge, MA: Belknap Press of Harvard University Press, 1992); Ann Shola Orloff and Theda Skocpol, "Why Not Equal Protection? Explaining the Politics of Public Social Welfare in Britain and the United States, 1880s–1920s," *American Sociological Review* 49 (1984): 726–750; Edwin Amenta and Bruce Carruthers, "The Formative Years of U.S. Social Security Spending Policies," *American Sociological Review* 53 (1989): 661–678; Theda Skocpol and Kenneth Finegold, "Explaining New Deal Labor Policy," *American Political Science Review* 84(4) (1989): 1297–1315.

15. Peter B. Evans, *Embedded Autonomy: States and Industrial Transformation* (Princeton: Princeton University Press, 1995); Evans, "Government Action, Social Capital and Development: Reviewing the Evidence on Synergy," in *State-Society Synergy: Government and Society*, ed. Peter B. Evans. Research Series 94 (Berkeley: University of California Press, 1997), 181–209; Gregory Hooks, "The Rise of the Pentagon and U.S. State Building: The Defense Program as Industrial Policy," *American Journal of Sociology* 96 (1990): 358–404; Hooks, "The Weakness of Strong Theories: The U.S. State's Dominance of the World War II Investment Process," *American Sociological Review* 58 (1993): 37–53.

16. Jeff Goodwin, *No Other Way Out: States and Revolutionary Movements, 1945–1991* (Cambridge, UK: Cambridge University Press, 2001); Theda Skocpol, *States and Social Revolutions: A Comparative Analysis of France, Russia, and China* (Cambridge, UK: Cambridge University Press, 1979).

17. Michael Goldfield, "Worker Insurgency, Radical Organization, and New Deal Labor Legislation," *American Political Science Review* 83(4) (1989): 1257–1282.

18. Skocpol and Finegold, "Explaining New Deal Labor Policy," 1303.

19. Skocpol, *Protecting Soldiers and Mothers*.

20. Ibid., 11–40.

21. Ibid., 41.

22. Ibid., 50.

23. Ibid.

24. Gregory Hooks, "From an Autonomous to a Captured State Agency: The Decline of the New Deal in Agriculture," *American Sociological Review* 55 (1990): 29–43.

25. Skocpol, "Bringing the State Back In," 14; original emphasis.

26. C. Edward Paul, "Moving Forward with State Autonomy and Capacity: Example from Two Studies of the Pentagon during W.W.II," *Journal of Political and Military Sociology* 28(1) (Summer 2000): 21–42.

27. G. William Domhoff, "The Death of State Autonomy Theory: A Review of Skocpol's *Protecting Soldiers and Mothers*," *Critical Sociology* 19(2) (2003): 103–116.

28. Hooks, "From an Autonomous to a Captured State Agency."

29. Bruce Carruthers, "When Is the State Autonomous? Culture, Organization Theory, and the Political Sociology of the State," *Sociological Theory* 12(1) (March 1994): 19–44.

30. Michael Mann, "The Autonomous Power of the State: Its Origins, Mechanisms, and Results," *Archives Européenes de Sociologie* 25 (1984): 185–213.

31. Ibid., 207.

32. Carruthers, "When Is the State Autonomous," 25.

33. Carmenza Gallo, "The Autonomy of Weak States: States and Classes in Primary Resource Economies," *Sociological Perspectives* 40(4) (1997): 639–660.

34. Behan, *Plundered Promise*; David A. Clary, *Timber and the Forest Service* (Lawrence: University of Kansas Press, 1986); Paul W. Hirt, *A Conspiracy of Optimism: Management of the National Forests since World War Two* (Lincoln: University of Nebraska Press, 1994); Robbins, *Lumberjacks and Legislators*; Robbins, *American Forestry*.

35. Clary, *Timber and the Forest Service,* 22.

36. Nelson, *Burning Issue,* 16.

37. Ibid., 161.

38. Carle, *Burning Questions,* 14.

39. Schiff, *Fire and Water,* 23.

40. Pyne, *Year of the Fires,* 261.

41. Pyne, *Fire in America,* 261.

42. Langston, *Forest Dreams, Forest Nightmares.*

43. William B. Greeley, "'Piute Forestry' or the Fallacy of Light Burning," *The Timberman* (March 1920): 38–39; Editorial, "Graves Terms Light Burning Piute Forestry," *The Timberman* (January): 35.

44. M. Nelson McGeary, *Gifford Pinchot: Forester Politician* (Princeton, NJ: Princeton University Press, 1960), 19.

45. Gregory Allen Barton, *Empire Forestry and the Origins of Environmentalism* (Cambridge: Cambridge University Press, 2002).

46. Ibid., 14.

47. James C. Scott, *Seeing Like a State* (New Haven: Yale University Press, 1998), 12.

48. Ibid.

49. Pyne, *Tending Fire,* 34.

50. Langston, *Forest Dreams, Forest Nightmares,* 253–257.

51. Ibid., 250; Carle, *Burning Questions,* 17–22; Pyne, *Fire in America,* 103–106.

52. Langston, *Forest Dreams, Forest Nightmares,* 251; Pyne, *Fire in America,* 103.

53. Pyne, *Fire in America,* 102.

54. Carle, *Burning Questions*; Pyne, *Fire in America,* 107; Schiff, *Fire and Water.*

55. "Indian vs. Pinchot Conservation," *The Oregonian* [Portland], January 26, 1911, 1; F. E. Olmsted, *Light Burning in the California Forests* (Washington, DC: USDA Forest Service, 1911); Stephen J. Pyne, "The Source," distinguished lecture in Forest and Conservation History, Joint Conference of the American Society for Environmental History and the Forest History Society, Durham, NC, 2001. Available at www.lib.duke.edu/forest. Events/lecture2001%20text.html; accessed April 12, 2005.

56. Carle, *Burning Questions,* 4.

57. "Colgan Cracks Down on Forest Service," *Southern Hardwood Bulletin* 58, May 10, 1947, 1–3. Box 54, Forest Historical Society, Memphis, TN.

58. Carolyn Merchant, *The Death of Nature: Women, Ecology, and the Scientific Revolution* (San Francisco: Harper, 1980), 20.

59. Nelson, *Burning Issue,* 4.

60. Langston, *Forest Dreams, Forest Nightmares,* 5.

61. Ibid.

62. Robert H. Nelson, "The Federal Land Management Agencies," in *A New Century for Natural Resources Management*, ed. Richard L. Knight and Sarah F. Bates (Washington, DC: Island, 1995), 54.

63. Gifford Pinchot, *Breaking New Ground* (New York: Harcourt, Brace, 1947), 261.

64. Klyza, "Window of Autonomy," 179.

65. Pyne, *Tending Fire*, 32.

66. Skocpol, "Bringing the State Back In," 10.

67. Steen, *U.S. Forest Service*, 63.

68. Char Miller, *Gifford Pinchot and the Making of Modern Environmentalism* (Washington, DC: Island, 2001), 157.

69. Steen, *U.S. Forest Service*, 63.

70. Pinchot, *Breaking New Ground*, 153.

71. Langston, *Forest Dreams, Forest Nightmares*, 98.

72. Klyza, "Window of Autonomy," 180.

73. Ibid., 181.

74. Hays, *Conservation and the Gospel of Efficiency*, 142.

75. Ibid., 144.

76. Pyne, *Year of the Fires*.

77. Ibid., 290.

78. The exceptions are Nelson, *Burning Issue*, and Randall O'Toole, *Reforming the Fire Service* (Bandon, OR: Thoreau Institute, 2002). Both of these books foreground the fact that fire suppression serves the USFS's budget-maximizing tendencies.

79. This funding model was reformed with the passage of the 2009 Federal Land Assistance, Management and Enhancement Act, which establishes a fund for emergency suppression.

80. Pyne, *Tending Fire*, 90.

81. Ibid., 90–91.

82. Behan, *Plundered Promise*; Clary, *Timber and the Forest Service*; Hirt, *Conspiracy of Optimism*; Robbins, *Lumberjacks and Legislators*; Robbins, *American Forestry*.

83. Herbert Kaufman, *The Forest Ranger: A Study in Administrative Behavior* (Baltimore: Johns Hopkins University Press, 1960); Paul J. Culhane, *Public Lands Politics: Interest Group Influence on the Forest Service and the Bureau of Land Management* (Baltimore: Johns Hopkins University Press, 1960).

84. Hirt, *Conspiracy of Optimism*, 306–309.

85. Klyza, "Window of Autonomy."

86. Pinchot, *Breaking New Ground*, 254–256.

87. Klyza, "Window of Autonomy," 181–183.

88. Ibid.

89. See especially Grant McConnell, *Private Power and American Democracy* (New York: Alfred A. Knopf, 1966).

90. Hirt, *Conspiracy of Optimism*; Robbins, *Lumberjacks and Legislators*; Ben W. Twight and Fremont J. Lyden, "Measuring Forest Service Bias," *Journal of Forestry* 87 (May 1989): 35–41; Twight, Lyden, and E. Thomas Tuchmann, "Constituency Bias in a Federal Career System? A Study of District Rangers of the U.S. Forest Service," *Administration and Society* 22 (November 1990): 358–389.

91. Miller, *Gifford Pinchot*, 278.

92. Raphael Zon, letter to Maj. George P. Ahern, September 19, 1929, 2–3. Box 6, Zon Papers, Archives of the Minnesota Historical Society, St. Paul.

93. Pyne, *Tending Fire,* 94.

94. Carle, *Burning Questions*; Schiff, *Fire and Water.*

95. Carle, *Burning Questions,* 57–79.

96. Evans, *Embedded Autonomy*; Hooks, "Rise of the Pentagon"; Goodwin, *No Other Way Out.*

CHAPTER 4: MANAGING IN THE WAKE OF THE AX

1. In the early twentieth century the term "forestry" was used in opposition to "timber mining." That is, forestry was the science and practice of growing trees for harvest on a continuous basis. I use the term "forestry" in this way, denoting a conservationist model of timber production.

2. A small body of literature treats management's purposes explicitly. From the standpoint of working out a framework for developing management goals, see Marion Clawson, *Forests: For Whom and For What?* (Baltimore: Resources for the Future by Johns Hopkins University Press, 1975). For a historical conflict perspective, see Behan, *Plundered Promise.* On the connections between managerial purpose and fire, see Steen, *U.S. Forest Service*; Robbins, *Lumberjacks and Legislators*; Robbins, *American Forestry.*

3. George P. Ahern, Robert Marshall, E. N. Munns, Gifford Pinchot, Ward Shepard, W. N. Sparhawk, and Raphael Zon, "A Letter to Foresters," *Journal of Forestry* 28(4) (April 1930): 456–458.

4. R. C. Hall, "Observations on the 'Letter,'" *Journal of Forestry* 28(4) (April 1930): 461.

5. Royal S. Kellogg, "As I See It," *Journal of Forestry* 28(4) (April 1930): 461–462.

6. F. W. Reed, "Is Forestry a Religion?" *Journal of Forestry* 28(4) (April 1930): 463.

7. C. Stowell Smith, "De-bunking Forestry," *Journal of Forestry* 28(4) (April 1930): 465–466.

8. E. W. Hartwell, letter to Raphael Zon, February 26, 1930, 12–13. Box 6, P1237 Zon Papers, Archives of the Minnesota Historical Society, St. Paul; original emphasis.

9. Gonzalez, *Corporate Power and the Environment,* 30–37.

10. Pinchot quoted in Miller, *Gifford Pinchot,* 111–112.

11. J. Girvin Peters, "The Possibilities and the Limitations of Government Cooperative Work with the Private Owner," presentation to the Society of American Foresters, December 22, 1904, 1. Record Group 95–68: Administration—Office of Cooperative Forestry, National Archives, Washington, DC.

12. Pinchot, *Breaking New Ground,* 140.

13. Ibid., 142.

14. Hays, *Conservation and the Gospel of Efficiency*; Robbins, *Lumberjacks and Legislators*; Robbins, *American Forestry.*

15. Gifford Pinchot, "The Forester and the Lumberman," *Forestry and Irrigation* 9 (April 1903): 176. Interestingly, in connection with the colonial roots of American forestry's goals and as testimony to the favors exchanged by Pinchot and Roosevelt, Pinchot closed this speech with a plug for Roosevelt's invasion and occupation of the Philippines. He spoke glowingly of the lumbering opportunities ("when the Filipinos have learned to work, as they will readily learn under the instruction of the Americans, there is going to be an enormous expansion of the lumber trade in the islands . . . It is the finest opportunity for practical forestry that I have ever had anything to do with"; 176) as well as of the US military's fine conduct: "As a man sees what the Americans are doing out there in the islands, he cannot help being prouder and prouder of being an American, of belonging to a nation that is dealing with a problem so enormous and difficult in so thoroughly fine a way" (176).

16. Theodore Roosevelt, "The Importance of Practical Forestry," *Forestry and Irrigation* 9 (April 1903): 170.

17. Ibid., 171.

18. Robbins, *Lumberjacks and Legislators*.

19. Henry S. Graves, "New Relationship between the Government and the Lumber Industry," *West Coast Lumberman* 20(15) (1915): 39.

20. Ibid.

21. Henry S. Graves, "The Study and Practice of Silviculture," *The Forester* 7 (May 1901): 108–109.

22. Cited in American Forestry Association, *Proceedings of the American Forest Congress: Held at Washington, D.C., January 2 to 6, 1905, Under the Auspices of the American Forestry Association* (Washington, DC: Suter, 1905), 99.

23. Gonzalez, *Corporate Power and the Environment*, 37.

24. Allen quoted in Robbins, *American Forestry*, 60.

25. See, for example, R. A. Colgan, "Selling Lumber and Our American Way," address to the National Association of Commission Lumber Salesman, Inc., 1950. Box 46, Forest History Society; Wilson Compton, Annual Report of the Secretary and Manager, National Lumber Manufacturers Association, April 5, 1922, 22–23. Box 146, Forest History Society; Emanuel Fritz, Federal Regulation Imperils National Strength, June-December 1946. California State Archives, Sacramento; Glassow, Remarks of A. J. Glassow; George F. Jewett, letter to John B. Woods, May 1936. Box 2-34, David T. Mason Papers, Archives of the Oregon Historical Society, Portland; Jewett, letter to the Executive Committee, Board of Directors, National Lumber Manufacturers Association, January 31, 1938. Box 36, Forest History Society; Jewett, letter to Wilson Compton, June 23, 1938. Box 36, Forest History Society; Jewett, letter to Earle H. Clapp, acting chief, United States Forest Service, April 20, 1940. Box 63, Forest History Society; Jewett, letter to Ward Shepard, August 28, 1940. Box 36, Forest History Society; James Stevens, letter to Young and Rubican, Inc., August 22, 1946. Box 8, Folder 28, Papers of the West Coast Lumbermen's Association, Oregon Historical Society, Portland.

26. L. C. Boyle, letter to Dr. Wilson Compton, October 21, 1918. Box 110, Forest History Society.

27. David T. Mason, "Present Trends in Private Forest Ownership." Address to the Annual Meeting of the Society of American Foresters, Portland, OR, December 14, 1936. Box 5, Folder 8, David T. Mason Papers, Oregon Historical Society, Portland.

28. Robbins, *American Forestry*.

29. Scott, *Seeing Like a State*, 19. Scott uses the example of German forestry in the nineteenth century to make his case. However, he takes pains to note the coincidence of interest between bureaucratic and commercial forestry—the maximization of a revenue stream produced from the land. It is this maximizing tendency (in the case of state forestry) and requirement (in the case of capitalist forestry) that leads to the simplification of ecosystems.

30. Others disagree on this point—see, for example, Dean Bavington, "Managerial Ecology and Its Discontents: Exploring the Complexities of Control, Careful Use and Coping in Resource and Environmental Management," *Environments* 30(3) (2002): 3–22; and Mark Hudson, "Branches for Roots: Recalling the Context of Environmental Management," *Environments* 30(3) (2002): 23–36, for an exchange.

31. Henry S. Graves, "Fundamentals of the Fire Problem," *American Forestry* 16(11) (November 1910): 629.

32. Steen, *U.S. Forest Service*; Robbins, *American Forestry*; Robbins, "The Good Fight," 270–289.

33. Robbins, "The Good Fight," 277; George T. Morgan, "Conflagration as Catalyst: Western Lumbermen and American Forest Policy," *Pacific Historical Review* 47(2) (1978): 176.

34. Quoted in Charles S. Cowan, *The Enemy Is Fire! The History of Forest Protection in Big Timber Country* (Seattle: Superior Publishing, 1961), 41–42.

35. Quoted in Clyde S. Martin, "History and Influence of the Western Forestry and Conservation Association on Cooperative Forestry in the West," *Journal of Forestry* 43 (1945): 165.

36. Morgan, "Conflagration as Catalyst," 174.

37. Ibid., 173n16.

38. Robbins, "The Good Fight."

39. Morgan, "Conflagration as Catalyst," 185.

40. Carle, *Burning Questions*.

41. Nelson, *Burning Issue*.

42. Clary, *Timber and the Forest Service*, 147–149.

43. Ibid.; Hirt, *Conspiracy of Optimism*.

44. Henry Clepper, *Professional Forestry in the United States* (Baltimore: Johns Hopkins University Press, 1971), 135–136.

45. James O'Connor, "The Second Contradiction of Capitalism," *Capitalism, Nature, Socialism* 1 (October 1988): 1–30.

46. Ibid.; O'Connor, *Natural Causes*.

47. Karl Polanyi, *The Great Transformation* (Boston: Beacon, 1944), 72–73.

48. O'Connor, *Natural Causes*, 148.

49. Clary, *Timber and the Forest Service*. While the threat of timber famine was indeed a steady drumbeat from the Forest Service until the 1950s, I concur with Hirt's (*Conspiracy of Optimism*, 305) assessment that it was less this "quasi-religious" belief in the need for the state to keep the timber flowing and more the USFS's need to accommodate and facilitate the process of capitalist accumulation that provided the main force behind the agency's actions.

50. Pinchot, *Fight for Conservation*, 15.

51. Henry S. Graves, "Private Forestry," *Journal of Forestry* 17(2) (February 1919): 113–121.

52. Committee for the Application of Forestry, Society of American Foresters, "Forest Devastation: A National Danger and a Plan to Meet It," *Journal of Forestry* 17(8) (1919): 911.

53. Ibid., 913.

54. Quoted in "Senate Special Forestry Committee Hears Chief Forester and Others on Reforestation Problems," *American Lumberman,* April 7, 1923, 55.

55. Cited in Henry A. Wallace, letter from Secretary of Agriculture Henry A. Wallace, transmitting a report of the Forest Service pursuant to Senate Resolution 175, 72nd Congress, 1st Session. Region 8, Office for Information, State and Private Forestry, United States Forest Service, Atlanta, GA.

56. USDA, Statement by Secretary Wallace before the Joint Committee of Congress on Forestry, January 17, 1939, 1291–40–9. Box 91, Forest History Society.

57. "Watts and Compton Debate Public Regulation of Forest Lands," *California Lumber Merchant*, October 15, 1943, 26. Box 144, Forest History Society; Lyle F. Watts, letter to Wilson Compton, June 24, 1944. Box 54, Forest History Society.

58. Quoted in Hirt, *Conspiracy of Optimism*, 46.

59. "Watts and Compton Debate Public Regulation," 26.

60. Hirt, *Conspiracy of Optimism*, 139.

61. USDA Forest Service, *Douglas-Fir Supply Study: Alternative Programs for Increasing Timber Supplies from National Forest Lands* (Portland, OR: Pacific Northwest Forest and Range Experiment Station, 1969).

62. Dana and Fairfax, *Forest and Range Policy*, 198.

63. Clary, *Timber and the Forest Service*; Hirt, *Conspiracy of Optimism*.

64. Henry S. Graves, letter to R. S. Kellogg, May 29, 1919. Box 143, Forest History Society.

65. Graves, "Private Forestry," 113.

66. Steen, *U.S. Forest Service*, 176.

67. Royal S. Kellogg, "A Discussion of Methods," *American Forests* 25 (August 1919): 1282–1283.

68. Committee for the Application of Forestry, "Forest Devastation," 915.

69. Gifford Pinchot, "The Lines Are Drawn," *Journal of Forestry* 17(8) (December 1919): 899–900.

70. Committee for the Application of Forestry, "Forest Devastation," 941.

71. Ibid., 941–942.

72. Karl Marx, *Capital*, vol. 1 (London: Penguin Classics, 1990 [1867]), 638; William Leiss, *The Domination of Nature* (Boston: Beacon, 1974).

73. William B. Greeley, "Self-Government in Forestry," *Journal of Forestry* 18 (February 1920): 103–105.

74. Pinchot, "The Lines Are Drawn."

75. Gifford Pinchot, letter to J. Girvin Peters, U.S. Forest Service, September 21, 1920. E. T. Allen Papers, Oregon Historical Society, Portland.

76. Ibid.

77. Ibid.

78. William B. Greeley, letter to Gifford Pinchot, October 6, 1920. E. T. Allen Papers, Oregon Historical Society, Portland.

79. Ibid.

80. Gifford Pinchot, letter to William B. Greeley, United States forester, October 22, 1920. E. T. Allen Papers, Oregon Historical Society, Portland; emphasis added.

81. Ibid.

82. Ralph Hosmer, "The National Forestry Program Committee, 1919–1928," *Journal of Forestry* 45 (September 1947): 636.

83. Royal S. Kellogg, letter to "Elwood," October 31, 1962. Royal S. Kellogg Letter File, Manuscripts Collection, Forest History Society.

84. E. T. Allen, "Federal Forest Legislation," unpublished monograph, n.d. E. T. Allen Papers, Oregon Historical Society, Portland.

85. Ibid.

86. E. T. Allen, letter to Royal S. Kellogg, January 10, 1921. Box 1, National Forestry Program Committee Papers, Manuscripts and Archives, Cornell University Library, Ithaca, NY; emphasis added.

87. E. T. Allen, letter to William B. Greeley, February 20, 1922, and letter to Royal S. Kellogg, February 21, 1922. Both in Box 2, National Forestry Program Committee Papers, Manuscripts and Archives, Cornell University Library, Ithaca, NY; William B. Greeley, letter to E. T. Allen, March 4, 1922. Box 2, National Forestry Program Committee Papers, Manuscripts and Archives, Cornell University Library, Ithaca, NY; Hosmer, "National Forestry Program Committee," 632.

88. William B. Greeley, letter to Royal S. Kellogg, June 1, 1921. Box 1, National Forestry Program Committee Papers, Manuscripts and Archives, Cornell University Library, Ithaca, NY.

89. Royal S. Kellogg, letter to E. T. Allen, November 21, 1921. Box 1, National Forestry Program Committee Papers, Manuscripts and Archives, Cornell University Library, Ithaca, NY.

90. E. T. Allen, letter to Royal S. Kellogg; Wilson Compton, letter to Royal S. Kellogg, September 15, 1922. Box 2, National Forestry Program Committee Papers, Manuscripts and Archives, Cornell University Library, Ithaca, NY.

91. E. T. Allen, letter to Bill Greeley, November 14, 1921. Box 1, National Forestry Program Committee Papers, Manuscripts and Archives, Cornell University Library, Ithaca, NY.

92. Allen, letter to Royal S. Kellogg (1922).

93. Allen, letter to William B. Greeley (1922).

94. Ibid.

95. E. T. Allen, letter to Harris A. Reynolds, September 25, 1920. Box 2, National Forestry Program Committee Papers, Manuscripts and Archives, Cornell University Library, Ithaca, NY.

96. Ibid.

97. Cited in "Senate Special Forestry Committee Hears Chief Forester," 55.

98. USDA Forest Service, Minutes of 962nd Meeting of the Service Committee, January 19, 1922. Record Group 95–8, 1919–1935, National Archives, Washington, DC.

99. Allen, letter to Harris A. Reynolds.

100. Steen, *U.S. Forest Service,* 185–188.

101. Wilson Compton, Speech to the Annual Meeting of the American Forestry Association, Chicago, reprinted in the *Saginaw News Courier,* January 24, 1924. Box 144, Forest History Society.

102. Greeley, *Forests and Men.*

103. Steen, *U.S. Forest Service,* 186–187.

104. Ibid., 188–189.

105. Kellogg, letter to "Elwood."

106. "One More Step toward Sound Forestry," *American Lumberman* 2561, June 14, 1924, 36.

107. William B. Greeley, Address at the Clarke-McNary Conference, October 15, 1926, Washington, DC, 3. Record Group 95–97, National Archives, Washington, DC.

108. O'Connor, *Natural Causes.*

109. Scott Stephens and Lawrence W. Ruth, "Federal Forest-Fire Policy in the United States," *Ecological Applications* 15(2) (2005): 533.

110. Western Forestry and Conservation Association, "A Report on the Clarke-McNary Law and Its Application in the Five Western States of Oregon, Washington, Idaho, Montana, and California," February 5, 1948. Box 17, WFCA Archive, Oregon Historical Society Library, Portland.

111. E. A. Sherman, letter to Francis Cuttle, January 31, 1925. Box 2, Record Group 95, Acc. no. 56-A-254, FRC San Bruno, CA; emphasis added.

112. House Committee on Agriculture, 66th Congress, Third Session, Hearings on H.R. 15327, January 26, 1921, 31 (Washington, DC: Government Printing Office, 1921).

113. Ibid.

114. "Senate Special Forestry Committee Hears Chief Forester and Others."

115. Greeley, letter to E. T. Allen.

116. E. T. Allen, letter to A. W. Laird, August 30, 1926. Box 13, Records of the Western Forestry and Conservation Association, Oregon Historical Society, Portland.

117. "Cooperators Confer with President Coolidge to Cut Down Forest Fire Loss," *American Forests and Forest Life* 32 (November 1926): 679.

118. Greeley, Address at Clarke-McNary Conference.

119. Ward Shepard, "Cooperative Control: A Proposed Solution to the Forest Problem," *Journal of Forestry* 28(2) (1930): 113.

120. Robbins, *Lumberjacks and Legislators*.

121. Shepard, "Cooperative Control," 118.

122. "Facts Needed to Determine Lumber-Forestry Policy," *American Lumberman,* January 4, 1930, 29; Wilson Compton, letter to Hon. Walter H. Newton, secretary of the president, March 18, 1930. Presidential Papers, National Timber Conservation Board, Herbert Hoover Presidential Library, West Branch, IA.

123. "Facts Needed to Determine Lumber-Forestry Policy," 29.

124. Wilson Compton, letter to E. T. Allen, November 22, 1930. Box 5, Records of the Western Forestry and Conservation Association, Oregon Historical Society, Portland; Raphael Zon, "A Warning (Not for Publication): Conservation of Natural Resources Threatened," 1930, 2. Box 6, Zon Papers, Archives of the Minnesota Historical Society, St. Paul.

125. Frederick Fairchild, letter to Dr. Wilson Compton, November 12, 1931. Box 77, Forest History Society.

126. Robbins, *Lumberjacks and Legislators,* 164.

127. Wallace, letter from Secretary of Agriculture Henry A. Wallace, 1.

128. Ibid.

129. Ovid Butler, "Forest Situation Exposed," *American Forests* (May 1933): 204.

130. Quoted in Edgar B. Nixon, ed., *Franklin D. Roosevelt and Conservation: 1911–1945* (Hyde Park, NY: General Services Administration, National Archives and Records Service, Franklin D. Roosevelt Library, 1957), 130.

131. Butler, "Forest Situation Exposed," 204.

132. Robert Young Stuart, Memorandum for the Secretary, April 18, 1933. Box 11, Forest History Society.

133. Clepper, *Professional Forestry,* 152.

134. Quoted in Nixon, *Franklin D. Roosevelt,* 132.

135. Ibid.

136. Ibid., 130.

137. Raphael Zon, letter to Gifford Pinchot, May 24, 1933. Box 7, Zon Papers, Archives of the Minnesota Historical Society, St. Paul.

138. Ward Shepard, letter to Robert Y. Stuart, April 28, 1933. Box 7, Zon Papers, Archives of the Minnesota Historical Society, St. Paul.

139. Quoted in Nixon, *Franklin D. Roosevelt,* 150.

140. Raphael Zon, letter to Gifford Pinchot, May 23, 1933. Box 7, Zon Papers, Archives of the Minnesota Historical Society, St. Paul.

141. Ibid.

142. Zon, letter to Gifford Pinchot (May 24, 1933).

143. Zon, letter to Maj. George P. Ahern.

144. Mason, "Present Trends."

145. Tugwell, Rexford. Memorandum to President Franklin D. Roosevelt, May 17, 1934. Official File 1c, Box 9, Franklin D. Roosevelt Papers, Franklin D. Roosevelt Presidential Library, Hyde Park, NY.

146. Mason, "Present Trends."

147. Steen, *U.S. Forest Service,* 226.

148. Cited in Robert Marshall, letter to Raphael Zon, April 2, 1934. Box 8, Zon Papers, Archives of the Minnesota Historical Society, St. Paul.

149. USDA Forest Service, Minutes of the 1468th Meeting of the Service Committee, November 16, 1933. Record Group 95–8, 1919–1935, National Archives, Washington, DC.

150. F. A. Silcox, "Foresters Must Choose," *Journal of Forestry* 33 (March 1935): 199.

151. Ibid., 202.

152. Ibid.

153. Ibid.

154. Joint Committee of Conservation, Minutes of the Joint Committee of Conservation Conference, Cosmos Club, Washington, DC, February 28, 1935. Box 2-32, David T. Mason Papers, Oregon Historical Society, Portland.

155. George F. Jewett, letter to the president (note to Allen attached), February 14, 1935. Box 4, Records of the Western Forestry and Conservation Association, Oregon Historical Society, Portland.

156. Joint Committee of Conservation, Minutes of the Joint Committee of Conservation Conference.

157. Western Forestry and Conservation Association, Proceedings of the Forest Policy Conference, December 8–10, 1937, Portland, OR. Oregon State University Library, Corvallis.

158. National Forest Products Association, Minutes of a Conference with Chief Forester F. A. Silcox, February 23, 1938. Box 22, Forest History Society.

159. Ibid.

160. John B. Woods, letter to David Mason, March 17, 1938. Box 36, Forest History Society.

161. David Mason, letter to G. F. Jewett, March 16, 1938. Box 36, Forest History Society.

162. George F. Jewett, letter to John B. Woods, March 21, 1938. Box 36, Forest History Society.

163. John B. Woods, letter to David Mason, August 16, 1938. Box 2-32, David T. Mason Papers, Oregon Historical Society, Portland.

164. Cited in William B. Greeley, Notes on Meeting of NLMA Conservation Committee, Chicago, IL, July 19–20, 1938, 1. Box 27, Forest History Society.

165. I. N. Tate, letter to Captain John B. Woods, April 4, 1938. Box 4, Forest History Society.

166. Woods, John B., letter to David Mason, March 13, 1936. Box 2–21, David T. Mason Papers, Oregon Historical Society, Portland.

167. Jewett, Statement to the Joint Congressional Committee on Forestry.

168. C. S. Chapman, Statement to the Joint Congressional Committee on Forestry, January 16, 1940, 2. Box 91, Forest History Society.

169. Wilson Compton, Statement in Behalf of the Lumber and Timber Products Industries before the Congressional Joint Forestry Committee, January 17, 1940, 15. Box 91, Forest History Society.

170. Ibid.

171. Ibid., 16.

172. Wellington R. Burt, Analysis of Hearings of Joint Congressional Committee on Forestry before the Forest Industries Conference, December 28, 1939. Box 69, Forest History Society.

173. Joint Congressional Committee on Forestry, *Forest Lands of the United States, Report of the Joint Committee on Forestry*. 77th Congress, 1st Session, Document 32 presented to the US Congress (Washington, DC: Government Printing Office, March 1941), 5.

174. Ibid., 20.

175. Ibid., 28–29.

176. "Editorial: Presented by Mr. Bankhead—Outline for New Forest Policy," *The Timberman* 42 (May 1941): 48.

177. Ibid.

178. Nixon, *FDR and Conservation,* 550.

179. Bureau of the Budget, Memorandum for the President, December 4, 1942. Box 1, Official File 446, Franklin D. Roosevelt Papers, Franklin D. Roosevelt Presidential Library, Hyde Park, NY.

180. Quoted in Nixon, *Franklin D. Roosevelt,* 550–551.

181. Quoted in "Watts and Compton Debate Public Regulation," 26.

182. Steen, *U.S. Forest Service,* 266.

183. Quoted in "Watts and Compton Debate Public Regulation," 27.

184. Ibid.

185. Ibid.

186. Steen, *U.S. Forest Service,* 256.

187. Zon, letter to F. E. Olmsted.

188. Steen, *U.S. Forest Service,* 261.

189. Ovid Butler, *Annual Report for 1942, the American Forestry Association* (Washington, DC: American Forestry Association, 1942).

190. Stuart Moir, letter to Lyle Watts, chief forester, October 6, 1943. Box 1, A-F, Stuart Moir Collection, Oregon Historical Society, Portland.

191. National Lumber Manufacturers Association, Action Program (confidential), n.d. Box 152, Forest Historical Society.

192. Steen, *U.S. Forest Service,* 267.

193. Ibid.

194. National Lumber Manufacturers Association, Suggested Program and Outline of Specific Activities in Opposition to Proposals for Federal Forest Regulation, n.d. Box 2, Forest History Society.

195. Western Forestry and Conservation Association, Regulationists Would Control Our Business, 1949. Box 1, A-F, Stuart Moir Papers, Oregon Historical Society, Portland.

196. R. A. Colgan, letter to A. J. Glassow, June 27, 1949. Box 2, Forest History Society.

197. S. V. Fullaway Jr., letter to Walter S. Johnson, March 28, 1952; Walter S. Johnson, letter to Harry T. Kendall, March 21, 1952; and Stuart Moir, letter to Clyde S. Martin, April 17, 1952; all in Box 28, Forest History Society.

198. Steen, *U.S. Forest Service,* 270.

CHAPTER 5: OUT OF THE FRYING PAN: CATASTROPHIC FIRE AS A "CRISIS OF CRISIS MANAGEMENT"

1. William B. Greeley, "Forest Conservation Program for the United States," 1931, 1. Unpublished manuscript. Box 16, Greeley Papers, University of Oregon Special Collections, Eugene.

2. Wilson Compton, letter to F. C. Peterson, March 12, 1938. Box 83, Forest History Society.

3. William B. Greeley, letter to Hon. Rufus C. Holman, April 14, 1939, and John B. Woods, letter to Hon. Richard B. Russell Jr., chairman, Department of Agriculture Subcommittee, Committee on Appropriations, May 2, 1938, both in Box 83, Forest History Society.

4. Ovid Butler, letter to Wilson Compton, December 1, 1938. Box 83, Forest History Society.

5. Western Forestry and Conservation Association (WFCA), Resolutions. Meeting of the WFCA, Portland, OR, December 15–16, 1939. Box 4, Records of the Western Forestry and Conservation Association, Oregon Historical Society, Portland.

6. William B. Greeley, "Looking Back Forty Years," address to the WFCA, Portland, OR, December 7–9, 1955. Box 8, William B. Greeley Papers, University of Oregon Special Collections, Eugene.

7. President of the United States, *Message of the President of the United States Transmitting the Budget, 1925* (Washington, DC: Government Printing Office, 1925), A84; President of the United States, *The Budget of the United States Government, 1956* (Washington, DC: Government Printing Office, 1956), 358.

8. R. E. McArdle, letter to Stuart Moir, undated [1948]. Box 1, Forest History Society.

9. Clyde S. Martin, letter to George M. Fuller, vice president, NLMA, January 3, 1950. Box 1, Forest History Society.

10. George M. Fuller, Memo to Consulting Foresters, June 15, 1949. Box 1, Forest History Society.

11. R. A. Colgan, "News about Lumber," NLMA press release, June 24, 1949. Box 1, Forest History Society.

12. Clyde S. Martin, letter to Henry Bahr, secretary, NLMA, December 19, 1949. Box 1, Forest History Society.

13. Steen, *U.S. Forest Service*, 264.

14. R. A. Colgan, Statement of R. A. Colgan Jr. on Behalf of the National Lumber Manufacturers Association and Affiliated Associations Relative to S. 282, S. 396, S. 1458, S.J. Res. 24 and H.R. 2296 before a Subcommittee of the Senate Committee on Agriculture and Forestry, May 25, 1949, 3–8; Truman Collins, Testimony of Mr. Truman Collins for the Western Pine Association, Portland, Oregon, before the Senate Committee on Agriculture and Forestry, May 25, 1949; George Flanagan, Statement in Behalf of West Coast Lumbermen's Association, Portland, Oregon, on H.R. 2296 (and Related Senate Bills) and S.J. Res. 24, presented by Mr. George Flanagan of Medford, Oregon, before the Senate Committee on Agriculture and Forestry (Ellender Subcommittee), May 25, 1949; Richard Wortham Jr., Statement of Richard Wortham Jr. for the Southern Pine Association in Opposition to S. 1458 and H.R. 2296 before a Subcommittee of the Senate Committee on Agriculture and Forestry, May 25, 1949, 5; all in Box 1, Forest History Society.

15. Bernard L. Orell, letter to R. E. McArdle, April 2, 1958. Box 28, Forest History Society.

16. National Lumber Manufacturers Association (NLMA), Memo to NLMA Committee on Forest Conservation and NLMA Forestry Committee, January 14, 1953, and NLMA, letter to Hon. Carl Hayden, May 27, 1959, both in Box 8, Forest History Society.

17. Pyne, *Tending Fire*, 90–91.

18. Michael Perelman, *The Perverse Economy: The Impact of Markets on People and the Environment* (New York: Palgrave Macmillan, 2003).

19. James O'Connor, *The Fiscal Crisis of the State* (New York: St. Martin's, 1973).

20. Wilderness Society, *The Economics of Fuel Treatment: Can We Afford to Treat Everywhere?* Science and Policy Brief 5, Ecology and Economics Research Department (Washington, DC: Wilderness Society, 2003), 1.

21. K. M. Schmidt, J. P. Menakis, C. C. Hardy, W. J. Hann, and D. L. Bunnell, "Development of Coarse-Scale Spatial Data for Wildland Fire and Fuel Management." USDA General Technical Report RMRS–87, 2002. Available at www.treesearch.fs.fed.us/pubs/4590; accessed April 5, 2011.

22. Gerald W. Williams, *The Forest Service: Fighting for Public Lands* (Westport, CT: Greenwood, 2007), 194.

23. Mark A. Finney, R. C. Seli, C. W. McHugh, A. A. Ager, B. Bahro, and J. K. Agee, "Simulation of Long-Term Landscape-Level Fuel Treatment Effects on Large Wildfires," *International Journal of Wildland Fire* 16(6) (2007): 712–727. My thanks to an anonymous reviewer for directing me to this research.

24. All interviewees were assigned pseudonyms to maintain confidentiality.

25. See, for example, John B. Foster, "Marx's Theory of Metabolic Rift: Classical Foundations for Environmental Sociology," *American Journal of Sociology* 105(2) (1999): 366–405; Foster, *Marx's Ecology: Materialism and Nature* (New York: Monthly Review Press, 2000); Brett Clark and Richard York, "Carbon Metabolism: Global Capitalism, Climate Change, and the Biospheric Rift," *Theory and Society* 34 (2005): 391–428; Rebecca Clausen and Brett Clark, "The Metabolic Rift and Marine Ecology," *Organization and Environment* 18(4) (December 2005): 422–444; Jason W. Moore, "Environmental Crises and the Metabolic Rift in World-Historical Perspective," *Organization and Environment* 13(2) (June 2000): 123–157.

26. Foster, *Marx's Ecology,* 149–151.

27. John B. Foster and Brett Clark, "Ecological Imperialism: The Curse of Capitalism," in *The Socialist Register 2004,* ed. L. Panitch and Colin Leys (London: Merlin, 2003), 186–201.

28. Moore, "Environmental Crises."

29. Ibid., 124.

30. Ibid.

31. Clark and York, "Carbon Metabolism."

32. Clausen and Clark, "Metabolic Rift."

33. Ibid.

34. Clark and York, "Carbon Metabolism," 391.

35. Clausen and Clark, "Metabolic Rift."

36. Clark and York, "Carbon Metabolism."

37. Dana Backer, Sara Jensen, and Gary McPherson, "Impacts of Fire Suppression Activities on Natural Communities," *Conservation Biology* 18(4) (August 2004): 937–946; Wilderness Society, *Forest Fires.*

38. Donato et al., "Post-Wildfire Logging," 1; Beschta et al., "Postfire Management," 957–967. For a review of the literature on post-fire logging as of 1998, see McIver and Starr, "Environmental Effects of Postfire Logging," 23–25.

39. Jessica Halofsky and David Hibbs, "Controls on Early Post-Fire Woody Plant Colonization in Riparian Areas," *Forest Ecology and Management* 258(7) (September 15, 2009): 1350–1358.

40. USDA Forest Service, "Overview of Fiscal Year 2006 President's Budget," 2005, B2. Available at http://www.fs.fed.us/; accessed November 18, 2006.

41. Offe, *Contradictions of the Welfare State,* 35–64.

42. Ivan Illich, *Celebration of Awareness* (London: Calder and Boyas, 1971); Illich, *Tools for Conviviality* (Berkeley: Heyday Books, 1973); Illich, *Medical Nemesis* (Berkeley: Heyday Books, 1976); Illich, *Towards a History of Needs* (Berkeley: Heyday Books, 1977).

43. John McKnight, *The Careless Society: Community and Its Counterfeits* (New York: Basic Books, 1995).

44. Dean Bavington, *The Iatrogenic Effects of Environmental Management: Servicing a Needy Nature?* (Toronto: York University, Faculty of Environmental Studies Occasional Paper Series, 1998); Bavington, "Managerial Ecology and Its Discontents," 3–22.

45. Offe, *Contradictions of the Welfare State,* 45.

46. Fred H. Buttel, "Environmental Sociology and the Explanation of Environmental Reform," *Organization and Environment* 16(3) (2003): 306–344.

47. Hays, *Conservation and the Gospel of Efficiency*; Hays, *A History of Environmental Politics since 1945* (Pittsburgh: University of Pittsburgh Press, 2000); Miller, *Gifford Pinchot*; M. E. Kraft, *Environmental Policy and Politics,* 2nd ed. (New York: Longman, 2001).

48. Buttel, "Environmental Sociology," 318.

49. Ibid.

50. Hays, *History of Environmental Politics*; Kraft, *Environmental Policy.*

51. Buttel, "Environmental Sociology," 316.

52. Ibid., 318.

53. Offe, *Contradictions of the Welfare State,* 39.

54. Ibid.

CHAPTER 6: THE WEIGHT OF PAST WEAKNESS: PROSPECTS FOR ECOLOGICAL MODERNIZATION IN FIRE MANAGEMENT

1. Arthur P.J. Mol and Gert Spaargaren, "Ecological Modernisation Theory in Debate: A Review," in *Ecological Modernisation around the World: Perspectives and Critical Debates,* ed. Arthur P.J. Mol and D. Sonnenfeld (New York: Frank Cass, 2000), 36.

2. The Environmental Kuznets Curve (EKC) describes a hypothesized relationship between environmental damage and economic growth. An EKC (plotting the relationship between, for example, rates of deforestation in a given country and its per capita gross national income) would rise initially as environmental damage increased along with growth, up to a certain point, at which point environmental damage (normally measured as a rate or an amount of pollution per unit of output) begins to fall. The EKC is named after economist Simon Kuznets, who postulated a similar inverted U-shaped curve describing the relationship between gross domestic product and inequality. For EMT and empirical work on the EKC, see Karen Ehrhardt-Martinez, Edward M. Crenshaw, and J. Craig Jenkins, "Deforestation and the Environmental Kuznets Curve: A Cross-National Investigation of Intervening Mechanisms," *Social Science Quarterly* 83(1) (March 2002): 238; Maurie J. Cohen, "Risk Society and Ecological Modernisation: Alternative Visions for Post-Industrial Nations," *Futures* 29(2) (1997): 109; Mol and Spaargaren, "Ecological Modernisation Theory in Debate," 42–43; Buttel, "Ecological Modernization as Social Theory," 57–65; Arthur P.J. Mol, *The Refinement of Production* (Utrecht: Van Arkel, 1995), 46–47; J. Timmons Roberts and Peter E. Grimes, "Carbon Intensity and Economic Development 1962–91: A Brief Exploration of the Environmental Kuznets Curve," *World Development* 25(2) (1997): 196.

3. Buttel, "Ecological Modernization as Social Theory," 57.

4. Farnham, "Forest Service Budget Requests," 253–267; Timothy J. Farnham and Paul Mohai, "National Forest Timber Management over the Past Decade: A Change in Emphasis for the Forest Service?" *Policy Studies Journal* 23(2) (1995): 268–280; Timothy J. Farnham, Cameron Proffitt Taylor, and Will Callaway, "A Shift in Values: Non-Commodity Resource Management and the Forest Service," *Policy Studies Journal* 23(2) (1995): 281–295; Paul Mohai, "The Forest Service since the National Forest Management Act: Assessing the Bureaucratic Response to External and Internal Forces for Change," *Policy Studies Journal* 23(2) (1995): 247–252.

5. Farnham and Mohai, "National Forest Timber Management," 269.

6. USDA Forest Service, "Fiscal Year 2011 President's Budget: Budget Justification," 2011, 25. Available at http://www.fs.fed.us/; accessed April 3, 2011.

7. Farnham and Mohai, "National Forest Timber Management," 270.

8. Farnham, Taylor, and Callaway, "Shift in Values."

9. USDA Forest Service, "Protecting People and Sustaining Resources in Fire-Adapted Ecosystems: A Cohesive Strategy. Forest Service Management Response to General Accounting Office Report GAO/RCED–99–65," October 13, 2000. Available at http://www.fs.fed.us/publications/2000/cohesive_strategy10132000.pdf; accessed November 27, 2005; USDA Forest Service, "Fire and Fuels Policy Position Paper," 2005. Available at http://www.fs.fed.us/publications/policy-analysis/fire-and-fuels-position-paper.pdf; accessed November 25, 2005; USDA/USDI, *Federal Wildland Fire Management Policy and Program Review Report*.

10. For 2000, 2002, and 2003, see Calkin et al., "Forest Service Large Area Burned," 179; for 2004 and 2005, see USDA Forest Service, "Fiscal Year 2006 President's Budget: Budget Justification Overview," 2006, B–3. Available at http://www.fs.fed.us/; accessed May 15, 2009; for 2007–2008, see USDA Forest Service, "Fiscal Year 2009 President's Budget," D–2; for 2009, see USDA Forest Service, "Fiscal Year 2011 President's Budget," 11-7.

11. Calkin et al., "Forest Service Large Area Burned."

12. Ibid.

13. Parsons, "Challenge of Restoring Natural Fire to Wilderness," 276.

14. Inglasbee, "Begging the Question," 1.

15. A wildland fire use plan is required for any national forest administration that wants to allow naturally ignited fires to burn. The plans only exist for wilderness areas.

16. Parsons, "Challenge of Restoring Natural Fire to Wilderness," 277.

17. Dale Bosworth, Statement of Dale Bosworth, chief, US Forest Service, United States Department of Agriculture, before the United States Senate Committee on Energy and Natural Resources Subcommittee on Public Lands and Forests Concerning Healthy Forests Restoration Act Implementation, July 19, 2006. Available at http://energy.senate.gov/public/index.cfm?FuseAction=Hearings.Testimony&Hearing_ID=1574&Witness_ID=1426; accessed January 5, 2007.

18. Machlis et al., *Burning Questions*.

19. Julie Cart and Bettina Boxall, "Air Tanker Drops in Wildfires Are Often Just for Show," *The Los Angeles Times*, July 29, 2008. Available at http://www.latimes.com/news/local/la-me-wildfires29–2008jul29,0,5666042.story; accessed April 3, 2009.

CHAPTER 7: CONCLUSION: THE CHRONIC PAROLEE

1. Jenks Cameron, *The Development of Governmental Forest Control in the United States* (Baltimore: Johns Hopkins University Press, 1928), 378.

2. Ibid., 381.

3. Reda M. Denis Parks, "Healthy Forest Restoration Act—Will It Really Protect Homes and Communities?" *Ecology Law Quarterly* 31 (2004): 639–664.

4. Buttel, "Environmental Sociology," 306–344.

5. O'Connor, *Natural Causes,* 155.

6. Karl Marx, *The Eighteenth Brumaire of Louis Bonaparte* (Moscow: Progress, 1937). Available at http://www.raggedclaws.com/criticalrealism/archive/brumaire_iv.html; accessed January 30, 2007.

7. This monopoly, however, is becoming diluted as other players enter the field of fire management. The nonprofit Nature Conservancy has recently become a key player in disseminating knowledge about returning fire to its ecological role.

8. Dana Fisher and William Freudenberg, "Ecological Modernization and Its Critics: Assessing the Past and Looking toward the Future," *Society and Natural Resources* 14 (2001): 701–709; Richard York and Eugene A. Rosa, "Key Challenges to Ecological Modernization Theory," *Organization and Environment* 16(3) (March 2003): 1–16.

9. O'Connor, *Natural Causes*, 152–155.

References

Ad Council, National Association of State Foresters, United States Forest Service. "Only You Can Prevent Wildfires." Press release, Washington, DC, April 23, 2001.

Agee, James. *Fire Ecology of the Pacific Northwest Forests.* Washington, DC: Island, 1993.

Ahern, George P., Robert Marshall, E. N. Munns, Gifford Pinchot, Ward Shepard, W. N. Sparhawk, and Raphael Zon. "A Letter to Foresters." *Journal of Forestry* 28(4) (April 1930): 456–458.

Allen, Edward T. "Federal Forest Legislation." Unpublished monograph, n.d. E. T. Allen Papers, Oregon Historical Society, Portland.

———. Letter to Harris A. Reynolds, September 25, 1920. Box 2, National Forestry Program Committee Papers, Manuscripts and Archives, Cornell University Library, Ithaca, NY.

———. Letter to Bill Greeley, November 14, 1921. Box 1, National Forestry Program Committee Papers, Manuscripts and Archives, Cornell University Library, Ithaca, NY.

———. Letter to Royal S. Kellogg, January 10, 1921. Box 1, National Forestry Program Committee Papers, Manuscripts and Archives, Cornell University Library, Ithaca, NY.

———. Letter to Royal S. Kellogg, February 21, 1922. Box 2, National Forestry Program Committee Papers, Manuscripts and Archives, Cornell University Library, Ithaca, NY.

———. Letter to William B. Greeley, February 20, 1922. Box 2, National Forestry Program Committee Papers, Manuscripts and Archives, Cornell University Library, Ithaca, NY.

———. Letter to A. W. Laird, August 30, 1926. Box 13, Records of the Western Forestry and Conservation Association, Oregon Historical Society, Portland.

Amenta, Edwin. "State-Centered and Political Institutional Theory: Retrospect and Prospect." In *The Handbook of Political Sociology*, ed. T. Janoski, Robert Alford, Alexander Hicks, and Mildred Schartz. New York: Cambridge University Press, 2005, 94–114.

Amenta, Edwin, and Bruce Carruthers. "The Formative Years of U.S. Social Security Spending Policies." *American Sociological Review* 53 (1989): 661–678.

American Forests and Paper Association. "AF&PA Hails Passage of Healthy Forests Restoration Act." Press release, November 23, 2003. Available at http://www.afandpa.org/Template.cfm?Section=Press_Releases1&template=/PressRelease/PressReleaseDisplay.cfm&PressReleaseID=251&PressReleaseCategoryID=10&ShowArchives=0; accessed November 5, 2005.

———. "AF&PA Praises Forest Emergency Recovery and Research Act: Bipartisan Legislation Seen as Vital to Long Term Forest Health." Press release, November 3, 2005. Available at http://www.afandpa.org/Template.cfm?Section=Press_Releases1&template=/PressRelease/PressReleaseDisplay.cfm&PressReleaseID=757&PressReleaseCategoryID=10&ShowArchives=0; accessed November 5, 2005.

American Forestry Association. *Proceedings of the American Forest Congress: Held at Washington, D.C., January 2 to 6, 1905, under the Auspices of the American Forestry Association*. Washington, DC: Suter, 1905.

American Lands Alliance. *After the Fires: Do No Harm in America's Forests*, 2005. Available at http://www.americanlands.org/documents/1130855803_AftertheFiresFinalEmail.pdf; accessed January 23, 2006.

Arno, Stephen F., and Steven Allison-Bunnell. *Flames in Our Forest: Disaster or Renewal?* Washington, DC: Island, 2002.

Backer, Dana, Sara Jensen, and Gary McPherson. "Impacts of Fire Suppression Activities on Natural Communities." *Conservation Biology* 18(4) (August 2004): 937–946.

Barton, Gregory Allen. *Empire Forestry and the Origins of Environmentalism*. Cambridge: Cambridge University Press, 2002.

Bavington, Dean. *The Iatrogenic Effects of Environmental Management: Servicing a Needy Nature?* Toronto: York University, Faculty of Environmental Studies Occasional Paper Series, 1998.

———. "Managerial Ecology and Its Discontents: Exploring the Complexities of Control, Careful Use and Coping in Resource and Environmental Management." *Environments* 30(3) (2002): 3–22.

Beale, John. "Cooperative Forest Fire Protection: Report to the 38th Annual Meeting of the National Association of State Foresters, September 13–15, 1960." Box 216, Records of the National Association of State Foresters, Denver Public Library, Denver, CO.

Behan, Richard W. *Plundered Promise: Capitalism, Politics, and the Fate of the Federal Lands*. Washington, DC: Island, 2001.

Beschta, Robert L., Jonathan J. Rhodes, J. Boone Kaufmann, Robert E. Gresswell, G. Wayne Minshall, James R. Karr, David A. Perry, F. Richard Hauer, and Christopher A. Frissell. "Postfire Management on Forested Public Lands of the Western United States." *Conservation Biology* 18(4) (August 2005): 957–967.

Bosworth, Dale. Statement of Dale Bosworth, chief, U.S. Forest Service, United States Department of Agriculture, before the United States Senate Committee on Energy and Natural Resources Subcommittee on Public Lands and Forests Concerning Healthy Forests Restoration Act Implementation, July 19, 2006. Available at http://energy.senate.gov/public/index.cfm?FuseAction=Hearings.Testimony&Hearing_ID=1574&Witness_ID=1426; accessed January 5, 2007.

Boyle, L. C. Letter to Dr. Wilson Compton, October 21, 1918. Box 110, Archive of the National Forest Products Association, Forest History Society, Durham, NC.

Brunson, Mark, and Bruce Shindler. "Geographic Variation in Social Acceptability of Wildland Fuels Management in the Western United States." *Society and Natural Resources* 17(8) (2004): 661–678.

Bunker, Page S. Letter to the regional forester, USFS, Atlanta GA, November 23, 1938. Box 144, Record Group 95, CCC Cooperation Agreements, SCS 1939, National Archives, Washington, DC.

Bureau of the Budget. Memorandum for the President, December 4, 1942. Box 1, Official File 446, Franklin D. Roosevelt Papers, Franklin D. Roosevelt Presidential Library, Hyde Park, NY.

Burt, Wellington R. Analysis of Hearings of Joint Congressional Committee on Forestry before the Forest Industries Conference, December 28, 1939. Box 69, Archive of the National Forest Products Association, Forest History Society, Durham, NC.

Busenberg, George. "Wildfire Management in the United States: The Evolution of a Policy Failure." *Review of Policy Research* 21(2) (2004): 145–156.

Butler, Ovid. "Forest Situation Exposed." *American Forests* (May 1933): 204–206, 236.

———. Letter to Wilson Compton, December 1, 1938. Box 83, Archive of the National Forest Products Association, Forest History Society, Durham, NC.

———. *Annual Report for 1942, the American Forestry Association.* Washington, DC: American Forestry Association, 1942.

Buttel, Fred H. "Ecological Modernization as Social Theory." *Geoforum* 31 (2000): 57–65.

———. "Environmental Sociology and the Explanation of Environmental Reform." *Organization and Environment* 16(3) (2003): 306–344.

Calkin, David E., Krista M. Gebert, J. Greg Jones, and Ronald P. Neilson. "Forest Service Large Area Burned Suppression Expenditure Trends, 1970–2002." *Journal of Forestry* 103(4) (June 2005): 179–183.

Cameron, Jenks. *The Development of Governmental Forest Control in the United States.* Baltimore: Johns Hopkins University Press, 1928.

Carle, David. *Burning Questions: America's Fight with Nature's Fire.* Westport, CT: Praeger, 2002.

Carruthers, Bruce. "When Is the State Autonomous? Culture, Organization Theory, and the Political Sociology of the State." *Sociological Theory* 12(1) (March 1994): 19–44.

Castree, Noel. "Marxism and the Production of Nature." *Capital and Class* 72 (Autumn 2000): 2–34.

Chapman, C. S. Statement to the Joint Congressional Committee on Forestry, January 16, 1940. Box 81, Archive of the National Forest Products Association, Forest History Society, Durham, NC.

Clark, Brett, and Richard York. "Carbon Metabolism: Global Capitalism, Climate Change, and the Biospheric Rift." *Theory and Society* 34 (2005): 391–428.

Clary, David A. *Timber and the Forest Service.* Lawrence: University of Kansas Press, 1986.

Clausen, Rebecca, and Brett Clark. "The Metabolic Rift and Marine Ecology." *Organization and Environment* 18(4) (December 2005): 422–444.

Clawson, Marion. *Forests: For Whom and For What?* Baltimore: Resources for the Future by Johns Hopkins University Press, 1975.

Clepper, Henry. *Professional Forestry in the United States.* Baltimore: Johns Hopkins University Press, 1971.

Cohen, Maurie J. "Risk Society and Ecological Modernisation: Alternative Visions for Post-industrial Nations." *Futures* 29(2) (1997): 105–119.

"Colgan Cracks down on Forest Service." *Southern Hardwood Bulletin* 58, May 10, 1947. Box 54, Archive of the National Forest Products Association, Forest History Society, Durham, NC.

Colgan, R. A. Letter to A. J. Glassow, June 27, 1949. Box 2, Archive of the National Forest Products Association, Forest History Society, Durham, NC.

———. "News about Lumber." NLMA press release, June 24, 1949. Box 1, Archive of the National Forest Products Association, Forest History Society, Durham, NC.

———. Statement of R. A. Colgan Jr. on Behalf of the National Lumber Manufacturers Association and Affiliated Associations Relative to S. 282, S. 396, S. 1458, S.J. Res. 24, and H.R. 2296 before a Subcommittee of the Senate Committee on Agriculture and Forestry, May 25, 1949. Box 1, Archive of the National Forest Products Association, Forest History Society, Durham, NC.

———. "Selling Lumber and Our American Way." Address to the National Association of Commission Lumber Salesmen, Inc., 1950. Box 46, Archive of the National Forest Products Association, Forest History Society, Durham, NC.

Collins, Truman. Testimony of Mr. Truman Collins for the Western Pine Association, Portland, Oregon, before the Senate Committee on Agriculture and Forestry, May 25, 1949. Box 1, Archive of the National Forest Products Association, Forest History Society, Durham, NC.

Commission on Presidential Debates. Debate Transcripts, the Second Bush-Kerry Debate (October 8, 2004), Washington University, St. Louis, MO. Available at http://www.debates.org/pages/trans2004c.html; accessed December 12, 2006.

Committee for the Application of Forestry, Society of American Foresters. "Forest Devastation: A National Danger and a Plan to Meet It." *Journal of Forestry* 17(8) (1919): 911–945.

Compton, Wilson. Annual Report of the Secretary and Manager, National Lumber Manufacturers Association, April 5, 1922. Box 146, Archive of the National Forest Products Association, Forest History Society, Durham, NC

———. Letter to Royal S. Kellogg, September 15, 1922. Box 2, National Forestry Program Committee Papers, Manuscripts and Archives, Cornell University Library, Ithaca, NY.

———. Speech to the Annual Meeting of the American Forestry Association, Chicago, IL, reprinted in *The Saginaw News Courier*, January 24, 1924. Box 144, Archive of the National Forest Products Association, Forest History Society, Durham, NC.

———. Letter to E. T. Allen, November 22, 1930. Box 5, Records of the Western Forestry and Conservation Association, Oregon Historical Society, Portland.

———. Letter to Hon. Walter H. Newton, secretary of the president, March 18, 1930. Presidential Papers, National Timber Conservation Board, Herbert Hoover Presidential Library, West Branch, IA.

———. Letter to F. C. Peterson, March 12, 1938. Box 83, Archive of the National Forest Products Association, Forest History Society, Durham, NC.

———. Statement in Behalf of the Lumber and Timber Products Industries before the Congressional Joint Forestry Committee, January 17, 1940. Box 91, Archive of the National Forest Products Association, Forest History Society, Durham, NC.

"Cooperators Confer with President Coolidge to Cut Down Forest Fire Loss." *American Forests and Forest Life* 32 (November 1926): 679–680.

Cowan, Charles S. *The Enemy Is Fire! The History of Forest Protection in Big Timber Country*. Seattle: Superior Publishing, 1961.

Culhane, Paul J. *Public Lands Politics: Interest Group Influence on the Forest Service and the Bureau of Land Management*. Baltimore: Johns Hopkins University Press, 1981.

Dana, Samuel Trask, and Sally Fairfax. *Forest and Range Policy: Its Development in the United States,* 2nd ed. New York: McGraw-Hill, 1980.

DellaSala, Dominick A., Jack E. Williams, Cindy Deacon Williams, and Jerry R. Franklin. "Beyond Smoke and Mirrors: A Synthesis of Fire Policy and Science." *Conservation Biology* 18(4) (2004): 976–986.

Domhoff, G. William. "The Death of State Autonomy Theory: A Review of Skocpol's *Protecting Soldiers and Mothers*." *Critical Sociology* 19(2) (2003): 103–116.

Donato, Daniel C., J. B. Fontaine, John L. Campbell, W. Douglas Robinson, J. Boone Kauffman, and Beverly E. Law. "Post-wildfire Logging Hinders Regenerations and Increases Fire Risk." *Science Express* 5 (January 2003), 1. Available at http://www.sciencexpress.org; accessed February 12, 2007.

DuBois, Coert. *Systematic Fire Protection in the California Forests*. Washington, DC: Government Printing Office, 1914.

Editorial. "Graves Terms Light Burning Piute Forestry." *The Timberman* (January 1920): 35.

Editorial. "Presented by Mr. Bankhead—Outline for New Forest Policy." *The Timberman* 42 (May 1941): 9, 48.

Ehrhardt-Martinez, Karen, Edward M. Crenshaw, and J. Craig Jenkins. "Deforestation and the Environmental Kuznets Curve: A Cross-National Investigation of Intervening Mechanisms." *Social Science Quarterly* 83(1) (March 2002): 226–243.

Evans, Peter B. *Embedded Autonomy: States and Industrial Transformation.* Princeton: Princeton University Press, 1955.

———. "Government Action, Social Capital and Development: Reviewing the Evidence on Synergy." In *State-Society Synergy: Government and Society*, ed. Peter B. Evans. Research Series, vol. 94. Berkeley: University of California Press, 1997, 181–209.

"Facts Needed to Determine Lumber-Forestry Policy." *American Lumberman,* January 4, 1930, 29.

Fairchild, Frederick. Letter to Dr. Wilson Compton, November 12, 1931. Box 77, Archive of the National Forest Products Association, Forest History Society, Durham, NC.

Farnham, Timothy J. "Forest Service Budget Requests and Appropriations: What Do Analyses of Trends Reveal?" *Policy Studies Journal* 23(2) (1995): 253–267.

Farnham, Timothy J., and Paul Mohai. "National Forest Timber Management over the Past Decade: A Change in Emphasis for the Forest Service?" *Policy Studies Journal* 23(2) (1995): 268–280.

Farnham, Timothy J., Cameron Proffitt Taylor, and Will Callaway. "A Shift in Values: Non-commodity Resource Management and the Forest Service." *Policy Studies Journal* 23(2) (1995): 281–295.

Finney, Mark A., R. C. Seli, C. W. McHugh, A. A. Ager, B. Bahro, and J. K. Agee. "Simulation of Long-Term Landscape-Level Fuel Treatment Effects on Large Wildfires." *International Journal of Wildland Fire* 16(6) (2007): 712–727.

"First Things First" (editorial). *American Forests* 44 (July 1938): 313.

Fisher, Dana, and William Freudenberg. "Ecological Modernization and Its Critics: Assessing the Past and Looking toward the Future." *Society and Natural Resources* 14 (2001): 701–709.

Flanagan, George. Statement in Behalf of West Coast Lumbermen's Association, Portland, Oregon, on H.R. 2296 (and Related Senate Bills) and S. J. Res. 24, presented by Mr. George Flanagan of Medford, Oregon, before the Senate Committee on Agriculture and Forestry (Ellender Subcommittee), May 25, 1949. Box 1, Archive of the National Forest Products Association, Forest History Society, Durham, NC.

Folkman, William. "Butte County, California Residents: Their Knowledge and Attitudes about Forest Fires Reassessed." Research Note PSW–297. Berkeley: USDA Forest Service, Pacific Southwest Research Station, 1973.

Foster, John B. "Marx's Theory of Metabolic Rift: Classical Foundations for Environmental Sociology." *American Journal of Sociology* 105(2) (1999): 366–405.

————. *Marx's Ecology: Materialism and Nature*. New York: Monthly Review Press, 2000.

Foster, John B., and Brett Clark. "Ecological Imperialism: The Curse of Capitalism." In *The Socialist Register 2004*, ed. L. Panitch and Colin Leys. London: Merlin, 2003, 186–201.

Fritz, Emanuel. "Federal Regulation Imperils National Strength," June–December 1946. California State Archives, Sacramento.

Fullaway, S. V., Jr. Letter to Walter S. Johnson, March 28, 1952. Box 28, Archive of the National Forest Products Association, Forest History Society, Durham, NC.

Fuller, George M. Memo to Consulting Foresters, June 15, 1949. Box 1, Archive of the National Forest Products Association, Forest History Society, Durham, NC.

Gallo, Carmenza. "The Autonomy of Weak States: States and Classes in Primary Resource Economies." *Sociological Perspectives* 40(4) (1997): 639–660.

Gantenbein, Douglas. *A Season of Fire: Four Months on the Firelines in the American West*. New York: Jeremy P. Tarcher/Penguin, 2003.

Glassow, A. J. Remarks of A. J. Glassow, president, NLMA, May 12, 1949, Shoreham Hotel, Washington, DC. Box 46, Archive of the National Forest Products Association, Forest History Society, Durham, NC.

Goldfield, Michael. "Worker Insurgency, Radical Organization, and New Deal Labor Legislation." *American Political Science Review* 83(4) (1989): 1257–1282.

Gonzalez, George A. *Corporate Power and the Environment: The Political Economy of U.S. Environmental Policy*. Lanham, MD: Rowman and Littlefield, 2001.

Goodwin, Jeff. *No Other Way Out: States and Revolutionary Movements, 1945–1991*. Cambridge: Cambridge University Press, 2001.

Graves, Henry S. "The Study and Practice of Silviculture." *The Forester* 7 (May 1901): 102–115.

————. "Fundamentals of the Fire Problem." *American Forestry* 16(11) (November 1910): 629–631.

————. "Protection of Forests from Fire." *USDA Forest Service Bulletin* 32. Washington, DC: Government Printing Office, 1910.

————. "New Relationship between the Government and the Lumber Industry." *West Coast Lumberman* 20(15) (1915): 39–40.

————. Letter to R. S. Kellogg, May 29, 1919. Box 143, Records of the Society of American Foresters, Forest History Society, Durham, NC.

————. "Private Forestry." *Journal of Forestry* 17(2) (February 1919): 113–121.

Greeley, William B. Letter to Gifford Pinchot, October 6, 1920. E. T. Allen Papers, Oregon Historical Society, Portland.

————. "'Piute Forestry' or the Fallacy of Light Burning." *The Timberman* (March 1920): 38–39.

————. "Self-Government in Forestry." *Journal of Forestry* 18 (February 1920): 103–105.

———. Letter to Royal S. Kellogg, June 1, 1921. Box 1, National Forestry Program Committee Papers, Manuscripts and Archives, Cornell University Library, Ithaca, NY.

———. Letter to E. T. Allen, March 4, 1922. Box 2, National Forestry Program Committee Papers, Manuscripts and Archives, Cornell University Library, Ithaca, NY.

———. Address to the Clarke-McNary Conference, Washington, DC, October 15, 1926. Record Group 95–97, National Archives, Washington, DC.

———. "Forest Conservation Program for the United States," 1931. Unpublished manuscript. Box 16, Greeley Papers, University of Oregon Special Collections, Eugene.

———. Notes on Meeting of NLMA Conservation Committee, Chicago, IL, July 19–20, 1938. Box 27, Archive of the National Forest Products Association, Forest History Society, Durham, NC.

———. Letter to Hon. Rufus C. Holman, April 14, 1939. Box 83, Archive of the National Forest Products Association, Forest History Society, Durham, NC.

———. *Forests and Men*. Garden City, NY: Doubleday, 1951.

———. "Man-Made Fires." *Perkins Glue Line* 33 (September 1954). Box 40, Archive of the National Forest Products Association, Forest History Society, Durham, NC.

———. "Looking Back Forty Years." Address to the WFCA, Portland, OR, December 7–9, 1955. Box 8, William B. Greeley Papers, University of Oregon Special Collections, Eugene.

Hall, R. C. "Observations on the 'Letter.'" *Journal of Forestry* 28(4) (April 1930): 459–461.

Halofsky, Jessica, and David Hibbs. "Controls on Early Post-Fire Woody Plant Colonization in Riparian Areas." *Forest Ecology and Management* 258(7) (September 15, 2009): 1350–1358.

Hanson, Chad. "The Big Lie: Logging and Forest Fires." *Earth Island Journal* 15(1) (Spring 2000): 12–13.

Hartwell, E. W. Letter to Raphael Zon, February 26, 1930. Box 6, P1237 Zon Papers, Archives of the Minnesota Historical Society, St. Paul.

Hays, Samuel P. *Conservation and the Gospel of Efficiency: The Progressive Conservation Movement, 1890–1920*. New York: Atheneum, 1969.

———. *A History of Environmental Politics since 1945*. Pittsburgh: University of Pittsburgh Press, 2000.

Hidy, Ralph, Frank Ernest Hill, and Allen Nevins. *Timber and Men: The Weyerhauser Story*. New York: Macmillan, 1963.

Hirt, Paul W. *A Conspiracy of Optimism: Management of the National Forests since World War Two*. Lincoln: University of Nebraska Press, 1994.

Hooks, Gregory. "From an Autonomous to a Captured State Agency: The Decline of the New Deal in Agriculture." *American Sociological Review* 55 (1990): 29–43.

———. "The Rise of the Pentagon and U.S. State Building: The Defense Program as Industrial Policy." *American Journal of Sociology* 96 (1990): 358–404.

———. "The Weakness of Strong Theories: The U.S. State's Dominance of the World War II Investment Process." *American Sociological Review* 58 (1993): 37–53.

Hosmer, Ralph. "The National Forestry Program Committee, 1919–1928." *Journal of Forestry* 45 (September 1947): 627–645.

House Committee on Agriculture. 66th Congress, Third Session, Hearings on H.R. 15327, January 26, 1921. Washington, DC: Government Printing Office, 1921.

Hudson, Mark. "Branches for Roots: Recalling the Context of Environmental Management." *Environments* 30(3) (2002): 23–36.

Illich, Ivan. *Celebration of Awareness*. London: Calder and Boyas, 1971.

———. *Tools for Conviviality*. Berkeley: Heyday Books, 1973.

———. *Medical Nemesis*. Berkeley: Heyday Books, 1976.

———. *Towards a History of Needs*. Berkeley: Heyday Books, 1977.

Ingalsbee, Timothy. "Wildfire Paradoxes." *Oregon Quarterly* 82(2) (Winter 2002): 18–23.

———. "Begging the Question: Appropriate Management Response as a Toolbox vs. Tautology: Integrating Safety, Ethical, and Ecological Sideboards into AMR." Paper presented at Fire in the Southwest: Integrating Fire Management into Changing Ecosystems, Association for Fire Ecology, Tucson, AZ, January 30, 2008.

Jeffers, D. S. Letter to H. H. Chapman, October 15, 1934. Box 50, Archive of the Society of American Foresters, Forest History Society.

Jewett, George F. Letter to the president, February 14, 1935. Box 4, Records of the Western Forestry and Conservation Association, Oregon Historical Society, Portland.

———. Letter to John B. Woods, May 1936. Box 2-34, David T. Mason Papers, Archives of the Oregon Historical Society, Portland.

———. Letter to the Executive Committee, Board of Directors, National Lumber Manufacturers Association, January 31, 1938. Box 36, Archive of the National Forest Products Association, Forest History Society, Durham, NC.

———. Letter to John B. Woods, March 21, 1938. Box 36, Archive of the National Forest Products Association, Forest History Society, Durham, NC.

———. Letter to Wilson Compton, June 23, 1938. Box 36, Archive of the National Forest Products Association, Forest History Society, Durham, NC.

———. Letter to Earle H. Clapp, acting chief, United States Forest Service, April 20, 1940. Box 63, Archive of the National Forest Products Association, Forest History Society, Durham, NC.

———. Letter to Ward Shepard, August 28, 1940. Box 36, Archive of the National Forest Products Association, Forest History Society, Durham, NC.

———. Statement to the Joint Congressional Committee on Forestry, January 16, 1940, Washington, DC. Box 91, Archive of the National Forest Products Association, Forest History Society, Durham, NC.

Johnson, Walter S. Letter to Harry T. Kendall, March 21, 1952. Box 28, Archive of the National Forest Products Association, Forest History Society, Durham, NC.

Joint Committee of Conservation. Minutes of the Joint Committee of Conservation Conference, Cosmos Club, Washington, DC, February 28, 1935. Box 2-32, David T. Mason Papers, Oregon Historical Society, Portland.

Joint Congressional Committee on Forestry. *Forest Lands of the United States, Report of the Joint Committee on Forestry.* 77th Congress, 1st Session. Document 32 presented to the US Congress. Washington, DC: Government Printing Office, March 1941.

Kauffman, J. Boone. "Death Rides the Forest: Perceptions of Fire, Land Use, and Ecological Restoration of Western Forests." *Conservation Biology* 18(4) (August 2004): 878–882.

Kaufman, Herbert. *The Forest Ranger: A Study in Administrative Behavior.* Baltimore: Johns Hopkins University Press, 1960.

Kellogg, Royal S. "A Discussion of Methods." *American Forests* 25 (August 1919): 1282–1283.

———. Letter to E. T. Allen, November 21, 1921. Box 1, National Forestry Program Committee Papers, Manuscripts and Archives, Cornell University Library, Ithaca, NY.

———. "As I See It." *Journal of Forestry* 28(4) (April 1930): 461–462.

———. Letter to "Elwood," October 31, 1962. Royal S. Kellogg Letter File, Manuscripts Collection, Forest History Society, Durham, NC.

Klyza, Christopher McGrory. "A Window of Autonomy: State Autonomy and the Forest Service in the Early 1900s." *Polity* 25(2) (Winter 1992): 173–196.

Koch, Elers. "The Passing of the Lolo Trail." *Journal of Forestry* 33(2) (February 1935): 98–104.

Kraft, M. E. *Environmental Policy and Politics,* 2nd ed. New York: Longman, 2001.

Kriz, Margaret. "Fighting Fire with Logging." *National Journal* 34(28) (2002): 2092–2093.

Langston, Nancy. *Forest Dreams, Forest Nightmares: The Paradox of Old Growth in the Inland West.* Seattle: University of Washington Press, 1995.

Leiss, William. *The Domination of Nature.* Boston: Beacon, 1974.

Machlis, Gary E., Amanda B. Kaplan, Seth P. Tuler, Kathleen A. Bagby, and Jean E. McKendry. *Burning Questions: A Social Science Research Plan for Federal Wildland Fire Management.* Contribution 943, Idaho Forest, Wildlife, and Range Experiment Station. Moscow: College of Natural Resources, University of Idaho, 2002.

Mann, Michael. "The Autonomous Power of the State: Its Origins, Mechanisms, and Results." *Archives Européenes de Sociologie* 25 (1984): 185–213.

Marshall, Robert. Letter to Raphael Zon, April 2, 1934. Box 8, Zon Papers, Archives of the Minnesota Historical Society, St. Paul.

Martin, Clyde S. "History and Influence of the Western Forestry and Conservation Association on Cooperative Forestry in the West." *Journal of Forestry* 43 (1945): 165–169.

———. Letter to Henry Bahr, secretary, NLMA, December 19, 1949. Box 1, Archive of the National Forest Products Association, Forest History Society, Durham, NC.

———. Letter to George M. Fuller, vice president, NLMA, January 3, 1950. Box 1, Archive of the National Forest Products Association, Forest History Society, Durham, NC.

Marx, Karl. *The Eighteenth Brumaire of Louis Bonaparte*. Moscow: Progress, 1937. Available at http://www.raggedclaws.com/criticalrealism/archive/brumaire_iv.html; accessed January 30, 2007.

———. *The German Ideology*. Moscow: Progress, 1976.

———. *Capital*, vol. 1. London: Penguin Classics, 1990; vol. 2. New York: Vintage, 1979 [1867].

Mason, David T. "Present Trends in Private Forest Ownership." Address to the Annual Meeting of the Society of American Foresters, Portland, OR, December 14, 1936. Box 5, Folder 8, David T. Mason Papers, Oregon Historical Society, Portland.

———. 1938. Letter to G. F. Jewett, March 16, 1938. Box 36, Archive of the National Forest Products Association, Forest History Society, Durham, NC.

McArdle, R. E. Letter to Stuart Moir, undated, 1948. Box 1, Archive of the National Forest Products Association, Forest History Society, Durham, NC.

McConnell, Grant. *Private Power and American Democracy*. New York: Alfred A. Knopf, 1966.

McGeary, M. Nelson. *Gifford Pinchot: Forester Politician*. Princeton: Princeton University Press, 1960.

McIver, James D., and Lynn Starr. "Environmental Effects of Postfire Logging: Literature Review and Annotated Bibliography," 2000. General Technical Report PNW-GTR-486, USDA Forest Service, PNW Research Station, Portland, OR.

McKnight, John. *The Careless Society: Community and Its Counterfeits*. New York: Basic Books, 1995.

Merchant, Carolyn. *The Death of Nature: Women, Ecology, and the Scientific Revolution*. San Francisco: Harper, 1980.

Miller, Char. *Gifford Pinchot and the Making of Modern Environmentalism*. Washington, DC: Island, 2001.

Mohai, Paul. "The Forest Service Since the National Forest Management Act: Assessing the Bureaucratic Response to External and Internal Forces for Change." *Policy Studies Journal* 23(2) (1995): 247–252.

Moir, Stuart. Letter to Lyle Watts, chief forester, October 6, 1943. Box 1, A–F, Stuart Moir Collection, Oregon Historical Society, Portland.

———. Letter to Clyde S. Martin, April 17, 1952. Box 28, Archive of the National Forest Products Association, Forest History Society, Durham, NC.

Mol, Arthur P.J. *The Refinement of Production*. Utrecht: Van Arkel, 1995.

Mol, Arthur P.J., and Gert Spaargaren. "Ecological Modernisation Theory in Debate: A Review." In *Ecological Modernisation around the World: Perspectives and Critical Debates*, ed. Arthur P.J. Mol and D. Sonnenfeld. New York: Frank Cass, 2000, 17–49.

Moore, Jason W. "Environmental Crises and the Metabolic Rift in World-Historical Perspective." *Organization and Environment* 13(2) (June 2000): 123–157.

Morgan, George T. "Conflagration as Catalyst: Western Lumbermen and American Forest Policy." *Pacific Historical Review* 47(2) (1978): 167–188.

Morris, William G. "Forest Fires in Western Oregon and Washington." *Oregon Historical Quarterly* 35 (December 1934): 313–339.

National Forest Products Association. Minutes of a Conference with Chief Forester F. A. Silcox, February 23, 1938. Box 22, Archive of the National Forest Products Association, Forest History Society, Durham, NC.

National Interagency Fire Center. "2005 End of Season Report Charts and Tables," 2005. Available at http://www.nifc.gov/nicc/predictive/intelligence/2005_statssumm/2005Stats&Summ.html; accessed March 16, 2006.

———. "Wildland Fire Historical Statistics, Total Fires and Acres, 1960–2005," 2005. Available at http://www.nifc.gov/stats/wildlandfirestats.html; accessed March 16, 2006.

———. "2008 Year-to-Date Report on Fires and Acres Burned by State," 2009. Available at http://www.nifc.gov/fire_info/ytd_state_2008.htm 2005b; accessed April 3, 2009.

National Lumber Manufacturers' Association. Action Program (confidential), n.d. Box 152, Archive of the National Forest Products Association, Forest History Society, Durham, NC.

———. Suggested Program and Outline of Specific Activities in Opposition to Proposals for Federal Forest Regulation, n.d. Box 2, Archive of the National Forest Products Association, Forest History Society, Durham, NC.

———. Memo to NLMA Committee on Forest Conservation and NLMA Forestry Committee, January 14, 1953. Box 8, Archive of the National Forest Products Association, Forest History Society, Durham, NC.

———. Letter to Hon. Carl Hayden, May 27, 1959. Box 8, Archive of the National Forest Products Association, Forest History Society, Durham, NC.

Nelson, Robert H. "The Federal Land Management Agencies." In *A New Century for Natural Resources Management*, ed. Richard L. Knight and Sarah F. Bates. Washington, DC: Island, 1995, 37–54.

———. *A Burning Issue: A Case for Abolishing the U.S. Forest Service.* Lanham, MD: Rowman and Littlefield, 2000.

Nixon, Edgar B., ed. *Franklin D. Roosevelt and Conservation: 1911–1945.* Hyde Park, NY: General Services Administration, National Archives and Records Service, Franklin D. Roosevelt Library, 1957.

Nordlinger, Eric A. *On the Autonomy of the Democratic State.* Cambridge: Harvard University Press, 1981.

O'Connor, James. *The Fiscal Crisis of the State.* New York: St. Martin's, 1973.

———. "The Second Contradiction of Capitalism." *Capitalism, Nature, Socialism* 1 (October 1988): 1–30.

———. *Natural Causes: Essays in Ecological Marxism.* New York: Guilford, 1998.

Offe, Claus. *Contradictions of the Welfare State.* London: Hutchinson, 1984.

Olmsted, F. E. *Light Burning in the California Forests.* Washington, DC: USDA Forest Service, 1911.

"One More Step toward Sound Forestry." *American Lumberman* 2561, June 14, 1924.

Orell, Bernard L. Letter to R. E. McArdle, April 2, 1958. Box 28, Archive of the National Forest Products Association, Forest History Society, Durham, NC.

Orloff, Ann Shola, and Theda Skocpol. "Why Not Equal Protection? Explaining the Politics of Public Social Welfare in Britain and the United States, 1880s–1920s." *American Sociological Review* 49 (1984): 726–750.

O'Toole, Randall. "Memo to President Clinton: The Forest Service Has Already Been Reinvented," n.d. Available at http://www.ti.org/history.html; accessed July 19, 2006.

———. *Reforming the Fire Service*. Bandon, OR: Thoreau Institute, 2002.

Paige, Sean. "Uncle Sam Gets Burned Out West." *Insight Magazine* (June 2000). Available at http://www.cei.org/gencon/019,03091.cfm; accessed March 30, 2006.

Parks, Reda M. Denis. "Healthy Forest Restoration Act—Will It Really Protect Homes and Communities?" *Ecology Law Quarterly* 31 (2004): 639–664.

Parsons, David J. "The Challenge of Restoring Natural Fire to Wilderness." USDA Forest Service Proceedings RMRS-P-15, vol. 5 (2000): 276–282.

Paul, C. Edward. "Moving Forward with State Autonomy and Capacity: Example from Two Studies of the Pentagon during W.W. II." *Journal of Political and Military Sociology* 28(1) (Summer 2000): 21–42.

Perelman, Michael. *The Perverse Economy: The Impact of Markets on People and the Environment*. New York: Palgrave Macmillan, 2003.

Peters, J. Girvin. "The Possibilities and the Limitations of Government Cooperative Work with the Private Owner." Presentation to the Society of American Foresters, December 22, 1904. Record Group 95–68: Administration—Office of Cooperative Forestry, National Archives, Washington, DC.

Pinchot, Gifford. "The Forester and the Lumberman." *Forestry and Irrigation* 9 (April 1903): 176–178.

———. *The Fight for Conservation*. New York: Doubleday Page, 1910.

———. "The Lines Are Drawn." *Journal of Forestry* 17(8) (December 1919): 899–900.

———. Letter to J. Girvin Peters, U.S. Forest Service, September 21, 1920. E. T. Allen Papers, Oregon Historical Society, Portland.

———. Letter to William B. Greeley, United States forester, October 22, 1920. E. T. Allen Papers, Oregon Historical Society, Portland.

———. *Breaking New Ground*. New York: Harcourt, Brace, 1947.

Polanyi, Karl. *The Great Transformation*. Boston: Beacon, 1944.

President of the United States. *Message of the President of the United States Transmitting the Budget, 1925*. Washington, DC: Government Printing Office, 1925.

———. *The Budget of the United States Government, 1956*. Washington, DC: Government Printing Office, 1956.

———. *Healthy Forests: An Initiative for Wildfire Prevention and Stronger Communities*, 2002. Available at http://www.whitehouse.gov/infocus/healthyforests/Healthy_Forests_v2.pdf; accessed February 15, 2006.

———. "President Thanks Work Crews and Firefighters." Office of the Press Secretary, August 22, 2002. Available at http://www.whitehouse.gov/news/releases/2002/08/20020822-2.html; accessed March 31, 2006.

Pyne, Stephen J. *Fire in America: A Cultural History of Wildland and Rural Fire.* Seattle: University of Washington Press, 1982.

———. *America's Fires: Management on Wildlands and Forests.* Durham, NC: Forest History Society, 1997.

———. "The Source." Distinguished lecture in Forest and Conservation History, Joint Conference of the American Society for Environmental History and the Forest History Society, Durham, NC, 2001. Available at www.lib.duke.edu/forest.Events/lecture2001%20text.html; accessed April 12, 2005.

———. *Year of the Fires: The Story of the Great Fires of 1910.* New York: Viking Penguin, 2001.

———. "Pyromancy: Reading Stories in the Flames." *Conservation Biology* 18(4) (August 2004): 874–877.

———. *Tending Fire: Coping with America's Wildland Fires.* Washington, DC: Island, 2004.

Quadrennial Fire and Fuels Review Integration Panel. "Quadrennial Fire and Fuel Review Report," 2005. Available at www.nifc.gov/nimo/backgrnd/qffr_report.pdf; accessed February 16, 2006.

Reed, F. W. "Is Forestry a Religion?" *Journal of Forestry* 28(4) (April 1930): 462–464.

Robbins, William G. *Lumberjacks and Legislators: Political Economy of the U.S. Lumber Industry, 1890–1941.* College Station: Texas A&M University Press, 1982.

———. *American Forestry: A History of National, State, and Private Cooperation.* Lincoln: University of Nebraska Press, 1985.

———. "The Good Fight: Forest Fire Protection in the Pacific Northwest." *Oregon Historical Quarterly* 102(3) (Fall 2001): 270–289.

Roberts, J. Timmons, and Peter E. Grimes. "Carbon Intensity and Economic Development 1962–91: A Brief Exploration of the Environmental Kuznets Curve." *World Development* 25(2) (1997): 191–198.

Rodgers, Andrew Denny, III. *Berhard Eduard Fernow: A Story of North American Forestry.* New York: Hafner, 1968.

Roosevelt, Theodore. "The Importance of Practical Forestry." *Forestry and Irrigation* 9 (April 1903): 169–173.

Rothman, Hal K. *A Test of Adversity and Strength: Wildland Fire in the National Park System.* Washington, DC: Department of the Interior, n.d.

Schiff, Ashley L. *Fire and Water: Scientific Heresy in the Forest Service.* Cambridge: Harvard University Press, 1962.

Schlich, Sir William. *Schlich's Manual of Forestry.* London: Bradbury, Agnew, 1904.

Schmidt, K. M., J. P. Menakis, C. C. Hardy, W. J. Hann, and D. L. Bunnell. "Development of Coarse-Scale Spatial Data for Wildland Fire and Fuel Mangament," 2002.

USDA General Technical Report RMRS–87. Available at www.treesearch.fs.fed. us/pubs/4590; accessed April 5, 2011.

Scott, James C. *Seeing Like a State*. New Haven: Yale University Press, 1998.

"Senate Special Forestry Committee Hears Chief Forester and Others on Reforestation Problems." *American Lumberman*, April 7, 1923, 55.

Shepard, Ward. "Cooperative Control: A Proposed Solution to the Forest Problem." *Journal of Forestry* 28(2) (1930): 113–120.

———. Letter to Robert Y. Stuart, April 28, 1930. Box 7, Zon Papers, Archives of the Minnesota Historical Society, St. Paul.

Sherman, E. A. Letter to Francis Cuttle, January 31, 1925. Box 2, Record Group 95, Acc. no. 56-A–254, Federal Records Center, San Bruno, CA.

Sierra Club. *Forest Fires: Beyond the Heat and Hype*. Washington, DC: Sierra Club, n.d. Available at http://www.sierraclub.org/forests/report01/ecl01_forestfires.pdf; accessed March 30, 2006.

Silcox, F. A. "Foresters Must Choose." *Journal of Forestry* 33 (March 1935): 198–204.

Skocpol, Theda. *States and Social Revolutions: A Comparative Analysis of France, Russia, and China*. Cambridge: Cambridge University Press, 1979.

———. "Bringing the State Back In: Strategies of Analysis in Current Research." In *Bringing the State Back In*, ed. Peter B. Evans, Dietrich Rueschemeyer, and Theda Skocpol. New York: Cambridge University Press, 1985, 4–37.

———. *Protecting Soldiers and Mothers: Political Origins of Social Policy in the United States*. Cambridge: Belknap Press of Harvard University Press, 1992.

Skocpol, Theda, and Kenneth Finegold. "Explaining New Deal Labor Policy." *American Political Science Review* 84(4) (1990): 1297–1315.

Smith, C. Stowell. "De-bunking Forestry." *Journal of Forestry* 28(4) (April 1930): 464–470.

Smith, Neil. *Uneven Development*. Oxford: Blackwell, 1984.

Sparhawk, William N. "The History of Forestry in America." *Yearbook of Agriculture*. Washington, DC: Government Printing Office, 1949, 702–714.

Spivak, Randi. "The Politics of FERRA." Paper presented at the Public Interest Environmental Law Conference, University of Oregon School of Law, March 4, 2006, Eugene.

Standardization Committee. Proceedings of the Standardization Committee, Western Forestry and Conservation Association, April 24–25, 1919, Portland, OR.

Steen, Harold K. *The U.S. Forest Service: A History* (centennial edition). Durham, NC, and Seattle: Forest History Society and University of Washington Press, 2004.

Steinberg, Ted. *Acts of God: The Unnatural History of Natural Disaster in America*. Oxford: Oxford University Press, 2000.

Stepan, Alfred. *The State and Society: Peru in Comparative Perspective*. Princeton: Princeton University Press, 1978.

Stephens, Scott, and Lawrence W. Ruth. "Federal Forest-Fire Policy in the United States." *Ecological Applications* 15(2) (2005): 532–542.

Stevens, James. Letter to Young and Rubican, Inc., August 22, 1946. Box 8, Folder 28, Papers of the West Coast Lumbermen's Association, Oregon Historical Society, Portland.

Stevens, James, and Robert E. Mahaffay. "The Lumber Business." Unpublished manuscript, 1946. Box 8, Folder 29, Records of the West Coast Lumbermen's Association, Oregon Historical Society, Portland.

Strategic Issues Panel on Fire Management. "Large Fire Suppression Costs: Strategies for Cost Management." Report to the Wildland Fire Leadership Council, 2004. Available at http://www.fireplan.gov/reports/2004/costmanagement.pdf; accessed December 3, 2005.

Stuart, Robert Young. Memorandum for the Secretary, April 18, 1933. Box 11, Archive of the National Forest Products Association, Forest History Society, Durham, NC.

Tate, I. N. Letter to Captain John B. Woods, April 4, 1938. Box 4, Archive of the National Forest Products Association, Forest History Society, Durham, NC.

Trachtman, Paul. "Fire Fight." *Smithsonian* 34(5) (August 2003): 42–51.

Tugwell, Rexford. Memorandum to President Franklin D. Roosevelt, May 17, 1934. Official File 1c, Box 9, Franklin D. Roosevelt Papers, Franklin D. Roosevelt Presidential Library, Hyde Park, NY.

Twight, Ben W., and Fremont J. Lyden. "Measuring Forest Service Bias." *Journal of Forestry* 87 (May 1989): 35–41.

Twight, Ben W., Fremont J. Lyden, and E. Thomas Tuchmann. "Constituency Bias in a Federal Career System? A Study of District Rangers of the U.S. Forest Service." *Administration and Society* 22 (November 1990): 358–389.

USDA (US Department of Agriculture). Statement by Secretary Wallace before the Joint Committee of Congress on Forestry, January 17, 1939, 1291-40-9. Box 91, Archive of the National Forest Products Association, Forest History Society, Durham, NC.

USDA Forest Service. *The Use of the National Forest Reserves: Regulations and Instructions*, 1905. Available at http://www.lib.duke.edu/forest/Research/usfscoll/publications/1905_Use_Book/1905_use_book.pdf; accessed March 24, 2006.

———. Minutes of 962nd Meeting of the Service Committee, January 19, 1922. Record Group 95–8, 1919–1935, National Archives, Washington, DC.

———. Minutes of the 1468th Meeting of the Service Committee, November 16, 1933. Record Group 95–8, 1919–1935, National Archives, Washington, DC.

———. *Report of the Chief of the Forest Service*. Washington, DC: Government Printing Office, 1934.

———. *Report of the Chief of the Forest Service*. Washington, DC: Government Printing Office, 1936.

———. *Douglas-Fir Supply Study: Alternative Programs for Increasing Timber Supplies from National Forest Lands*. Portland, OR: Pacific Northwest Forest and Range Experiment Station, 1969.

———. "Protecting People and Sustaining Resources in Fire-Adapted Ecosystems: A Cohesive Strategy. Forest Service Management Response to General Accounting

Office Report GAO/RCED–99–65," October 13, 2000. Available at http://www.fs.fed.us/publications/2000/cohesive_strategy10132000.pdf; accessed November 27, 2005.

———. "Fire and Fuels," 2004. Available at http://www.fs.fed.us/projects/four-threats/documents/firefuels-fs.pdf; accessed April 7, 2006.

———. "Fire and Fuels Policy Position Paper," 2005. Available at http://www.fs.fed.us/publications/policy-analysis/fire-and-fuels-position-paper.pdf; accessed November 25, 2005.

———. "Fiscal Year 2006 President's Budget: Budget Justification Overview," 2006, B–3. Available at http://www.fs.fed.us/; accessed May 15, 2009.

———. "Overview of Fiscal Year 2006 President's Budget," 2005, B2. Available at http://www.fs.fed.us/; accessed November 18, 2006.

———. "Fiscal Year 2011 President's Budget: Budget Justification," 2011. Available at http://www.fs.fed.us/; accessed April 3, 2011.

USDA Office of Information. "Fire Toll in National Forests Held to Low Level This Year." Press release, October 5, 1933. File 144, Record Group 95, ECW Information, 1933, National Archives, Washington, DC.

USDA/US Department of the Interior (USDI). *Federal Wildland Fire Management Policy and Program Review Report*, 1995. Available at http://www.fs.fed.us/land/wdfirex.htm; accessed December 21, 2004.

———. *FY 2002 Performance Report: National Fire Plan*. Washington, DC: USDA/USDI, 2002.

United States General Accounting Office (GAO). "Forest Service: A Framework for Improving Accountability." Report to the Subcommittee on Interior and Related Agencies, Committee on Appropriations, House of Representatives, 1999. GAO/RCED/AIMD–00–2. Available at http://www.gao.gov/new.items/r100002.pdf; accessed November 23, 2005.

———. *Forest Service: Information on Appeals and Litigation Involving Fuels Reduction Activities*. Washington, DC: GAO, 2003.

Vaughn, Jacqueline, and Hanna J. Cortner. *George W. Bush's Healthy Forests: Reframing the Environmental Debate*. Boulder: University Press of Colorado, 2005.

Vitas, George. *Forest and Flame in the Bible*. A program aid of the Cooperative Forest Fire Prevention Campaign sponsored by the Ad Council, State Foresters, and the USDA Forest Service. Washington, DC: Government Printing Office, 1937; reprinted 1961.

Wallace, Henry A. Letter from Secretary of Agriculture Henry A. Wallace, Transmitting a Report of the Forest Service Pursuant to Senate Resolution 175, 72nd Congress, 1st Session, 1933. Office for Information, Region 8, State and Private Forestry, USFS, Atlanta, GA.

"Watts and Compton Debate Public Regulation of Forest Lands." *California Lumber Merchant*, October 15, 1943, 26–28. Box 144, Archive of the National Forest Products Association, Forest History Society, Durham, NC.

Watts, Lyle F. Letter to Wilson Compton, June 24, 1944. Box 54, Archives of the National Forest Products Association, Forest History Society, Durham, NC.

Weber, Max. *Economy and Society: An Outline of Interpretive Sociology.* 2 vols. Edited by Guenther Roth and Claus Wittich. New York: Bedminster, 1968.

Western Forestry and Conservation Association (WFCA). Proceedings of the Forest Policy Conference, December 8–10, 1937, Portland, OR. Oregon State University Library, Corvallis.

———. Resolutions. Meeting of the WFCA, December 15–16, 1939, Portland, OR. Box 4, Records of the Western Forestry and Conservation Association, Oregon Historical Society, Portland.

———. A Report on the Clarke-McNary Law and Its Application in the Five Western States of Oregon, Washington, Idaho, Montana, and California, February 5, 1948. Box 17, Records of the West Coast Lumbermen's Association, Oregon Historical Society, Portland.

———. "Regulationists Would Control Our Business," 1949. Box 1, A-F, Stuart Moir Papers, Oregon Historical Society, Portland.

Weyerhaeuser, George H., Jr. "The Three Impediments: Time, Fire and Taxes." In *Forest Policy for Private Forestry: Global and Regional Challenges*, ed. Lawrence Teeter, Ben Cashore, and Daowei Zhang. New York: CABI, 2003, 61–66.

Wiebe, Robert. *The Search for Order, 1877–1920.* New York: Hill and Wang, 1967.

Wilderness Society. *Forest Fires: Beyond the Heat and Hype.* Washington, DC: Wilderness Society, n.d.

———. *The Economics of Fuel Treatment: Can We Afford to Treat Everywhere?* Science and Policy Brief 5, Ecology and Economics Research Department. Washington, DC: Wilderness Society, 2003.

Wildland Fire Leadership Council. *Guidance for Implementation of Federal Wildland Fire Management Policy*, 2009. Available at http://www.fusee.org; accessed March 31, 2009.

Williams, Gerald W. "Wildland Fire Management in the 20th Century." *Fire Management Today* 60(4) (Fall 2000): 15–20.

———. *The Forest Service: Fighting for Public Lands.* Westport, CT: Greenwood, 2007.

Winter, Greg, and Jeremy Fried. "Homeowner Perspectives on Fire Hazard, Responsibility, and Management Strategies at the Wildland-Urban Interface." *Society and Natural Resources* 13(1) (2000): 33–49.

Woods, John B. Letter to David Mason, March 13, 1936. Box 2–21, David T. Mason Papers, Oregon Historical Society, Portland.

———. Letter to David Mason, March 17, 1938. Box 36, Archive of the National Forest Products Association, Forest History Society, Durham, NC.

———. Letter to David Mason, August 16, 1938. Box 2-32, David T. Mason Papers, Oregon Historical Society, Portland.

————. Letter to Hon. Richard B. Russell Jr., chairman, Department of Agriculture Sub-committee, Committee on Appropriations, May 2, 1938. Box 83, Archive of the National Forest Products Association, Forest History Society, Durham, NC.

Wortham, Richard, Jr. Statement of Richard Wortham Jr. for the Southern Pine Association in Opposition to S. 1458 and H.R. 2296 before a Subcommittee of the Senate Committee on Agriculture and Forestry, May 25, 1949. Box 1, Archive of the National Forest Products Association, Forest History Society, Durham, NC.

Wuerthner, George. "Out of the Ashes." *National Parks* 76(7-8) (September-October 2002). Retrieved from Academic Search Elite database, April 17, 2005.

York, Richard, and Eugene A. Rosa. "Key Challenges to Ecological Modernization Theory." *Organization and Environment* 16(3) (March 2003): 1–16.

Zon, Raphael. Letter to F. E. Olmsted, May 24, 1919. Box 3, Zon Papers, Archives of the Minnesota Historical Society, St. Paul.

————. Letter to Maj. George P. Ahern, September 19, 1929. Box 6, Zon Papers, Archives of the Minnesota Historical Society, St. Paul.

————. "A Warning (Not for Publication): Conservation of Natural Resources Threatened," 1930. Box 6, Zon Papers, Archives of the Minnesota Historical Society, St. Paul.

————. Letter to Gifford Pinchot, May 23, 1933. Box 7, Zon Papers, Archives of the Minnesota Historical Society, St. Paul.

————. Letter to Gifford Pinchot, May 24, 1933. Box 7, Zon Papers, Archives of the Minnesota Historical Society, St. Paul.

INDEX